THE SCIENTIFIC
INFORMER

THE SCIENTIFIC INFORMER

By

ROBERT J. FERGUSON, JR.

Polygraph Representative and Security Control Specialist
Keeler Institute Graduate
Member of the American Polygraph Association
Officer-Consultant to the American Academy of Registered Criminologists
Minneapolis, Minnesota

CHARLES C THOMAS · PUBLISHER
Springfield · Illinois · U.S.A.

Published and Distributed Throughout the World by

CHARLES C THOMAS • PUBLISHER

BANNERSTONE HOUSE

301-327 East Lawrence Avenue, Springfield, Illinois, U.S.A.

NATCHEZ PLANTATION HOUSE

735 North Atlantic Boulevard, Fort Lauderdale, Florida, U.S.A.

© *1971, by* CHARLES C THOMAS • PUBLISHER

Library of Congress Catalog Card Number: 79-135930

With THOMAS BOOKS *careful attention is given to all details of manufacturing and design. It is the Publisher's desire to present books that are satisfactory as to their physical qualities and artistic possibilities and appropriate for their particular use.* THOMAS BOOKS *will be true to those laws of quality that assure a good name and good will.*

Printed in the United States of America
N-1

This book is proudly dedicated to the many tireless professional, private, law enforcement, and governmental champions of justice who unceasingly struggle to preserve the rights of the individual, as well as society as a whole. There is a vital difference between youthful idealism and practical adult realism.

PREFACE

I HAVE TRIED TO BE very careful in presenting *The Scientific Informer* so that its contents may not only be interesting and informative reading but also reach every level of understanding.

This work seeks to establish an undeniable foundation upon which all future judicial, legislative and professional discussions and considerations of polygraphy may more intelligently be approached.

Another purpose of this book is once and for all to disprove the unjust criticisms of polygraphy heretofore expounded upon through baseless witch hunts and with reckless abandon by the uninformed and misinformed.

Now, a curious question automatically presents itself. Does this book belong to the author?

Somehow, I think not.

In reality, I believe I have only compiled and put together some years of frustration, sacrifice, heartbreak and toil, success and defeat, unwarranted criticism, and professional dedication of but a handful of men whom I proudly call American champions of justice.

The real authors are the nation's dedicated law enforcement officers and investigators from every source—the brilliant attorneys, writers, and statesmen—whose personal experiences, as they lived them, make up the ingredients of this text.

Some time ago I wrote a letter to Erle Stanley Gardner, world famous author, attorney, avid proponent of polygraphy, co-originator of the Court of Last Resort, whose efforts and deeds will forever live in the halls of human appreciation because of his life-long devotion to protection of the innocent and falsely accused.

I respectfully told Mr. Gardner of my plans to write a book which might conceivably become a dramatic breakthrough resulting in greater recognition of the efficacy and reliablity of the polygraph technique.

He enthusiastically responded and sent me one of the few remaining copies of his *The Court of Last Resort,* published in 1952 by William Sloane Associates, New York.

I studied this book quite closely. The magnitude of its contents became the inspiration and guideline for *The Scientific Informer.*

It suddenly dawned on me that there was an unlimited harvest of scientifically nurtured fruit just waiting to be plucked. On advice from Mr. Gardner I began writing to champions of justice throughout this nation, including a highly specialized group called the American Polygraph Association. I asked each of them for real live cases wherein only the results of a polygraph test, specifically, became the deciding factor in protecting the innocent as well as ferreting out the guilty.

And they, for the most part, readily responded. Unfortunately, some of them couldn't because of other commitments and restrictions. Even so, they still belong to this work, and hopefully its sequel, as much as do the original contributors.

Then, utilizing the theme contained in *The Court of Last Resort,* I touched upon legal concepts in America today, letting the actual cases reveal the existence of modern judicial complacency and plain ignorance, inadequate prosecutors and defense counsels, the tragic lack of proper court facilities and the apathy of misled "do-gooders," further illustrating how often the defense stands alone.

This book takes a firm stand against any and all "moonbeam reasoning" decisions of some district, state and Supreme Courts which have resulted in protection of the guilty or conviction of the innocent, offering no redress for those who have suffered in both areas, apparently with little regard to "justice or judging."

To permit a few, through incompetent judicial decisions, to escape their just dues because of legal loopholes and outdated precedent compounded into precedent, may be some way of projecting the image of American justice to the entire world.

But, to let the honest, law-abiding suffer at the expense of a few is little more than plain asininity.

How swings the pendulum?

It is time we stopped kidding ourselves. It is time to balance the scales of justice. It is time for a reaffirmation of trust in America. It is time for a new awakening in the faith that has made this the greatest and most prosperous nation in the world.

To improve upon the "faults" of America is sorely needed. But, to "change" our basic Constitutional safeguards and the American way of providing incentive for those who sincerely aspire would be little more than utter catastrophe, subjugating our children and theirs to a form of monotonous slavery from which there is no escape or return.

It is time for the "Silent American" to speak up, and act!

While exploring the chapters herein, it is hoped the reader will feel this call for a new awakening within himself. If so, let it be in the form of a cry for the equitable kind of justice that inherently belongs to the American system of jurisprudence.

Polygraphy seeks only the truth at all levels, fairly, impartially and objectively, without concern about race, creed, color, religion or political affiliations.

When I think of justice, and in particular the word "truth," I remember a once close and beautiful association with the Reverend Peter J. and Alvina Nickel, life long Alaskan missionaries, now ministering along the wilderness of the Kenai Penninsula.

One of Reverend Nickel's favorite expressions was a brief biblical quote from St. John, Chapter 8, Verse 32:

> And ye shall know the truth and
> the truth shall make you free.

Is this not the reason why Erle Stanley Gardner and the many other champions of justice have given most of their adult lives and energies, each in his own way, towards maintaining some balance of the scales of justice?

Because of these dedicated champions, *The Scientific Informer* was conceived, born, and now has become the reality of truth as it exists in this book, in this day and time.

A EULOGY

On wednesday, march 11, 1970, Erle Stanley Gardner passed away at his ranch home in Temecula, California, at the age of 80.

He left behind him literary legacies and legal legends that will live forever, henceforth creating inspiration for those striving to balance the scales of justice.

"Uncle Erle," as he was affectionately called by all who knew him, was a staunch proponent attesting to the efficacy of the polygraph technique. While leading the famous Court of Last Resort, he frequently utilized polygraph's reliability to help free many innocent persons unjustly imprisoned.

On the day of his death, his widow, Jean Bethell Gardner, asked that in lieu of flowers for his funeral, donations be sent to the American Polygraph Association's Case Review Committee so that her husband's life-long dedication to protection of the innocent might be carried on in capable hands.

Erle Stanley Gardner, the lawyer. Erle Stanley Gardner, the author of 165 books read by millions. Erle Stanley Gardner, avid sportsman, traveler and explorer, intimately aware of the constant need for a specific balance between right and wrong, and nature itself. Erle Stanley Gardner, an American.

He spent a lifetime supplying answers to real and fictional problems, but he never quite solved the problem which bothered him the most: Why does a man become a slave to the very thing he hoped would set him free?

Erle Stanley Gardner searched to find a truth on earth—and now the truth has set him free.

ACKNOWLEDGMENTS

Wᴛʜᴏᴜᴛ ᴛʜᴇ ᴄʜᴀᴍᴘɪᴏɴꜱ of Justice noted below, along with other appreciated assistance, *The Scientific Informer* might never have been created.

The American Polygraph Association.

Erle Stanley Gardner, lawyer and famous writer; cooriginator of The Court of Last Resort. Honorary member of The American Polygraph Association. Mr. Gardner was in the process of writing the Foreword to this book just prior to his untimely death.

Harry Steeger, Argosy Magazine. Cooriginator and long-time benefactor of The Court of Last Resort.

Alex Greggory, Detroit, Michigan, one of the first polygraph examiners teamed with The Court of Last Resort.

Dee E. Wheeler, Chief Polygraph Examiner, Fort Worth Crime Laboratory, Fort Worth, Texas.

Warren D. Holmes, Holmes Polygraph Service, Inc., Miami, Florida.

C. B. Hanscom, Director, Department of Police, University of Minnesota, Minneapolis, Minn.

Richard O. Arther, B.S., M.A., New York, *The Journal of Polygraph Studies.* Director National Training Center of Lie Detection, a national polygraph authority.

Lincoln M. Zonn, President of Lincoln M. Zonn, Inc., New York, the world's largest private polygraph and security control consulting firm, servicing the entire nation and many foreign countries.

L. R. Wynne, Captain and Polygraph Examiner, Amarillo Police Department, Amarillo, Texas.

Warren King, Lieutenant, Burbank Police Department, Burbank, California.

H. A. Albert, Texas Department of Public Safety; polygraphist and former Chairman of the Board licensing polygraph examiners in the State of Texas.

John A. Charney, polygraphist, Long Beach Police Department, Long Beach, California.

Frederick C. Martin, polygraphist for the Orange County District Attorney, Orange County, California.

Leonard Harrelson, President, The Keeler Polygraph Institute, Chicago, Illinois.

Stephen L. Gardella, polygraphist, San Diego, California Police Department. Charter member of the California Association of Polygraph Examiners in Law Enforcement.

Alec E. Greene, deceased, polygraphist, Hollywood, California. Former Executive Director of The American Polygraph Association.

Benjamin Malinowski, Chief Warrant Officer, C.I.D., retired; former polygraph instructor at the Army's Fort Gordon School of Polygraphy.

John E. Reid and Associates, Chicago, Illinois.

Wallace R. Rash, licensed Texas polygraphist with Truth Verification, Inc., Dallas, Texas.

The Cleve Backster Research Foundation, Inc., New York City, N. Y.

J. D. Williams, Director of Security, The Zale Corp., Dallas, Texas.

The Hon. Olin E. Teague, Congressman, Texas.

John Murren, Personnel Director, Foremost-McKesson.

Major General Carl C. Turner, TPMG, United States Army.

Leo J. Mulcahy, Commissioner, Connecticut State Police.

Roger Alton Pfaff, Judge (retired), Consolidated Domestic Relations and Concilliation Court, Los Angeles, Calif.

Edward Bennett Williams, attorney at law, Washington, D.C.

Duncan Gault, attorney at law, Mineral Wells, Texas; U.S. Commissioner as well as a brilliant defense counsel.

Dr. G. H. Lawrence, Assistant Professor, Neuropsychiatric Department, St. Louis University School of Medicine, St. Louis, Missouri.

Gene Miller, Staff Reporter, *Miami Herald,* Pulitzer Prize winner.

The Editorial Staff, *Fort Worth Star-Telegram,* Fort Worth, Texas.

F. Lee Bailey, attorney at law, Boston, Mass.

William Sloane and Associates, New York, *The Court Of Last Resort,* 1952, by Erle Stanley Gardner.

William Morrow & Company, Inc., New York, *The Case Of The Careless Cupid,* by Erle Stanley Gardner.

If, per chance, proper credits have not been given elsewhere, such occurred only through oversight, certainly not intentional in any manner.

CONTENTS

THE SCIENTIFIC
INFORMER

I

A TIME FOR ARMAGEDDON

THE PROCEDURAL SAFEGUARDS of our Constitution are designed to prevent the innocent from unjust or erroneous prosecution and conviction. They were surely not meant to allow the guilty to delay or evade their just deserts, except insofar as is absolutely necessary to protect the innocent.

In its emphasis upon such safeguards, our United States Supreme Court has, however, seemingly lost sight of this fundamental principle and has, in effect, said the laws are to be interpreted so that the guilty have the maximum opportunity to escape the punishment the law decreed.

As we shall most vividly see in this book, there are two sides of the same coin.

While the Supreme Court also has the interpretative responsibility of making certain that every accused receives due process of law, in recent years the Court has injected into its opinions question that it is making laws which invariably end up circumventing the basic purpose of the law, itself, thereby creating malfeasance of due process.

No doubt, there are a number of innocent people in prisons today. Nevertheless, literally thousands of unquestionably guilty criminals are free because of minute legal loopholes made possible by confusion in the thoughts of lawyers and judges as they try to interpret the Court's interpretations of precedent compounded upon precedent.

Because of this, along with many other causes, the pendulum of due process seems to have capsized in favor of the dishonest and the criminal, at the expense of society as a whole.

We are not discussing only people whose guilt is in doubt, but also murderers who have led police to a body after the murder and

3

drug peddlers who have been caught with large quantities of drugs in their possession.

We are referring to rapists who have made written statements and turned stained clothing for analysis over to the police.

These are people who were freed and turned loose again on society on nothing but legal technicalities.

In May of 1967, a high government official was quoted as saying, "The level of crime has risen a 'little bit,' but there is no wave of crime in the country."

To say the least, this was and is a bit confusing.

We have seen our cities convulsed with mindless destruction in the name of "civil rights," universities shut down by self-styled revolutionaries in the name of "academic rights," sedition and draft evasion by cowards and overeducated milquetoasts in the name of "morality," militants and radicals openly advocating guerrilla warfare and anarchy in order to disrupt the democratic process and overthrow the government in the name of "freedom," a youth culture anesthetized and sustained by drugs in the name of "self-expression," hippies and flower children aimlessly wandering and littering the streets in the name of "love and peace," an unprecedented, steadily rising crime rate, five times faster than the population, the assassination of political leaders, and finally, a shambles of primitive lawlessness in the nation's capital in the name of "the right to equal shares for everybody."

At the heart of this problem is an age-old moral dilemma with which every healthy society must come to terms. It is that of balancing the rights of the individual against the good of society as a whole, drawing the fine line between the function of government and the obligation of the citizen to himself and to his country.

No society can long tolerate a breakdown of its laws and expect to survive. Dissent is healthy when it acts as a catalyst for needed improvement and change. But constructive change must come about as a steady, slow, and sure evolution; it cannot take place violently.

Reform by anarchy and guerrilla tactics, using fear and crime as weapons, is self-defeating. Without laws, and more importantly, without the enforcement of those laws, there can neither be justice nor freedom.

"Human rights" is a meaningless phrase when there are no laws to define them, and no means to safeguard them. Law and order is the only thing that protects the rights of the individual from tyranny—a tyranny in which strength is measured by brute force and the laws of the jungle, not by the laws of justice.

That so much coercion and violation of the law has been allowed is, we believe, due in part to an unspoken assumption that because there are social reasons for it, somehow it isn't crime. In part it is due simply to the spineless response of our national leaders. They have excused themselves by perpetrating the myth that violence is an inevitable result of just grievances and civil rights issues—that riots are spontaneous expressions of grief and rage for centuries of oppression.

But, is this not also true at the local level? For example, in February 1969 former Chief of Police Cato Hightower, Fort Worth, Texas, reported to the City Council that a new breed of hoodlum had become the cause of a wave of armed robberies.

In Januuary 1969, the city of Fort Worth officially logged 103 reported armed robberies—a 50 percent increase. Chief Hightower said a high percentage of the robberies were being committed by people who are very young and who have no police records, their ages ranging from 16 to 24, unemployed and apparently pulling the robberies on the "spur of the moment."

He explained, "They are the type who used to mug people in parks and other secluded places at night, and they have graduated to armed robbery."

Here begin the roots of the hard-core criminal.

At the same meeting, a concerned community area representative urged the Council to adopt a 1968 Tarrant Grand Jury recommendation that two-man police patrol units be used at night. The City Council received the report but took no action.

It is sheer folly to condone lawlessness in the belief that it is a form of social unrest which must have an outlet; or out of fear that to counter with surmounting force would result in more violence. That is to admit the criminal has become stronger than the law. The real oppressor is ignorance. To sacrifice the social order and the right of the majority for the sake of pacifying a few depraved, warped minds is the epitome of misguided humanitarianism at best. At worst, it approximates social suicide.

The real breakdown of law and order is in the individual. The frenzied aimless search for values, for Utopia and for absolutes indicates that the evil protested by the militants and the radicals is not so much in society as in themselves. It is manifested in the cries for instant change but the inability to say specifically what kind of change; in the preoccupation with personal desires in the name of rights; the quest for material goods at the expense of spiritual autonomy; the eagerness to generalize blame onto the government, or "the establishment," or "the system," as a scapegoat for all social ills; the trend to make the government take over obligations which should belong to the individual; the philosophy that the world owes me a living; twisting liberty into license from law; and finally, in the failure to recognize that freedom and responsibility to one's country are two sides of the same coin.

Present crime rates are a grave threat and of great concern. But a greater danger lies in a complacent attitude and false sense of security in the face of the root cause of widespread lawlessness, a breakdown in the administration of justice; a failure to administer the minimum and maximum set punishments for violation of specific laws; the presence of a staggering preponderance of jurisprudence literally enmeshed with interpretations of portions of other portions of interpretations, again compounded upon outdated precedent; the failure of courts to establish a firm approach based on new precedent which upholds the law and the purposes of justice; the virtual prohibition of use of scientific law enforcement tools designed to aid the investigation in acquiring irrefutable evidence of guilt or innocence; the decadence in state laws which prevent the falsely convicted and confined from speedy remedies to freedom; the absence of recourse or compensation for the victims or henious crimes as well as the victims of incompetent investigation and prosecution.

The courts (and lawyers) must bear an abundant share of the blame for the rising crime wave, because of the excruciating slowness with which "justice" is sometimes administered, and because of the highly technical rulings which, for example, have let loose convicted criminals because somewhere along the legal line some-body didn't dot an "i" ar cross a "t" to the satisfaction of per-snickety judges.

Take the case of Richard Speck, who in the fall of 1966 killed eight nurses in Chicago—frightful slaughter for the sake of slaughter. At his trial it took six weeks just to pick a jury, but he was convicted and sentenced to death in the spring of 1967.

More than a year and a half later, his appeal was rejected by the Illinois Supreme Court and now the sentence has been indefi-nitely postponed because in the meantime, in another case, the U.S. Supreme Court said that a defendant's rights were impaired if he was convicted by a jury from which those who did not believe in capital punishment were rejected.

Dr. Martin Luther King, Jr., was assassinated in April of 1968, and his alleged killer apprehended in June. His trial was delayed until March of 1969.

Senator Robert Kennedy was assassinated in June 1968. The accused assassin was arrested on the spot. It was February of 1969 before his trial got underway, beset by a series of technical maneuvers.

In the summer of 1965, FBI agents trailed William Spinelli for several days following a reliable tip that he was bookmaking and involved in illegal gambling operations. After confirming the pattern of his comings and goings they obtained a search warrant, alleging under oath they expected to find gambling paraphernalia in Spinelli's apartment.

One August afternoon they nabbed Spinelli and searched his apartment, finding the tools of bookmaking. A jury trial followed; Spinelli was convicted of violating federal gambling laws, and sentenced to three years in prison, plus a $5,000 fine.

Spinelli appealed his case, attacking the validity of the contents of the search warrant. Later, the entire Eighth Circuit Court of Appeals, sitting *en banc,* voted 6-2 to uphold the warrant and to sustain the conviction.

During late January, 1969, in a most dismaying opinion, the Supreme Court voted 5-3 to set Spinelli free.* The opinion, was

*Spinelli v. U.S., 393 US 410, 21 L Ed 637, 89 S Ct 584.

a triumph of pettifoggery over common sense; it was a shocking manifestation of the Court's kid-glove solicitude for criminal defendants.

If these nit-pickers and bleeding hearts continue with such monstrous opinions, one despairs of seeing a return to sanity in our criminal law.

The majority's objection was that the FBI had failed to establish "probable cause" for the search warrant to be issued. Heaven forbid! Every criminal defense lawyer in the country must have danced with joy on reading this conclusion.

If the farfetched principles laid down by the Court in the *Spinelli* case should be applied retroactively, our prison wardens might as well toss away their keys.

Obviously, the *Spinelli* decision will place new burdens upon our overburdened law enforcement officers. It will provide a hundred new legalistic loopholes for the big fish of organized crime to swim around in.

No one questions the vital place that the Fourth Amendment occupies in the palladium of our liberties: "The right of people to be secure in their persons, houses, papers, and effects, against unreasonable searches and seizures, shall not be violated, and no warrants shall be issued but upon probable cause, supported by oath or affirmation, and particularly describing the place to be searched and the persons or things to be seized."

The Court's opinion in June of 1968, in *Bumber v. North Carolina,* was bad enough. In that case, the Court reversed the conviction of a brutal rapist on a moonbeam line of reasoning, claiming the evidence (a gun that had figured in the crime taken from his grandmother's home, where the suspect lived) as to the warrant was not clear. Apparently it didn't matter that rape had actually taken place.

This decision is far more damaging than the Bumber case. It goes far beyond the previous landmark case of *Aguilar v. Texas,* decided several years ago. In the *Spinelli* case, Justice Black filed a blistering dissent and was joined by two other justices. He quoted Appeals Judge Floyd R. Gibson who had said in this case:

"I am disturbed by these decisions that appear to relentlessly

chip away at the ever-narrowing area of effective police operation
. . . . Moreover, if we become increasingly technical and rigid in
our demands upon police officers I fear we make it increasingly
easy for criminals to operate, detected but unpunished."*

From the bench, Justice Black angrily asserted:

"It seems to me it's time for us to sit up and take notice of
where we are going and what for."

If this judicial and criminal holocaust continues, the President,
the whole Federal Government, state and local police and prosecutors, everybody, can wage a telling war against crime—and much
of all this can be in vain if the courts continue to nit-pick these
cases to futility.

Another contributor to lack of respect for law and order comes
via the senseless attacks by the "do-gooders"—unaware they are
often the mouthpieces of Communist-sponsored subversives—uninformed and misinformed clergy, gullible fraternal, business and
professional groups. These attacks are directed against every
scientific instrument, test, device, or invention, designed to help
law enforcement prove that a person has been guilty of committing
a crime.

We see this quite clearly in the some thirty years of attempts to
keep fingerprints from being admitted into evidence. The same
problem occurred with laboratory analysis of blood and various
other substances associated with a criminal act. There is still much
consternation and proposed legislation against bugging and wire-
tapping, the opponents screaming "invasion of privacy."

This goes on, notwithstanding the fact that law enforcement
has never made it a practice of promiscuously bugging just anyone's home or business. These devices have only been used to listen
in on or tap the conversations of those known to be violating the
law, or purporting to undermine our national security.

Even though a picture speaks for itself, unless falsified—which
investigative agencies are not about to do—photography, ballistics,
polygraphy, drunkometers—the use of informers—have run the
gauntlet of blasphemy from those who would deny all scientific
tools which aid in ferreting out the guilty.

---

*U. S. Supreme Court Reports 21 L Ed 2d (393 US 433) .

A sad public misconception frequently heard is that just as soon as the police use what scientific methods are now available, they will be better able to cope with the crime problem. This is almost utter nonsense when we see every effort being made to prevent their use.

Some television shows and movies with their super sleuths have led the public to believe that all the police need to do when there is a rape in an alley, or a murder, or an assault on a street, or theft of top-secret government information, is to use "scientific methods" to search for clues in tracking down the perpetrator of the crime. This is pure fiction, even though there are a few cases in which this can be done.

Scientific methods—investigative tools—can help establish a case, but only when a suspect is discovered. When there are no clues, with no place to go, only the human or scientific informer can ferret out a perpetrator. However, once this information is secured, if law enforcement is not permitted to interrogate, if irrefutable evidence is thrown out of court on technicalities, all the money and all the scientific equipment in the world is not going to prevent criminals from being turned loose on society.

Before the individual or group screams for banishment of any scientific informer, a long look at the increasing crime rate in this country should receive attention. Ironically, a great number of perpetrators adding to this increase do not come from the uneducated, the poverty-stricken, the ghettos, the underprivileged or what have you, but from the educated, intelligent, employed, supervisory, political and professional sources, and, of course, from organized crime.

Unlike several European countries which have maintained national crime statistics for well over a hundred years, we in this country have been keeping rather haphazardly since 1930 and only half credibly since 1958. As a result, most crime statistics in this country are scientifically unreliable, heretofore compiled by local police chiefs, determining on an original basis what is or is not a crime.

These statistics have been forwarded to the FBI. Aware that some police chiefs are chary of reporting crime increases—in many cases prima facie evidence of their incompetence—the agency carefully scrutinizes, judges, collates, and finally releases what it considers authentic figures, so that our national crime trends may be reasonably accurate.

In 1967 the President's Crime Commission hired three reliable research agencies to determine the extent of unreported crime in the nation. More than 10,000 households in Chicago, Boston and Washington, D.C. were surveyed. The person questioned was asked whether he or any member of his household had been a crime victim during the past year, whether the crime had been reported to the police, and, if not, why.

The survey revealed "that the actual amount of crime in the United States today is twice that reported in the uniform crime reports released by the FBI."

Until all investigative agencies are permitted to utilize the various scientific informers in bringing the dishonest to the bar of justice, crime will continue to increase.

Until all law-making agencies, jurists and jurors demand and enforce penalty commensurate with the offense committed, crime will continue to increase.

The idea of "preventive detention," which suggests that "dangerous, hard-core recidivists" be held in jail without bail until trial, will be a much-discussed topic for a long time to come. Even though filled with much merit, constitutional questions will be raised.

Does preventive detention, which amounts to a denial of bail, deprive a person of his liberty without due process of law? Should a person be confined in a jail on suspicion of crimes he has not yet committed?

The Constitutional questions remain to be answered. Opposition to the concept of preventive detention is expected from civil liberties spokesmen. How intense it will be probably will depend on how badly or narrowly the statute is drawn.

It might be instructive in this vein to reflect upon the fact that in Britain, the cradle of our liberties, an accused person is certainly assumed innocent—but he has no right to be released on bail if he is deemed likely to commit future offenses while free.

The British system is highly flexible and very much subject to a judge's discretion, and there doesn't seem to be too much controversy about it.

Essentially, the system simply requires the judge to do some judging: He weighs the record and decides whether the grant of bail in a particular case might endanger society. Clearly, there can be such a threat. There is no evading the fact that some hard-core repeaters, free on bail, proceed to commit new crimes, perhaps wounding or killing innocent victims in the process.

A man can do certain things that put limits on his freedom, just as he can follow financial practices that put limits on his credit. A person with a string of bad debts has a hard time getting credit. A person with a bad criminal record may have a hard time getting bail.

In England the burden is placed on the lawyer for the defendant to prove that his client is a good bail risk. It seems a logical enough procedure, and what ever the judge's decision, it can always be appealed.

Until Government bureaucracy disgorges its gluttonous contents, polices itself, eliminates its own corruption, makes available fair appeal procedures for Federal employees frequently accused on the flimsiest of excuses, crime will continue to increase.

Until firms or factories awarded defense contracts are prevented from charging the Federal Government almost prohibitive prices on items and materials readily available through other private industrial sources, cheaper by ten times, crime will continue to increase.

Until the Congress of the United States appropriates adequate funds to combat dishonesty, with emphasis on speedier court trials, additional court rooms, more judges and qualified prosecuting attorneys which will eliminate clogging of court calendars and permit more time to case preparation, crime will continue to increase.

As the late Senator Everett M. Dirksen, Illinois, said in January of 1969: "U. S. Attorneys are so overworked that people in their offices can devote an average of only forty-five minutes to the preparation of a case for presentation in court. That is a dreary state of affairs." He added, "You've got criminals running around on bail awaiting trial for as long as three years and in the interim they may commit two, three or four more crimes. As a result, they are tried on a variety of charges and generally get a concurrent sentence for all—a sentence shorter than would have been the case had each offense been treated separately."

Until parents, school teachers and the clergy refrain from irresponsible domestic conduct, radical strike demonstrations, devaluation of moral concepts and values which confuse and warp the minds of young people almost beyond the point of corrective channeling, crime will continue to increase.

Until city, county and state officials raise the pay of their law enforcement officers so they won't have to "moonlight" on the side barely to exist, and until police training schools are brought up to date and staffed with qualified instructors, crime will continue to increase.

Until adherence to the preservation of, and reaffirmation of, our democratic society—called Americanism—is revived, crime will continue to increase.

Men need to live by the guidance of rational principles and to resolve their differences peacefully. It is both immoral and impractical to abandon principles in times of crisis, and then hope to survive on the basis of pragmatic expediency and cowardly compromise.

Each time a violation of either individual or public rights is tolerated it serves as an invitation for future violations. A free society cannot survive unless men of objective reason rally to its defense. Until they do, crime will continue to increase.

While the role of the human informer has become vitally important to law enforcement, his purpose and even veracity has been so severely challenged, then limited, that admission of his testimony into record now faces almost insurmountable legal blockades. The human informer is also most reluctant to appear in court for fear of placing his life, or that of his family, in jeopardy.

Bugging, wire-tapping, and many other scientific informers have found themselves in even a more restricted situation.

The Supreme Court ruling that Government evidence obtained by electronic eavesdropping must be made available to defendants has left the Justice Department in a vise that could seriously hamper prosecution of criminals or interfere with counterespionage efforts by this country.

The court's intention, of course, is to strengthen the practice of democracy, but the effect of the ruling will be to weaken the Government's hand in protecting the nation from the enemies who would eliminate democracy.

The court laid down its rule in a case involving a Russian employed by a Soviet trading agency in New York and an American, both of whom the Justice Department accused of spying for Russia.

In a 5-3 decision, the court said that any criminal defendant has the right to see all transcripts of conversations by him that have been picked up on illegal Government listening devices, whether or not the information obtained is relevant. This is to allow the defense to determine if such information is being used improperly by the prosecution.

Congress, in 1968, authorized Federal "bugging" provided it was approved in advance by a Federal judge and the suspect or defendant was told he had been bugged within ninety days after the eavesdropping ended. Under this law, the judge could decide whether bugging transcripts would be shown the defendant "in the interest of justice."

The defendant can challenge the legality of a judge's order approving bugging. If the defendant wins and the bugging is declared illegal, the Supreme Court ruling presumably would apply.

The 1968 law also permits the President to authorize bugging for internal security surveillance, without going to a Federal judge or informing the suspect. It is also this kind of eavesdropping that is caught up in the court's decision and understandably has thrown the Justice Department into consternation.

For years, Federal agents have bugged places, including foreign embassies, to keep tabs on Communist-bloc plans and to have an early warning on any "unpleasantness" planned for the United States.

As luck would have it, some defendants in criminal cases totally unconnected with internal security matters have been overheard calling these bugged places about routine business. Under the recent court ruling, the Justice Department would have to disclose the transcripts of these calls and thereby reveal it was illegally listening in on foreign governments, or drop its criminal case.

Unless it is able to persuade the court to amend its ruling, it is believed the Justice Department will forego such prosecution in order to preserve the necessary secrecy for its counterespionage work.

This means the agency probably will drop its cases against several Chicago demonstrators because to proceed now would jeopardize its internal security surveillance.

After this Supreme Court ruling, a Government official said, "All a defendant in a routine tax case, or any other kind of Federal case, has to do now is to telephone a few foreign embassies, give his name, and we'll have to drop the case against him."

The court has acted to protect the rights of individuals on trial and thus buttressed the theory of democratic government. Yet no matter how hard it is to face and accept, a democracy such as ours, like less-libertarian systems, cannot grant all freedoms to individuals and leave none for itself to use in the interest of its own preservation.

Of all the scientific informers, only polygraphy (commonly called the lie detector) despite its attacks from many sources, has weathered the storms of criticism and appears to be coming out on top as a most effective investigative tool. Not even its most outspoken professional, private, and legislative critics have found a way to stop its widespread use.

In general, the judiciary has refused to permit polygraphy testimony into evidence, except in certain stipulated cases. Backed by witch-hunts initiated by Mob-infested labor unions, a few states have seen fit to enact flimsy antipolygraph legislation which has, for the most part, been totally ineffective. Other states, and the number is rapidly growing, have had the wisdom to legislate strict licensing laws resulting in professional status and recognition for this unique field of scientific endeavor.

Biased legislative subcommittee hearings in Washington, D.C., intent on seeking to outlaw polygraphy, turned out to be such a ridiculous farce that application of this scientific informer has tripled in Government, the military, law enforcement and private industry.

All polygraph schools have long waiting lists of applicants and many colleges and universities have incorporated polygraph studies into their curriculums.

One might ask: Why cannot this scientific informer be stopped?

The answer is so simple that even the most adamant adversaries of polygraphy are unable to cope with it.

Initially, men of reason backed by ideals of justice and equity, fairness and impartiality will not permit polygraph's banishment.

As we shall see in ensuing chapters, this "informer" plays a near perfect and vital role in offering undeniable protection for the innocent. Its role in ferreting out the guilty is universally accepted.

Although judicial recognition of polygraph results into evidence is surely and rightfully coming, such has not previously been materially relevant.

Polygraphy, with its numerous techniques and approaches, is nothing more than an investigative tool. It is not infallible, but its application has turned out to be 97 percent reliable. Incidental hereto, however, confessions and admissions obtained through polygraphy are usually admissible, as long as they meet other legal requirements.

Since no person can be forced to take a polygraph test, those who do must willingly volunteer. Valid test results cannot be obtained unless the volunteer cooperates with the administering polygraphist.

Another area, somewhat frustrating to the critical "rat-chasing" researchers is that they cannot find a method of group classification or categorization of this science. The reason is that polygraph test recordings are strictly psychophysiological in their final analysis, free of subjectivity, speculative theories or unfounded hypothesis, originating from the chemistry makeup of an individual's own brain and autonomic nervous system. No two persons can possibly produce an identical physiological response or reaction to the same stimulus.

In a very real sense, therefore, the "tattle-tale" science of polygraphy becomes almost pure objectivity.

Polygraph chart tracings originate from but one source—the body of the examinee. Needless to say, he "tattles on himself." No person can voluntarily control the function of his autonomic nervous system.

Strangely, even the most avid opponents of polygraphy call for its assistance when it may be to their own benefit, or when "the chips are down."

To ethical-minded polygraphists the world over, it is just as much a crime for a complacent society through ineffective laws, biased and prejudicial law enforcement investigation, incompetent and unconcerned prosecution and the appointment of inadequate defense counsels, to falsely accuse, convict and confine a person as it is for the individual to willfully commit rape, robbery, murder, or for that matter, any other dishonest act or crime.

The National Commission on Violence, Dr. Milton S. Eisenhower, Chairman, reported on November 1, 1969, that the nation now spends less on justice than on agriculture subsidies.

It is time to counter the trend of over-applying concepts such as freedom and rights to the point that they are no longer recognizable; time to reestablish the balance between the role of government and the responsibility of the individual. We must affirm the ethics of individual strength and substitute them for collective dependence. We should remind ourselves again, and teach our children, that the real power lies in moral strength and mental integrity. These qualities are hard-won products of a long process. They do not come from slogans, nor are they the prerogative of the young or underprivileged. They cannot be required or replaced by insolence, bad manners or violence. And we must never forget that freedom is not a right, automatically bestowed, but something not easily attained and difficult to keep.*

*Hon. Teague, Olin E., Texas, in The House of Representatives, Wednesday, September 4, 1968.

II

YOU DESERVE TO KNOW THE TRUTH

M AN IN GENERAL doesn't appreciate what he has until he is deprived of it. Then he starts to miss it. He takes good health for granted until sickness comes along. He takes three meals a day for granted until some unusual circumstance makes him go hungry. Liberty is only a term until he is deprived of it, and then he begins to realize what it means to have freedom of motion and freedom of choice.

Freedom is, after all, only relative. No man has absolute freedom. We are bound by economic chains, by ties of personal dependency. We are subject to greed and other personal desires, war, work, worry and taxes. More so, we are subject to the justice of our own making.

Under our theory of law, the people are superior to any department of the Government, legislative, executive or judicial. They must, of course, exercise their wishes in accordance with the methods prescribed in the Constitution, but once those methods have been complied with, the will of the people is the supreme law of the land.

This doesn't mean that in order to decide whether Bill Green has been wrongfully convicted, the people must pass an initiative measure, or, if we decided that Bill Green has been wrongfully convicted, the people need to present a Constitutional amendment to get him liberated.

But in criminal investigations and in subsequent trials, certain obvious truths are not always truths, per se, nor after an expert analysis of testimony are they obvious.

For example, police may not force the identification of a witness in the manner in which a good card magician forces the man from the audience to pick out one particular card from a

18

deck, but there can be no question that prior tactics used by police were such as to greatly influence the witness in making an identification.

Identification evidence, even when asserted with vehemence, should always be considered in the light of surrounding circumstances.

Some persons who are positive and opinionated will get on a witness stand and swear with every ounce of sincerity at their command that the defendant in the case is the person they saw at such-and-such a time and at such-and-such a place.

Unfortunately, the man who should be the most doubtful is, nine times out of ten, the man who is the most positive.

The fair man, whose testimony is apt to be accurate, is more likely to say, "Well, I can't be absolutely positive, but I 'think' that this is the man. Of course, it's been some time ago, but I think this is the man."

Defense attorneys are inclined to pounce upon such a witness and by showing that he isn't positive and only "thinks" the defendant is the man, sneeringly subject the witness to ridicule. In many instances such tactics are unfair.

On the other hand, jurors should not be too impressed by the testimony of the man who, after seeing some individual for a few seconds during the excitement attending the commission of a crime, swears positively that the man seated in the courtroom is the criminal. Jurors should consider all the facts.

Carefully conducted experiments show that it is rather difficult to make a positive identification, particularly where the individual was seen casually.

Let's look at the record of some police investigators and prosecutors. First, we go back to *Washington State v. Clarence Boggie* for brief reference.*

Clarence Boggie, prisoner #16587, was accused of killing Moritz Peterson, an elderly recluse, on Saturday night, June 26, 1933, at East 20th Street in Spokane.

Though Peterson clearly named his attacker to his daughter

*Gardner, Erle Stanley: *The Court of Last Resort,* 1952, William Sloane Associates, N.Y., pp. 27, 63, 85.

before he died—it certainly was not Boggie—a strange series of almost ridiculous circumstances began weaving a web of suspicion around Clarence Boggie and finally resulted in his receiving a life sentence in the State Penitentiary at Walla Walla.

Thirteen years later his case came before the Court of Last Resort. It launched an investigation with the assistance of Bill Gilbert, rector of St. Paul's Episcopal Church at Walla Walla, and also a part-time chaplain at the prison.

The Court of Last Resort found the case utterly incredible. Vague witness identification and evidence unrelated to the case had been admitted into record.

At the time of the trial, the prosecution had called a witness and the examination had been rather peculiar. She was never asked to identify Boggie as the man she had seen running away from the house the night of Peterson's murder; and when the attorney for the defense cross-examined her, he, probably fearing a trap, was careful not to give her any opportunity to make a positive identification.

What was the reason?

Her testimony from record intrigued the Court so much that its members sought to find her. When they did, they uncovered a shocking story.

This witness and her young son had seen the murderer emerge from the Peterson shack. They had followed as he ran down the street, not trying to overtake him but trying to keep him in sight. They had never seen his face. (None of the witnesses had ever seen the face of the fleeing man.)

A considerable time after the murder, and apparently at a time when Boggie was under arrest, this woman had seen a man prowling around the vicinity of the Peterson shack. The woman felt absolutely certain in her own mind that the man she saw was the same man she had seen running away from the scene of the murder.

She called police, telling them excitedly that the man who killed Moritz Peterson was outside and to come and pick him up.

The police told her to forget it, that the man who had killed

Moritz Peterson was Clarence Boggie, that Boggie had been arrested and was safe in jail awaiting trial.

The woman insisted that this man was the murderer, that in any event he was a prowler who had no business there, and she wanted police to come out and arrest him.

The police hung up. After a while the prowler went away.

Nor was this all. The day before Clarence Boggie was to be tried, the deputy prosecutor had gone to the school where this woman's twelve-year-old son was in attendance.

According to the woman, the deputy prosecutor painted a very glittering picture. Her boy was to be a very important witness. He was to be excused from school, and a big police car would come to get him. In court he was to stand up and be sworn as a witness, and for this he would receive witness fees which would be entirely his own money.

The deputy prosecutor, however, wanted him to be sure and identify Boggie. He wanted the boy to mention that he had seen the face of the murderer who was running away from the Peterson shack, and that this man was Boggie.

But the boy protested he "hadn't" seen the murderer's face.

The deputy prosecutor said, "But I want you to say that you saw the man's face. You know I am a public official. I wouldn't ask you to do anything that was wrong."

The perplexed, bewildered boy shook his head. He couldn't say he had seen the man's face because he hadn't.

Next, the deputy prosecutor warned the boy about saying anything to his mother about the conversation. So, the boy went home from school, a very troubled, worried young man who couldn't eat any supper.

An alarmed mother finally got the story from her tearful son. She was a good, straightforward American woman. She took the boy by the hand and walked up to the prosecutor's office.

"What," she indignantly demanded, "are you trying to do to my son?"

No wonder the prosecution had handled her with kid gloves.

More than fifteen years had passed from the time of the Peterson murder to the date the Court of Last Resort reached this woman. They couldn't talk to the boy because he had grown up to be a young man, had gone to war and had given his life for his country.

With evidence in favor of Boggie mounting, and with help from *The Seattle Times,* and *Argosy Magazine,* Governor Wallgren of the State of Washington finally granted Boggie a conditional pardon in December 1948. Boggie died a short time later.

A touch of irony enters here. After Boggie was sentenced, it was required by law that for the guidance of the sentencing and parole board the prosecutor shall make a statement concerning the facts of the case and the character of the defendant.

The prosecutor stated that Boggie was a cold-blooded murderer; that he had deliberately manufactured a deadly weapon; that he had lain in wait for an old man, had brutally bludgeoned him to death; that Boggie had had two previous convictions; that he was a desperate criminal. Evidently, the prosecutor felt Boggie should spend every last remaining minute of his life behind the walls of the penitentiary.

Subsequently, however, before Boggie was set free, that same deputy prosecutor had cut one corner too many, had been himself convicted of a crime and sent to prison.*

While the Clarence Boggie case has nothing to do with polygraphy, we have included it to help lay a foundation for past and present incompetency of a few investigating police officers, overzealous, sometimes sadistically inclined prosecutors, and unconcerned and unqualified judges.

The foregoing incident began some thirty-six years ago. Obviously it would be a present-day defense of police departments, judges and prosecutors to simply assert that times have changed for the better; that police investigators are more scientifically trained; that law schools and new legislation have resulted in more effective prosecution, and that judges are more mindful of a defendant's rights. For, after all, isn't this the latter part of the twentieth century?

Well?

---

*Gardner, Erle Stanley, *The Court Of Last Resort*. New York, William Sloan Associates, 1952, pp. 3, 17, 21, 38, 61.

On a Thursday in February, 1969, a man imprisoned three years on charges of raping the wife of a University of Pennsylvania professor was freed after his look-alike admitted to the crime following polygraphy. The resemblance was so striking that relatives of William J. Sealman, 22 (name fictitious) who had been serving a seven-and-a-half to twenty-year term were almost unable to tell the men apart.

Finally charged with the crime was Fred A. Benson, 22 (name fictitious) then serving two-to-ten years for another rape.

Sealman's lawyer, Bernard L. Lemisch, told Judge Alexander F. Barbieri that a chance encounter between some of Sealman's relatives and Benson at a Philadelphia police station in December 1967, led to the reopening of the case.

Lemisch said Benson was there for a hearing in his own case and Sealman already was in prison.

The relatives mistook Benson for Sealman and asked him what he was doing out of jail.

When Benson disavowed knowledge of who they were or what they were talking about, they told Lemisch of the incident and he presented a new case to the district attorney's office.

The rape victim, now living in California, was immediately flown back to Philadelphia and confronted Sealman and Benson at city hall. She was unable to tell them apart.

District Attorney Arlen Specter later told a court hearing that Benson submitted to polygraphy, confessed and described the crime in detail.

Judge Barbieri, who originally convicted and sentenced Sealman, told the falsely convicted man, "It's a pity. I wish I could undo it."

He was sorry.

What Erle Stanley Gardner's Court of Last Resort ran into a number of years ago is still most prevalent today. Times may have changed, but the tragedies still exist.

Polygraphy, with the help of remaining members of the Court of Last Resort, supported by the American Polygraph Association, along with new legal champions of the innocent, has intensified its struggle to bring about "a day of truth" at all levels of legal proceedings.

A great deal of discipline, research, and understanding is required to be enthusiastic about the portrayal of truth and accuracy in our court system. Most of us have been reared to think that our judicial system is dedicated to separating the innocent from the guilty, when such is not the case at all.

Sometimes one feels like asking, Are the people of today—are our courts—really interested in truth?

Because of outdated precedent, it seems our courts only separate out those against whom the evidence appears to be weighty from those against whom it appears to be thin. In other words, if a man commits a crime we are not going to put him in jail unless we can convict him with dignity. A great deal of attention, as well as apathy, has been directed towards the areas of human rights and dignity. At the moment, at least, the public majority is dissatisfied with our system of criminal justice. Correct or not, many from all walks of life feel it is a pretentious farce, inadequately administered so as to preserve law and order, and that so much attention has been paid to the rights of the criminal that the balance has swung against society and away from protection of the innocent.

The expert witness has even fallen into disrepute, primarily because of subjective analysis and evaluation lacking the scientific flavor long sought by both the judiciary and public at large.

As a result, polygraphy with its fairness, impartiality, and objectivity, is slowly beginning to receive the professional recognition and acceptance long denied it by the uneducated, uninformed, skeptic, and witch hunter.

For years polygraphy has been under attack by certain labor unions, writers of sorts, some professional egotists whose cry and hue for banishment has been based on their assertion that the technique is not one hundred percent perfect and, therefore, not infallible. Not one of these critics, many of whose articles contain the seeds of subsidy, has ever conducted a real polygraph test, has ever trained to be a polygraph examiner.

It got so bad at one point that Massachusetts decided, totally in uncontradicted testimony, that the polygraph "device," as they called it, was so inaccurate that it should be completely disregarded. In so doing, this magnanimous judging body cited the *Harvard Business Review* as authority, namely an article printed in early 1963 by psychologists Richard A. Sternbach, Lawrence A. Gustafson, and Ronald L. Colier. It was entitled, "Don't Trust The Lie Detector."

Study of this particular article lets one quickly realize that its authors probably know little or nothing about a polygraph instrument, much less anything about the technique.

As we shall see quite clearly in this text, it is entirely legal to convict and execute a person who is not guilty as charged, as long as he gets a "fair trial according to law." Thus far, he has not really been entitled to reliability or accuracy; only due process.

Though completely innocent, if he sits in prison for years and finds no legal trial error in his transcript, he may not file an action claiming he is innocent. Of course, there are minute exceptions but these appear to be rarely and reluctantly considered by the courts.

There are many obstacles of truth in our rules of evidence, purporting to make truth somewhat of a misnomer. The archaic theory of proof is designed to occur only when a jury of peers reach a unamious decision. If they are mistaken, proof still becomes relevant. Is it not reasonably true, in this country, that if a person is indicted, tried, even acquitted, the stigma comes close to that of psychological damnation henceforth?

If a man is innocent, he can frequently avoid trial by volunteering to polygraphy. This is the finest kind of objective clearance anyone can get.*

It is encouraging to note that many trial lawyers are using polygraphy to just advantage in becoming aware that the technique's greatest value is eliminating those falsely suspected or accused from a list of possibles in pre-trial.

Ironically, there are numerous cases of record in government, the military, and general law enforcement, where investigators

---

*Additional correlated reference material may be found in a speech by F. Lee Bailey, Attorney at Law, Boston, Mass., to the American Polygraph Association Seminar, Silver Spring, Maryland, August 21, 1968. Also see *American Polygraph Association Newsletter,* Vol. 3, No. 1, Jan.-Feb. 1969.

and prosecutors have not permitted the defendant—even at his request or insistance—to undergo polygraphy in an effort to prove his innocence. However, they readily use it when they think it is to their advantage. This situation is pathetic, particularly where public funds are involved. It certainly does not create faith, trust, or confidence in anyone involved. If polygraphy is available, conducted by an examiner schooled and trained on public funds, on an instrument paid for by public taxes, is it not the prerogative of any suspect to ask and be granted the right to attempt to clear himself?

In general, defense attorneys agree that their responsibility of protecting a client they "know" to be innocent rests heavily on their shoulders. But they also serve under their Cannons Of Ethics, and they further know that judges and jurys are but men, also, irrespective of their age or experience, and are swayed like other men by vehement prejudices. This is corruption, in reality, give it whatever name you so desire. A good judge should never boast of his power, because he should do nothing but what he can do justly; he is not the master but the minister of the law. His purpose is to judge rightly as of this time and place, and to realize that justice without wisdom is impossible.

The equal protection clause in our Constitution has occasionally been flaunted by merciless prosecuting attorneys and law enforcement officers who have decided for themselves, without ever giving a suspect a chance to establish the truth of his innocence. A prosecutor is elected or appointed to see that protection of the innocent is insured, particularly if there prevails the slightest doubt of guilt. In the same vein, is there not an equal responsibility resting on the shoulders of every judge, fees, prestige, and political aspirations not withstanding?

From a simple common-sense standpoint it would seem only just that judges should lend themselves to the availability of facts and truths which can be developed through the science of competent polygraphy. For the most part they have not, and much heartbreak has been the result. We illustrate in brief:

There is little problem in citing many cases wherein polygraphy has been considered by the courts. Likewise, it is doubtful that analyzation of these cases would be of any value to a present case at bar. Stare decisis is inherently retrospective and falls into a rather questionable category where scientific evidence is concerned. We believe few will disagree that science progresses from year to year, but has the judiciary forgotten that what a reviewing court may have found years ago as to a given scientific technique or instrument cannot be said, per se, to control a decision of today? The only way such a decision can still hold is because judges have failed to inform themselves on the main issues in question.

A basic example goes back almost fifty years to the first reported opinion relating to polygraphy (inadvertently called the lie detector) in the case of *Frye v. United States* (293 F. 1013). (In a subsequent chapter we shall again refer to other aspects of this ancient case.) This instance was a prosecution for murder, and the court held that the results of a systolic blood pressure test conducted by one William Marston were properly excluded when offered to establish Frye's denial of guilt.

There is little question that Marston's systolic recording instrument was a crude forerunner of modern polygraphy, yet truth and justice were thwarted by the exclusion. Frye was sentenced to life. He served three years before his innocence was proven by the confession of another person (N.Y. Judicial Council, Fourteenth Annual Report 265 (1948).

Justice Holmes said in 1895:

> An ideal system of law should draw its postulates and its legislative justification from science. As it is now, we rely on tradition, or vague sentiment, or the fact that we never thought of any other way of doing things, as our only warrant for rules which we enforce with as much confidence as if they embodied revealed wisdom . . . . ." (*Speeches,* Little, Brown & Co., Boston, 1918).

In 1923 was the science of polygraphy right in corroborating the claims that a defendant was innocent? Or, was the law right in excluding the offer of polygraphy (and science) from its trial mechanisms, whose avowed d'etre is to ferret out truth? Did the law, in the Frye case, misfire? Using this case as original precedent, how many other times has it since misfired?

Professor Richardson, in his recent and excellent treatise,

"Modern Scientific Evidence" (W. H. Anderson Co., Cincinnati, 1961) states the following (6.2, 6.3) :

> Through the years our courts have been called upon to recognize scientific discoveries and pass upon their legitimate function, if any, in judicial proceedings. In principle, the admission of scientific processes as legal evidence should properly be based upon the theory that the evolution in practical affairs of life, whereby the progressive and scientific tendencies of the age are manifest in every other department of human endeavor, cannot be ignored in legal procedure. And, that the law, in its efforts to enforce justice by demonstrating a fact in issue, will allow evidence of those scientific processes which are the work of educated and skillful men in their various fields of technical experience, and apply them to the demonstration of fact, leaving the weight and effect to be given to the effort and its results entirely to the jury or other fact-finding agency.

> ***** Thus, it will be seen that in order to be in a position to lay a foundation for the admission of scientific findings, the proponent must (1) be able to prove scientific acceptance, if not judicially noticed, of the particular scientific procedure by which the data is deduced, (2) that the test was properly controlled or the device was functioning properly and (3) that the operator or technician was the one possessing requisite skill by reason of training or experience.

That some courts have gone far beyond their powers, abusing their privileges, on passing upon the sufficiency of polygraphy by parroting or paralleling former unrelated decisions makes it rather sad to note such buffoonery contained in a decision rendered in *People v. Berkman* (307 Ill. 492, 139 N.E. 91 [1923]). In Berkman, the trial judge had admitted over objection of the defendant the testimony of a police ballistics expert who testified that in his opinion certain bullets came from a particular hand gun. In reversing the conviction for prejudicial error, the Supreme Court of Illinois said, in part, per Duncan J.:

> . . . . there is no evidence in the case, by which this officer claims to be an expert, that shows he knew anything about how Colt automatic revolvers are made, and how they are rifled. . . . the evidence of this officer is clearly absurd, besides not being based on any known rule that would make it admissible. If the real facts were brought out, it would undoubtedly show that all Colt revolvers of the same model and the same caliber are rifled precisely in the same manner, and the statement that one can know that a certain bullet

was fired out of a .32-caliber, where there are hundreds and perhaps thousands rifled in precisely the same manner and of precisely the same character is preposterous.

Temporarily, a proven scientific technique was dashed to pieces in an appellate tribunal "simply because the judges decreed it out of existence."

It is one thing to say that for one reason or another, grounded on legal principle, scientific evidence must be excluded; it is quite another for a court to inform science that it does not exist.

No doubt the "brilliance" of the drafter of the Berkman opinion, who pompously contributed his own ballistics expertise to buttress his opinion, would be enlightened to discover that there never has existed an "automatic revolver," Colt or otherwise.

The exposition of Judge Duncan in Berkman is unfortunately paralleled by Judge Irving Kaufman in *United States v. Stromberg* (179 F Supp. 279 [1959]) . In rejecting polygraphic evidence he stated:

> But a machine cannot be examined or cross-examined; its testimony as interpreted by an expert is, in that sense, the most glaring and blatant hearsay. Though the defendants cite in their brief certain articles which they contend establish the scientific accuracy of polygraph tests, I am not prepared to rule that the jury system is as yet outmoded. I still prefer the collective judgment of twelve men and women who have set through many weeks of trial and heard all the evidence on the guilt or innocence of a defendant.

We wonder if Judge Kaufman troubled himself to actually read the "certain articles" cited in defendants' brief or he would have had less concern with the testimony of machines or the abolition of the jury system. Here is a perfect instance of a judge who dared not even take a look at what could be a marvelous aid to accurate verdicts, but chose instead to turn on the defensive and snarl at a scientific offering which he apparently regarded as dangerous to his own job security.

Just as modern society must shake its head at the Berkman decision, it will in the not too distant future be forced to cast the same derisive look at Stromberg. When judges, who must by definition be the most objective and open-minded persons, snuff out by outrageous fiat truths which are essential to the heart of the system they represent, they shirk responsibility.

Professor McCormick, in his *Handbook on the Law of Evidence,* (West Publishing Co., 1954, p. 174) spoke out with conspicuous indigence on the refusal of the courts to make an objective evaluation of polygraphy:

> One reason usually given for these general pronouncements is that the tests have not yet won sufficient acceptance of their validity . . . . If we thus deflate the requirement to the normal standard which simply demands that the theory or device be accepted by a substantial body of scientific opinion, there can be little doubt that the lie detector technique meets this requirement. . . . In the light of past findings, it is believed that the courts' wholesale exclusion of lie detector test results, for want of scientific acceptability and proved reliability, is not supported by the facts. . . . In most of the cases where the results were held inadmissible no such foundation was laid, and the decisions may be explained on the ground, since the scientific facts were not so indisputable and readily verifiable as to enable the court to take judicial notice of them. . . .

Just where it is that courts get their information that polygraph tests are not scientifically recognized is somewhat puzzling, for there is substantial evidence to the contrary which is consistently ignored.

In the first reported survey on deception testing and the law (McCormick, Deception Tests and the Law of Evidence, 15 Calif. L. Rev. 484 [1927]) it was noted that only seven of thirty-eight leading psychologists queried expressed lack of faith in the polygraph. A more recent and comprehensive survey (Cureton, A consensus as to the Validity of Polygraph procedures, 22 Tenn. L. Rev. 728 [1953]) also reports wide scientific acceptance.

Dr. LeMoyne Snyder, one of the most repsected men in polygraph-medicolegal circles today, approached the subject of test reliability back in 1943 (15 Rocky Mtn. L. Rev. 162, 164) as follows:

> The next question is apt to be, "Is the machine infallible?" That question is exactly like asking whether a clinical thermometer, stethoscope, x-ray machine or compound microscope is infallible. A trained scientist may be mistaken in what he sees or hears by any one of these

devices. Like the thermometer and stethoscope the polygraph is simply an instrument for noting or recording physiological processes and it is possible for the operator to be mistaken in his interpretation of the recording. Even in the best of clinics the interpretation is not 100 percent accurate, but that does not imply that the machine should not be used. The same can be said for the polygraph.

As polygraphy reaches towards the threshold of judicial recognition it is expected that many will issue the old hue and cry that our trial system is about to be replaced by a battery of polygraphs, that men will be governed by machines, and that legal integrity is about to be destroyed if the polygraph is to be given a whit of recognition. These contentions can be answered quietly and logically.

It seems rather impossible that the testimony of any polygraphist will ever usurp the responsibility of any jury. Contrarily, an examiner's opinion may well help them arrive at truth, which is their sworn duty. They are helped by experts of all kinds, some of whom (such as psychiatrists) appear frequently on both sides of a given case, completely contradicting one another. It is unlikely that this will ever come to pass where polygraphists are concerned, since competent experts in this field will, in almost all cases, come to consistent conclusions.

The suggestion that jurys will blindly follow polygraph test results is a totally unfounded fear. Jurys are all too capable of disregarding any evidence—just or unjust—to which they do not take a shine. In fact, any court will be hard-put to recall a single instance within recent years where a person who has cleared a police polygraph test has ever been prosecuted.

The polygraph instrument does not detect lies in the strict sense at all. If it "detects" anything at all it is the truth. Its application is basic and narrow. The instrument does not believe or disbelieve as a juror must do. Its findings are not swayed by subjectivity. It only distinguishes between the whole truth and something less than the whole truth, and there its function ends as a diagnostic aide. It cannot testify but it can be used to provide the basis for expert opinion.

Under our system of criminal justice, the courts appear not

to be so concerned with those guilty who might escape punishment as they are with those who might be wrongfully punished, and rightfully so. Many defendants have escaped conviction because the state could not satisfy its burden of proof, or because despite very incriminating circumstances there remained in the mind of the trier of fact a reasonable doubt. Therefore, if equivocal polygraph tests results are admissible against a defendant, even on stipulation, unequivocal test results in his favor ought not to be excluded under any circumstances.*

We have written extensively on the necessity for truth verification in all legal proceedings. If truth is established, we have justice and freedom in that order. In daily life we search for truth if it really concerns us. Every individual believes he is entitled to justice as long as it is to his advantage. To the average person, freedom falls under many interpretations, depending on age, social position, education, and the times. Philosophically, let's take a brief look at each.

Truth is justice in action, inclusive of all virtues, older than sects and schools and, like charity, more ancient than mankind. Every man seeks for truth, but only God knows who has found it. The triumphs of truth are the most glorious, chiefly because they are the most bloodless of all victories, deriving their lustre from the number of the "saved," not the slain. Truth is a thing immortal and perpetual, and it gives to us a beauty that folds not away in time, nor does it take away the freedom of speech which proceeds from justice; but it gives to us the knowledge of what is just and lawful, separating from them the unjust and refuting them. Truth should be the first lesson of the child and the last aspiration of manhood; for it has well been said that the inquiry of truth, which is the enjoying of it, is the sovereign good of human nature. Loyalty to truth requires no competition. Truth in itself is also freedom, with liberty the parent of truth.

Justice is, itself, the great standing policy of civil society, and

---

*Portions of this chapter have been based on the trial and appellate record of Commonwealth of Massachusetts v. Angelo Fatalo, specifically before the Massachusetts Supreme Judicial Court, Middlesex County, No. 12956, May Sitting, 1963.

any departure from it, under any circumstances, lies under the suspicion of being no policy at all. Whenever there is a separation between liberty and justice, neither is safe. Nothing is high because it is in a high place, and nothing is low because it is in a low one. The philosophy of reasoning, to be complete, ought to comprise the theory of bad as well as good reasoning.

What a price we have paid for freedom! We have lived for it, bled for it, died for it, and now it is time we reclaimed it. Depend upon freedom because its lovers will be free. All special characters of freedom must be abrogated where the universal law of freedom is to flourish. Abraham Lincoln said in his conclusion, Second Annual Message to Congress: "In giving freedom to the slaves we assure freedom to the free—honorable alike in what we give and what we preserve."

Conformity to rules, regulations and laws does not mean a subjugation of freedom. Instead, it means an acceptance of moral responsibility and a dedication to the preservation of our progressive way of life. For example, one does not buy his brain. He acquires a "brain" through conformity to educational, social, religious and legal rules of conduct which, in turn, give him the exciting incentive to develop new information, knowledge and science.

Laxity in acknowledging the scientific principle and demanding conformity creates a permissive void which leads only along the paths of destruction. Ourselves and our courts appear to be the led, not the leaders. We have the common and statutory laws on the books. We have the power. We have the right, but we have not exercised it fully. The first obligation of the courts is to lay down the rules of law early, clearly, and positively, and then see they are enforced in no uncertain terms on both sides of the coin. Permissiveness is pure folly bordering on senility.

Because of what we have been blessed with today, do we not owe a tremendous obligation to the security of tomorrow?

III

WHEN THE DEFENSE STANDS ALONE

At the request of her attorney, a wealthy woman, under suspicion of murdering her husband by poisoning, submitted to polygraphy.

Present at the time were her attorney and a newspaper reporter, who watched the actual examination in progress through a one-way mirror.

The polygraphist (synonymous with examiner) established psychological rapport, read aloud the questions he intended to ask, made certain she understood each question, thoroughly probed for any immediate physical or mental problems—pills or medication—if any alcohol was consumed prior to the test, history of any previous nervous breakdowns, and anything else which physiologically could interfere with post-test chart interpretations, then applied instrument attachments to her body.

A standard medical blood-pressure cuff was wrapped around her right arm. This would record, through her brachial artery, relative blood pressure, heart beat and heart rate. In the chart tracing itself would be a dicrotic notch, coming from regurgitation of the blood against the closed aortic valve before vessel constriction forced the blood upward and outward into systemic circulation. Just below her breasts, he placed a pneumograph tube which would permit production of a respiratory tracing. On the first and third fingers of her left hand he attached galvanometer units. These would record changes in electrical energies as they occurred while nerve impulses ran along the nerve pathways, in turn affecting changes in bodily temperature. On the middle finger of her left hand, he placed a photo-optic plethysmograph which would analyze the blood volume and viscosity as it hit her fingertip prior to returning to the heart through venules and veins.

The chair she sat in contained air-filled bladders capable of transmitting to a recording pen her slightest toe, foot, leg or muscle movement. Two microphones sat on the examiner's desk. One would record, on a lined chart moving at six inches per minute, the amount of time consumed by each question he asked. The other would record the exact moment of her answer.

His final pretest instructions were as follows:

"Mrs. X, you will be on this chart for some two to three minutes. During that time, your right arm will commence to feel like it is halfway going to sleep because of the pressure on it. Please try to ignore the mild discomfort. It's not going to hurt you. Try not to flex the right arm muscle.

"Now (pointing specifically) no wiggling or moving of the toes, feet or fingers. No pressure on the hands or arms. No tightening up of the leg muscles. Sit still; relax. Nothing can hurt you. There is a small spot on the wall in front of you. Look straight at it. Blink your eyes normally. Do not stare. If you prefer, close your eyes. Breathe normally.

"Answer the questions with a simple 'Yes' or 'No' only. If you do not understand or hear a question, remain silent. However, no talking during the test, except 'Yes' or 'No'. Listen to each question and let it be completed before you answer. Do you understand? Do you have any questions?"

She had none.

The instrument was activated. Individual sections were adjusted. The test was underway.

"Sit perfectly still. Do not move. The test is about to begin. Answer the questions 'Yes' or 'No' only."

Ten seconds elapsed. It should now be noted that a minimum of ten seconds is allowed between all questions.

Do you live in Oregon?"

"No."

"Is this the month of September?"

"Yes."

"Do you intend to answer the questions truthfully?"

"Yes."

"Do you actually know what caused your husband's death?"

"No."

"Are you sitting in a chair?"

"Yes."

'Did you deliberately cause your husband's death?"

"No."

"Do you ever drink water?"

"Yes."

"Did you ever administer any poison to your husband?"

"No."

"Are you wearing shoes?"

"Yes."

'Was the poison administered to your husband ever in your possession?"

"No."

"Are you wearing a watch?"

"Yes."

"Did you work in collusion or plan with anyone else to poison your husband?"

"No."

"Are you wearing glasses?"

"Yes."

"Have you deliberately withheld any information concerning this matter from your attorney?"

"No."

"Have you ever drunk coffee?"

"Yes."

"Did you poison your husband?"

"No."

"Do you live in Bakersfield?"

"Yes."

"Have you deliberately lied to any question I've asked you during this test?"

"No."

"Sit perfectly still. I will release pressure in the arm cuff in just one moment."

The instrument was deactivated. The examiner, speaking in a soft monotone said, "Just relax, Mrs. X. We'll let your arm rest a few moments and then I'll conduct another chart using the same and perhaps other questions of relevancy."

A second, and then a third chart was conducted.

The examiner got up from behind his desk. He severed the last chart from its roll and removed instrument attachments from the subject's body. "Would you please step out and be seated in the waiting room, Mrs. X. I'll be with you shortly."

He quickly wrote out his interpretations and findings, then signaled the attorney and newspaper reporter into the examining room.

"Well?" the attorney asked.

"In my opinion, and there is no question in my mind, Mrs. X is telling the truth. She did not poison or kill her husband."

The reporter made a dash for the door.

Headlines across the front page of the morning paper read:

Widow Exonerated By Lie Detector Test

About 10:00 A.M., the District Attorney called Mrs. X's attorney. The conversation went thus:

Defense: Good morning. How's everything this morning?

D. A.: What the hell are you trying to do with all this publicity?

Defense: Counteract publicity given by the police that Mrs. X left town so she couldn't be questioned.

D. A.: You could have let the police question her.

Defense: Would the police have announced to the press that they considered her innocent?

D. A.: They don't consider her innocent and neither does my office, no matter how many lie detector tests she takes.

Defense: Come, come. Don't refer to this as a lie detector test because there is no such thing to begin with. You should know that it is only a scientific form of interrogation supported by the physiological recordings of a polygraph instrument.

D. A.: All right, all right. Very clever. But I call your attention to the fact that the courts are frowning upon use of publicity of this sort.

Defense: Of what sort?

D. A.:   Showing the results of a lie detector test.

Defense: I didn't know anyone had ever used it to establish in-
            nocence. When it's been used, it's usually been used
            by the police to establish guilt. When they don't get
            a confession, they call the test inconclusive and let it
            go at that. So, I'm starting something new. When
            there has been publicity concerning a case, I think the
            proper move is for the suspect to submit to scientific
            polygraphy, and give the public the results.

D. A.:   The courts won't let you do it.

Defense: What court is going to stop me?

D. A.:   You'll see. You'll be cited for contempt of court in
            connection with this stunt of yours.

Defense: In other words, the courts are going to stop a person
            from proclaiming his innocence to the world?

D. A.:   In this manner, yes.

Defense: Why?

D. A.:   The courts won't allow you to use a polygraph test to
            show that a suspect is guilty.

Defense: All right. How about a confession? Will they permit
            the publication of a confession?

D. A.:   No more. After a defendant has been arrested, if he
            confesses, the police won't allow that confession to be
            publicized.

Defense: All right. Now let's take the opposite end of the pic-
            ture. Suppose the suspect declares he's innocent. Are
            the courts going to prevent him from stating to the
            public that he is innocent?

D. A.:   Certainly not.

Defense: That's the situation in this case. The court could
            have prevented the publication of a polygraph test
            showing guilt after a person had been arrested. In this
            case, the person hasn't been arrested. A person volun-
            tarily submits to polygraphy. We have thought too
            much about using this science to establish guilt and
            not enough about it to prove innocence. A person
            whose reputation has been smeared by an innuendo

or an outright accusation has a right to have that reputation cleared.

D. A.: You haven't heard the last of this, and I may say that at the proper time and at the proper place, I'm going to ask the court to take action.

Defense: What court?

D. A.: The court in which Mrs. X will be tried.

Defense: Is she going to be tried?

D. A.: We have some evidence which we are evaluating at the present time. I believe it is quite likely she will be tried, despite the very obvious grandstand, flamboyant publicity which you have injected into the case.

Defense: Do you intend to make a statement to that effect to the press?

D. A.: I have already given the press the position of my office in a dignified manner consistent with the administration of justice.

Defense: In other words, you've tried to counteract my publicity.

D. A.: Not at all. I have been asked to define the position of my office and I have defined it.

Defense: When we get to court, if we do, I'll take a look at that statement and see if I consider there's anything in it to unfairly influence the public.

D. A.: You'll be in a sweet position to do that after all that blast of publicity on behalf of the defendant in the paper.

Defense: A person is always presumed innocent until he's proven guilty.

D. A.: Thank you for giving me an opportunity to brush up on fundamental criminal law.

Defense: Not at all. Call me anytime when you want to know something.*

How much power does a prosecuting attorney hold in his hands?

*Gardner, Erle Stanley, *The Case Of The Careless Cupid.* New York, William Morrow & Co., Inc., 1968, pp. 147-148.

The realization almost staggers the imagination.

Just about any prosecuting attorney can go to a prisoner and say, "Let's look at it this way, Joe. If you want to plead guilty to this crime I'll not plead your prior convictions and you can get out within a few years. If you stand trial I'll plead your priors, you'll be convicted, and that will mean you'll go up as a habitual criminal."

How many men have plead guilty under those circumstances, men who had nothing to do with the crime for which they are serving time?

A case in point comes out of the State of Washington. Several years ago, a man pleaded guilty to the charge of forging a check. He received a lengthy prison sentence.

The forgery was not isolated. It was part of a string of forgeries carried on with a well-defined modus operandi. The forgeries continued after the supposed culprit had pleaded guilty, been sentenced and incarcerated in prison.

Eventually, the right man was apprehended. There could be no question that he was the one who perpetrated the string of forgeries.

The prison board sent for the man who had pleaded guilty and said, "What on earth ever possessed you to plead guilty to a charge of which you were so manifestly innocent?"

He twisted his face in a cynical grin. "Because I was smart," he said.

They asked him to explain.

"The D.A. came to me and said, 'I've got you dead to rights. If I put you on trial you're going to be convicted. If you stand trial, I'll plead your priors and you'll go up for life as an habitual criminal.' That way I never would have stood any chance of getting out. This way I stood a chance after five years of getting out on parole. What would you have done?"

While there is obvious apathy in this illustration, not all the responsibility rests on the shoulders of overburdened prosecutors.

Equal blame presents itself in the method of case investigation by underpaid, uneducated and incompetent police officers who literally make the D.A.'s case for his prosecution. These incom-

petents become so blinded by the presence of hearsay and circumstantial evidence that they cannot see the truth even though it
may be right under their noses. They are convinced so-and-so is
guilty and nothing will change their minds. All these incompe-
tents want is a "solved" or "closed" case on their proficiency
record. It does not bother them in the slightest when an innocent
person takes the rap, because they have no conscience concerning
such matters.

Needless to say, the person with a criminal record becomes
easy prey to be set up as a scapegoat, sometimes through sadistic
efforts of certain police officers to "rid society of a no good
sonofabitch."

Similarly revolting are the politically ambitious deputy prosecutors who, knowing their case is poorly prepared and lacking irrefutable evidence, deliberately eliminate, through challenge,
analyticaly-minded and responsible persons from serving on a
jury.

Next, they inflame the thoughts of these jurors with presenta-
tions of a bunch of legal boondoggery acceptable at law, but containing no fact. And so, the innocent stands a good chance of getting convicted.

Who is going to take the trouble to determine whether he was
improperly convicted?

Certainly not the governor.

Governors these days are busy state executives. Every minute
of their time is consumed. They can't be bothered trying to determine whether some penniless unfortunate confined in prison
was wrongfully convicted.

So, those matters are largely delegated to advisory boards.

In some states, the parole board automatically passes upon applications for pardon and makes a "recommendation" to the
governor.

Human nature being what it is, there is an unfortunate tendency on the part of many such boards to feel that a prisoner who
makes application for a pardon to the governor is trying to "go
over their heads."

But even where there isn't this tendency, boards of parole are overworked organizations. They don't have the time to reopen a case and listen to the evidence, and they don't have the inclination. They feel, perhaps with cause, that once they open the door to readjudicate the facts they would be swamped with applications.

It must be remembered that a man who is in prison serving a fixed sentence has everything to gain and nothing to lose. Let's take an average case, a man convicted by a jury after a five-day trial. The transcript of testimony consists of 654 pages. Are members of a parole board going to read that transcript?

Another obstacle presents itself.

Sometimes fortuitous circumstances intervene. Perhaps someone else confesses to the crime, a key witness against the defendant finds himself dying and confesses that he committed perjury to send so-and-so to the penitentiary. Such things do happen.

Then what?

In many cases the prosecutor will ignore the confession. To admit its validity would be to acknowledge that he had convicted the wrong man. He rationalizes his position by claiming that it "would undermine public confidence in the process of justice," and he really feels the confession is spurious.

Of course, not all prosecutors are that way.

But when one has a confession corroborated with a wealth of detail which can be verified, when the man who was convicted of the crime is shown to be innocent, there will still be prosecutors sincere in their beliefs that they convicted the right man and that the confession is spurious.

Astonishingly enough, when one becomes aware of a miscarriage of justice, and approaches an attorney who defended the wrong client, he will not readily accept what is told him. In fact, in most instances he will even take an active part in fighting the new claim of innocence.

There are two reasons for this. (1) The defense attorney generally possesses guilt feelings because he did not detect that his client was actually innocent, and because his defense failed to free an innocent man, so he interprets the error as an indictment of his ability as a trial lawyer. (2) Unfortunately, many lawyers take a "holier-than-thou" respect for the judicial process, and cannot accept the fact that the system could have made an error. Even the most zealous criminal defense attorneys take a peculiar turn in their thinking when confronted with the fact that a miscarriage of justice has occurred, particularly if it was one of their clients.

Also, in attempting to secure freedom of the innocently convicted, more hurdles are encountered. Invariably, the state's attorney who prosecuted the case, or the judge who heard it, cannot be convinced an error has been made.

It is a terrible thing to say, but in many instances they would rather see the accused stay in prison than to admit they made a mistake.

Then there is a widespread belief that a convicted defendant can appeal to a higher court. This is perhaps the most fallacious of all the numerous erroneous popular beliefs about law.

A convicted defendant can appeal to a higher court asking it to review "questions of law." However, with very few technical exceptions, there can be no review of a "question of fact." If there has been an erroneous finding of fact, the defendant has no remedy. He is forever bound by the finding of the trial judge or jury.*

How many innocent people are in prison? And, for our purpose herein, how many innocent people are serving time or facing the death penalty for first degree murder?

We can do no more than make a statistical guess.

According to the President's Commission on Law Enforcement and the Administration of Justice, there are approximately 600,000 persons in prison for felony crimes.

If we consider that a mistake could be made in one out of a thousand cases—one tenth of 1 percent—this would mean that there are 600 people now in prison for crimes they did not commit. If we take the margin of error to be as high as five percent, as many jurists contend, this would mean there are approximately 30,000 persons imprisoned for crimes they did not commit.

As a rule, those imprisoned for murder comprise 12 percent of

*Gardner, Erle Stanley, *The Court of Last Resort.* New York, William Sloane Associates, 1952, pp. 81, 85, 118, 121.

our prison population. At the one-error-in-a-thousand cases rate, this would mean seventy-two men are in prison today for murders they did not commit, and at the higher 5 percent level of error, 3600 men may be in prison for murders they did not commit.

We do not agree that 5 percent of our prison population is innocent. We do believe, however, that mistakes are being made in at least one out of a thousand cases; seventy-two men now serving time or facing death for murder they did not commit seems to be a realistic, highly possible figure.

In cases of wrongful conviction, several common reasons are always found in the background:

1. Extreme community pressure to "solve" the murder.
2. The investigator (who built the case, or who obtained the confession) is generally a "bull-headed," dogmatic individual, very ego-involved, who cannot accept the possibility of being wrong.
3. The confession lacked specific details and was not corroborated by physical evidence.
4. Several points in favor of the accused were never reconciled, and were "explained away" by frivolous reasoning.
5. There was always evidence pointing to the real murderer, but he was a very persuasive individual and a prolific liar who "conned" the police into believing he was innocent.

Many contend that the judicial system in this country is an adversary system, lacking objectivity. The defense and the state each identify with their own particular side, "body and soul." It is tragic to say that in many instances they only seem interested in the truth if the truth is on "their" side.

For this, and various other rather obvious reasons, the American Polygraph Association, following its 1968 annual convention, issued the following statement:

> Men and women who have been convicted of capital crime are being offered a new opportunity for freedom by the American Polygraph Association.
>
> The opportunity is to be made available through the Association's recently established Case Review Committee, and will be open to individuals in prison who believe they have been convicted through

perjury, erroneous testimony, or mistaken identity, and who are able to successfully "clear" a polygraph examination.

The Case Review Committee will make teams of three polygraph examiners available to those imprisoned who can satisfy the review committee that there is a possibility that they were convicted in error.

All claimants will be screened very carefully before the polygraph will be used, and all examinations will be limited to matters of fact only. Cases involving Constitutional or legal interpretations are matters for lawyers and the courts, and will not be considered by the Review Committee. Any person convicted of a captial charge who establishes to the satisfaction of the Committee that he or she may be wrongfully imprisoned is eligible for the review service.

Requests for investigations of specific cases may be submitted by members of the judiciary, bar association, prosecution, and defense attorneys, officials of correctional institutions and agencies, and citizens' crime commissions.

When a case has been screened and accepted, a three-man team of expert polygraph examiners from across the country will be assigned to the case. If the team agrees that the imprisoned man or woman is telling the truth in his denial of guilt, the Review Committee, through the Association, will seek the cooperation of the legal profession and public officials for a reconsideration of the case. The Association will also ask witnesses who testified at the trial to volunteer for polygraph tests as well, if the situation warrants. In many instances, the Committee anticipates that some "non-polygraph" investigation procedures will be required, including the assistance of attorneys, legal aid bureaus, public defenders, psychologists, psychiatrists and other forensic disciplines.

The Case Review Committee Members, as of 1970, are as follows: Charles Zimmerman, Chairman, 261 Melrose Street, Auburndale, Massachusetts 02166; Robert S. Eichelberger, Washington, D.C.; C. B. Hanscom, University of Minnesota, Minneapolis, Minn.; Victor Kaufman, New York City, New York; Forrest Paull, Incline Village, Nevada, and Leonard Bierman, Miami, Florida.

Requests for consideration for review should be addressed to the Chairman.

A collateral tragedy to those falsely imprisoned represents itself in the form of those persons falsely accused.

For example, as early as 1956 the people of Texas recognized that a person wrongfully accused of a crime deserved some kind of restitution—something more than a mere "sorry, we made a mistake."

So, Texans wrote into their Constitution a provision that the Legislature may grant "aid and compensation" to a person who has paid a fine or served a sentence for an offense of which he was not guilty.

In 1965, the Texas Legislature spelled out the conditions and the amount ($25,000 to $50,000) of such compensation. But the law passed by the Legislature did not foresee all the circumstances under which a person could suffer injustice and damage by being wrongfully "accused" of a crime. The statute left a big gap.

During the early part of 1966, Ervin Byrd of Ft. Worth, Texas, spent five months and nineteen days in the Tarrant County jail, charged with a crime he did not commit.

It is to be noted that he was not convicted and therefore was not serving a sentence, one of the specifications of the law. There was nothing for which he could be pardoned, which is another requirement of the law before suit can be brought for compensation.

Though he suffered an economic loss estimated at $6,000, Mr. Byrd did not seek restitution. All he wanted was to have the blemish removed from his name—to have erased from police and FBI files the record of a wrongful and undeserved felony arrest.

Why shouldn't he be entitled to redress of both kinds?

The law aims at monetary compensation for "pain and suffering" resulting from erroneous conviction or imprisonment.

Mr. Byrd was unjustly imprisoned, just as much so as if he had been wrongly convicted and sentenced.

Authorities now say that expunging the arrest from the record is possible, if the effort is made to have it done. But why should the falsely accused pay additionally to have this done? Why shouldn't someone in official capacity be held responsible to pursue the matter and see that at this extent, at least, a wrong is set right?

Also, in all such cases it should be made mandatory that the reason for dismissal be a part of the court's dismissal order and of the notation that goes out to record-keeping agencies of law enforcement.

As for the polygraph test, which was refused Mr. Byrd at the beginning of his ordeal, we believe that should be the right of every criminal suspect who wants it. Granting this right should not be overburdensome to law enforcement agencies, for it is unlikely that many of the guilty would want to run the risk of exposure.

Exonerating the innocent is as much an obligation of law officers as convicting the guilty, and is due as much attention, diligence and effort; so also should be preservation of the good name of the law-abiding who are caught up in such unfortunate circumstances.

Throughout this book proof will be presented in various forms to show that already there is general scientific recognition and to further establish that the polygraph possesses efficacy, and that reasonable certainty can follow from polygraph tests.

It can be argued that if evidence of a polygraph test is admissible into trial evidence, a defendant's failure to submit to a test might lead a jury to believe that he must be guilty, or why would he not take a polygraph test? There may be some truth to this argument. But isn't it equally true that if a defendant fails to take the witness stand and submit to cross-examination, a jury might believe that he must be guilty, or why would he not take the stand and face his accusers under oath?

Who would seriously argue that a defendant ought to be denied the right to testify in his own behalf or denied the right not to testify? Why, therefore, should the right to present corroborating evidence be denied?

The important thing to remember is that defense counsel often represents a man whose only evidence is his own testimony. The prosecution might have several witnesses against such a defendant, including an informer on the prosecutor's payroll. How does an innocent man who lives alone prove that he was at home asleep at 2:00 A.M., at the time that a burglary or robbery of which he is accused was committed?

How does a woman, shopping alone in a department store, prove that she was not shoplifting when the department store's private detective and store manager both accuse her of carrying away some merchandise?

How does a business man or any other individual, who has had a conversation with two people who falsely accuse him of making oral statements during the conversation, prove that he did not make the oral statements in question?

How does a defendant ex-convict take the witness stand and thus allow his criminal record to be brought out, unless he can present some corroborating evidence that this time he happened to be innocent of the charges?

There is one way—through polygraphy.

Is there an experienced lawyer who cannot add other examples to this brief sampling of the kinds of cases where a lawyer and his client stand alone?*

Average citizens, and particularly the poor, often feel caught in an unfair administration of justice with nowhere to go for help. The poor, like the rich, can go to court but rarely have the money, and courts too often favor landlords and merchants against complaining tenants and customers.

The causes of alienation and lawlessness include landlords who charge exorbitant rents, racial block-busting takes advantage of buyer and seller, unscrupulous merchants, and a system of law that too often lets them get away with it.

*Arther, Richard O.: *The Journal of Polygraph Studies,* Vol. III, No. 3, Nov.-Dec., 1968.

IV

AND THE TRUTH SHALL MAKE YOU FREE

Wʜᴏ ᴀɴᴅ ᴡʜᴀᴛ may be termed a "competent polygraph examiner?"

We might simply describe him as a rare breed, dedicated to the welfare of his country, confident of his ability, well trained and educated; he is an experienced interrogator with a profound knowledge of the psychology of human behavior, thoroughly versed in law and physiology, compassionate and understanding, fair and impartial, ethically oriented. He has been around. He has lived.

Yet, in a manner of speaking, he frequently finds himself between the devil and the deep blue sea. He doesn't have the motherly protection of the American Medical Association. He lives in a world of objectivity, oblivious to subjectivity. In his chart interpretations and final test opinions he must be right.

Until the American Polygraph Association formed its Case Review Committee, the convicted innocents had no greater champions than Erle Stanley Gardner; Harry Steeger of *Argosy Magazine;* the late Leonarde Keeler who was known as the father of modern polygraphy; Alex Gregory, polygraphist emeritus; Le-Moyne Snyder, doctor of medicine and attorney at law; Raymond Schindler, brilliant private detective; and Tom Smith and Bob Rhay, former warden and staff subordinate at the Washington State Penitentiary, who made up the original Court of Last Resort.

It seems only natural for Mr. Gardner to open these chapters with a brief of one memorable case into which he and other Court of Last Resort members once inquired.

The warden of a state penitentiary telephoned long distance to tell the Court of Last Resort, entirely off the record, that during the ensuing week he was going to have to execute a man who might well be innocent.

Members of that court went to that state. They found a prisoner who was all but hysterically ill with fear. He couldn't eat or sleep. His execution was four days away. The man was highly emotional. After the crime had been committed, he had made the mistake of resorting to flight because he thought he might be suspected of another matter. The newspapers had literally crucified him before the trial.

Despite the man's "nervous" condition, Alex Gregory was finally able to establish sufficient rapport to conduct a fair and impartial test. Results indicated the convicted was telling the truth.

The governor of that state said, "If you people are sufficiently interested in the administration of justice to donate your valuable time in the interests of penniless unfortunates, my office will give you every opportunity to determine the facts. I'll grant this man a ninety-day reprieve so you can go to work."

A year or so later, the governor of that state called Erle Stanley Gardner and said, "We have been investigating the facts you people uncovered and the conclusions you reached and our office is now not only satisfied of this man's innocence, but we think we know the identity of the real murderer. I just want you to know that tomorrow morning the man is being granted an unconditional pardon."

*   *   *

On August 1, 1963, two young fishery employees pulled into a service station at Port St. Joe, Florida, and stopped by one of the commercial pumps. Attendants Jessie Burkett and Grover Floyd, Jr. came out to meet them.

While the four were exchanging pleasantries, Negroes Freddie Pitts, 19, a private in the United States Army; Wilbert Lee, 28; Lee's wife, Ella Mae; Dorothy Martin, Lee's sister-in-law; and one or two others, drove alongside the service station and parked near an outside pay phone booth. It was the nearest telephone to Lee's home.

The purpose of the telephone call was to notify Lee's relatives that his cousin, Arthur Leavins, had been shot to death during an argument. Willie Mae Lee, not related to Wilbert Lee, was also at the station.

While Lee was making his telephone call, Dorothy Martin asked one of the station attendants for a key to the "white" ladies' rest room. She was refused. Visiting from up North, Dorothy Martin became incensed. A violent argument erupted between her and the service station attendants, overheard by the two young fishery employees.

But the argument was also heard by a man whom no one had seen sneak into and hide in the men's rest room.

Wilbert Lee and Freddie Pitts also got into the argument. Finally, Burkett and Floyd ordered the entire group off the service station property.

Just a few hours later, the bodies of Burkett and Floyd were discovered by two women some distance from the service station. Both had been shot in the head. The news quickly spread. Lynch fever blossomed.

Investigating police discovered the service station cash register had been emptied. The wallets of both Burkett and Floyd were also empty.

To police, it was a clear case of robbery, kidnapping, and murder.

When word of the attendants' deaths reached the two young fishery employees, they immediately went to police and told their story of overhearing the violent argument. They described the car and occupants as best they could.

At 5:00 A.M., August 2nd, Pitts and Lee were arrested, without warrant, at Lee's home and taken to Port St. Joe jail. Not only were they accused of the murders, but began undergoing a vicious form of interrogation.

At 10:00 P.M. that day, Pitts was bodily removed from the jail by sheriff's deputies and placed in the rear of their car. For several hours the deputies drove around Gulf County, interrupting their questioning from time to time to strike Pitts with a blackjack. The blows to his head, and kidneys, caused extreme pain and produced contusions and swellings which remained visible for weeks. As a result of the beatings, Pitts was unable to eat as his jaw was swollen and his teeth loosened.

August 3, 1963: The interrogation of Lee continued all day. At midnight, Lee was released, having given a statement that he was innocent.

In the early morning hours, Pitts was returned to his cell. After further hours of interrogation containing brutal "prayer sessions," he made some generalized inculpatory admissions. The interrogation, physical and verbal abuse continued in an apparent effort by deputies to elicit corroborative detail.

Army Criminal Investigation Division representatives sought and were denied permission by the police to see Pitts.

August 4th: Lee remained home all day.

The interrogation of Pitts continued as before. He was transported to various locations in a vain search to corroborate his initial statements. Again, CID investigators were refused permission to see him.

August 5th: Lee stayed in Port St. Joe.

The interrogation of Pitts continued. Again CID was rebuffed in their efforts to see him.

August 6th: Lee was arrested, without warrant, at noon. From 3:00 P.M. through midnight, without food or rest, Lee was interrogated and accused of the murders.

The interrogation, and "prayer sessions" with Pitts continued. And, again, CID was not permitted to see him.

August 7th: At 12:30 A.M., after only one-half hour break in the prior night's questioning, the interrogation of Lee was resumed.

Police falsely stated to Lee that a laboratory analysis of his clothing proved he was at the crime scene and that his footprints had been there as well. The interrogation lasted 13 hours, was interrupted momentarily, and was then resumed for five hours, held in abeyance 20 minutes, and finally concluded at 4:30 the following morning.

The interrogation of Pitts also continued with the same vicious intensity.

August 8th: The evening session of the interrogation of Lee

began with a big fist driven into his kidney. "You are going to talk tonight," an officer grated, before smashing another fist into Lee's mouth. It went on until after midnight.

The interrogation of Pitts got rougher. Finally, he confessed. A written version of his statement, the details of which were provided by the police, was typed and Pitts signed it.

Then Pitts was permitted to see Army CID. To them, he promptly and fully retracted his confession. After CID departed, Pitts requested counsel. This was refused.

August 9th: The interrogation of Lee continued from the previous night. His wife was brought in. Officers then told Lee his wife would be executed if he didn't confess.

Lee confessed. Even so, his wife was held in custody.

August 14th: For the first time, Pitts and Lee were taken before a magistrate and informed of their rights to counsel and to remain silent. Attorney W. Fred Turner was appointed by the court to represent the accused, since both were financially insolvent.

August 15th: Attorney Turner had a second conference with his clients. At this time, two police officers and the State's chief witness were present.

Lee listened in silence, as ordered, while the witness, Willie Mae Lee, accused him and Pitts of the murders. At the conclusion of this statement, Lee protested his innocence. The police, the witness, and counselor Turner frankly stated they felt Lee was lying.

Believing he had no other choice, isolated and friendless, Lee confessed and agreed to plead guilty.

Pitts was then brought into the conference room and told to listen to a recorded statement of the State's chief witness. He listened in silence, as ordered and, at the conclusion of the statement, he protested his innocence.

The police, the witness, and counsel, also told Pitts that they knew he was lying. Turner then told Pitts he could not represent him because Lee had changed his plea to guilty and there was a conflict between Pitts and Lee.

Turner did not advise Pitts that the court would appoint another lawyer to represent him in such a purported conflict with Lee.

Pitts, afraid he would not be represented, confessed and agreed to plead guilty.

On August 17, 1963, Pitts and Lee pleaded guilty to first degree murder in the Fourteenth Judicial Circuit Court in Wewaihitchka, Florida. The Court adjudicated the two men guilty as charged. A jury was impaneled to decide whether mercy should be given.

The jury decided against mercy.

August 28, 1963: Still represented by attorney W. Fred Turner, Pitts and Lee stood before Circuit Judge W. L. Fitzpatrick and heard him say: (He spoke to them separately)

"You, Freddie L. Pitts . . .

"You, Wilbert Lee, alias Slingshot Lee . . .

". . . having entered a plea of guilty to the offense of murder in the first degree the Court adjudges you to be guilty of murder in the first degree; and the Court having impaneled a jury for the purpose of determining whether or not you are entitled to mercy and the jury having returned its verdict finding that you are not so entitled and the Court having determined that you are not so entitled, it is the judgment of the Court and the sentence of the law that you (Freddie L. Pitts and Wilbert Lee, alias Slingshot Lee) be remanded to the custody of the Sheriff of Gulf County, Florida, and by him delivered forthwith to the Superintendent of the Florida State Prison at Raiford, Florida, to be by him safely kept until the Governor of the State of Florida shall issue his warrant commanding your execution and designating an execution date and that at the time so designated the person lawfully authorized to do so shall cause to pass through your body a current of electricity of such intensity to cause your immediate death and the application of such current shall be continued until you are dead.

"And may God have mercy on your soul."

After sentencing, Pitts and Lee were transferred to Death Row in Raiford Prison.

Counsel for the convicted appealed.

Then began a strange chain of events.

On December 15, 1966, Warren Holmes, Holmes Polygraph Service, Inc., Miami, Florida, was contacted by Cecil Steward of the Broward County Sheriff's Department and asked to conduct a polygraph examination on one Mary Jean Akins.

She was jointly charged in an indictment with Curtis Adams, Jr. in Broward County for the murder of Floyd Earl McFarland.

The test was conducted on December 16, 1966, in the office of the State Attorney, Quentin Long. Present in a nearby office were Leonard Fleet, attorney for Mary Akins, and Charles Rich, attorney for Curtis Adams, Jr.

Mary Akins was polygraphed with the consent of her attorney.

At the conclusion of her test, Holmes advised the attorneys that he considered Mary Akin completely truthful in telling him that she knew about the murder of McFarland but was not present when Adams said he did it.

Then Holmes staggered the sensibility of his listeners. He told them that Mary Akins also told of how Curtis Adams, Jr. killed two service station attendants in Port St. Joe, Florida, for which two Negro males were convicted. Holmes let these attorneys listen to Mary Akins' tape-recorded statement.

Attorney Rich decided, in the interests of justice, that a possible miscarriage had occurred with respect to the St. Joe killings, and suggested that Curtis Adams, Jr. be polygraphed.

That test was conducted on December 21, 1966. Adams made a full confession to Holmes, including the confirmation that he, alone, had killed McFarland, as well as Jessie Burkett and Grover Floyd, Jr., the two gas station attendants in Port St. Joe, Florida.

Adams said he had been hiding in the men's rest room and overheard the argument between the attendants, Dorothy Morris, and the Pitts-Lee group. After they were ordered off the service station property, Adams said he held up Burkett and Floyd, and then forced them at gun-point to get into his car. He made Burkett drive, and ordered Floyd to sit in the front seat. Out on a country road he shot both of them to death.

On December 22, 1966, Holmes polygraphed Wilbert Lee and Freddie Pitts at Raiford Prison.

At the conclusion of the tests, he advised Maurice Rosen, attorney for Pitts and Lee, that his clients were indeed innocent.

Next began a detailed search of the Pitts and Lee trial transcript, followed by numerous appeals.

Rosen called in other champions of justice: Edward Bennett Williams, Washington, D.C.; Phillip A. Hubbart, Assistant Public Defender, Miami; Tobias Simon and Alfred Feinberg, also of Miami; and Jack Greenberg, James A. Nasrit, III, and Michael Meltsner of New York City.

Immediately they discovered a shocking story.

At the original trial, the Pitts and Lee confessions were never corroborated by a single piece of physical evidence.

Laboratory analysis conducted by the Florida Sheriff's Bureau strongly indicated innocence rather than guilt. The murder weapon was never recovered.

During the trial, defense counsel Turner filed no motions whatsoever in behalf of Pitts and Lee. Turner conducted no investigation of any kind, aside from talking to the police and prosecutor.

Turner advised Pitts and Lee to plead guilty because he was personally convinced they were guilty. He had prepared no defense.

At the trial which was conducted for the purpose of determining whether mercy should be granted, Turner presented no mitigating circumstances. He called no witnesses, although Pitts had a clean army record.

On the contrary, Turner placed Pitts and Lee on the stand and required them to repeat their prior false confessions.

After the conviction and sentence, Turner took an appeal to the Florida Supreme Court. His attitude toward Pitts and Lee was stated on page 1 of the three-page brief he filed:

> At the outset of this appeal, appellate counsel wishes the Court to know he was *directed* by the Circuit Judge to institute and perfect this appeal. The undersigned could find no evidence that the Defendants had been mistreated in any way at any stage of these proceedings. Their pleas were freely and voluntarily entered. The jury heard their testimony concerning the events of that fateful night in Gulf County where two men lost their lives.

Turner's appellate brief was only three pages long and cited no legal authority of any kind. The argument section of the brief contained four sentences.

On May 29, 1964, the Supreme Court of Florida affirmed the Pitts-Lee convictions.

March 1, 1965: The Supreme Court of the United States denied certiorari.

October 7, 1965: Pitt-Lee's defense team filed a Rule I proceeding petition with the Circuit Court. On October 19, 1965, Judge W. L. Fitzpatrick summarily denied the Rule I petition without granting a full evidentiary hearing.

July 21, 1966: The District Court of Appeals of Florida affirmed.

March 27, 1967: The Supreme Court of the United States denied certiorari.

Between July 1, 1966 and March 27, 1967, Pitts-Lee's defense team uncovered more startling facts.

On January 3, 1966, Broward County Deputy Sheriff Edward Clode received a message from Jesse Pait, a prison inmate at Raiford Penitentiary, that Pait wanted to see Clode. Deputy Clode responded and talked to Pait in prison.

Pait told Clode that Curtis Adams, Jr. had confessed to him that he had committed the Floyd-Burkett murders in Port St. Joe.

At the trial, Willie Mae Lee, after being subject to police coercion and intimidation, testified that she was with Pitts and Lee when they murdered Floyd and Burkett. However, no independent evidence verified her testimony.

In January 1967, Warren Holmes interviewed Willie Mae Lee at her home in Port St. Joe. "I lied," she cried. "I was afraid of the police. I've been waiting to tell the truth about this for over three years."

May 22nd, 1967: Pitts-Lee filed a petition for a writ of habeas corpus in the United States District Court for the Middle District of Florida.

July 27, 1967: Judge McRae of the United States Middle District Court transferred the case to the United States District Court for the Northern District of Florida.

September 11, 1967: Judge G. Harrold Carswell denied the petition for habeas corpus with leave to apply to the Florida State Courts for relief.

November 20, 1967: The Florida Supreme Court entered an order denying the petitioner's petition for habeas corpus without prejudice to apply for relief.

December 8, 1967: Counselor Phillip A. Hubbart, filed a Rule I Hearing brief on Motion To Vacate Judgment And Sentences of Freddie Pitts and Wilbert Lee, in the Circuit Court of the 14th Judicial Circuit in and for Gulf County, Florida, No. 519, 520.

Again it was denied.

They went back to the U.S. District and Florida Supreme Court and were told they had not exhausted all their remedies in the state courts.

Frustrating, to say the least, particularly with irrefutable proof of Pitts and Lee's innocence.

Now, Maurice Rosen took over. There was no place for him to go except back into the lion's den.

Rosen commenced a Rule I Proceeding in Gulf County on September 23, 1968. His petition was based on the fact that Pitts and Lee were innocent and their confessions had been beaten from them. He also argued that Pitts and Lee's defense lawyer, Turner, at the time of his representation, was incompetent.

The hearing lasted one week, becoming an incredible procedure which literally rocked the state of Florida. The judge did not immediately rule but decided he would wait for the transcript to be typed up and hold additional hearings for final arguments.

As of January 9, 1969, the transcript was completed. Concluding arguments were scheduled in February.

Rosen and his associates were hoping to win.

Pitts and Lee were praying to be set free.

Finally, on Tuesday, April 29, 1969, Circuit Judge Charles R. Holley set aside the convictions. For two men who for five years, eight months and one day had been condemned to die, Judge Holly voided the verdict of death. Legally, he made them innocent men.

In Judge Holly's ruling he said: "This court finds for Pitts and Lee on the issues of incompetent counsel and coerced confessions . . . "

They were removed from death row. They thought they were set free.

They were not. Decadence of precedent compounded into precedent stepped in, having little or no relevancy to the issue at bar.

Strangely, in the face of irrefutable evidence following Judge Holly's Rule 1 proceeding, the State Attorney from Gulf County appealed that ruling. The appeal was to be held before the Florida District Court on April 15, 1970. If Judge Charles R. Holly's ruling is upheld, Pitts and Lee will then get a new trial. If the District Court overturns Judge Holley's ruling, the counsel of Pitts and Lee will appeal to the Supreme Court or go directly to the Federal Courts.

Again!

Counsel for Pitts and Lee knew, or at least felt, justice would not be denied. Under case L-462, in the District Court of Appeal of Florida, First District, the brief of Appellees was entered:

> This is an appeal taken by the State of Florida from a judgment of the Circuit Court of the Fourteenth Judicial Circuit of Florida, Honorable Charles R. Holley sitting by designation, which judgment granted motions filed pursuant to the former Criminal Procedure Rule No. One and set aside judgments of guilt and death sentences imposed upon your appellees. In this brief, appellent will be referred to as "the State," appellees as "the defendants," or by their proper names. Citations to the record on appeal will be designated by reference to a "File No." and the page within that file, and the Appendix will be designated by the symbol "App."

We have already seen some of the facts of this case. Now we review this appeal's final conclusion by counsel for Pitts and Lee:

> The enormity of the injustice done to the defendants in this case is almost beyond belief. That such an event could happen in this country in this day and age is a reminder to all of us that injustice of enormous magnitude is still very much among us. No evasions, rationalizations or highly skilled legal arguments can quite obscure this simple truth. And it is to the courts of this country that the oppressed must turn for protection against injustice.

Mr. Justice Black in Chambers v. Florida, 309 U.S. 227, 241 (1940), put it most eloquently when he said:

> Under our constitutional system courts stand against any winds that blow as havens of refuge for those who might otherwise suffer because they are helpless, weak, outnumbered, or because they are non-conforming victims of prejudice and public excitement. Due process of law, preserved for all by our constitution, commands that no practice as that disclosed by this record shall send any accused to his death. No higher duty, no more solemn responsibility rests upon this court, than that of translating into living law and maintaining this constitutional shield deliberately planned and inscribed for the benefit of every human being subject to our constitution—of whatever race, creed or persuasion.

Judge Holley could not but be impressed and moved by the testimony and evidence which he heard in this case. In the name of Jusitce he set aside the convictions and sentences in this case. In this judgment, we believe he should be affirmed.*

Respectfully submitted,

BY: Phillip A. Hubbart
Irwin J. Block
Barry N. Semet
Maurice Rosen

Irrespective of the outcome, the Pitts-Lee case will create legal hassles for years to come as an outstanding example of pettifoggery in our courts today.

In this particular case it was not a question of Pitts' or Lee's innocence, but rather a challenge of the system of North Florida which apparently could not or would not admit to the state that they had sentenced two innocent Negroes to death.

---

*Case No. L-462, in The District Court of Appeal of Florida, First District. Citations: U.S. Constitution, Sixth Amend, Eighth Amend., Fourteenth Amend.; Florida Constitution, Art., I Sec. 16; 18 Am. Jur. 2d, Sec. 471; Canons of Prof. Ethics, Canon 5. 13 Fla. Jur. Evidence, Sec. 68, Sec. 418. Rule 1.850, Fla. Rules of Criminal Procedure. 355 U.S. 28, 2 L.Ed.2d 9 (1957); 386 S.S. 738 (1967); 331 F. 2d 842 (4th Cir. 1964); 344 F.2d 315 (2nd Cir. 1965); 89 S.Ct. 1709 (1969); 373 U.S. 83, 10 L.Ed2d 215 (1963); 393 F.2d 886 (5th Cir. 1968); 309 F.S. 227 (1940).

Nevertheless, it is a great victory for polygraphy, and Warren Holmes.

* * *

On February 23, 1959, Mary Meslener put her reddish blonde hair in a pony-tail and worked eight hours as a telephone reservation clerk at National Airlines near Miami International Airport. She had been working there just two weeks. At 7:36 P.M. that date she punched her time card and supposedly headed toward North Miami High Schol for a class in creative writing. She never made it.*

About 8:00 A.M. Wednesday, February 25, a warm and cloudy morning, Hugh Zeigler and his wife parked their jeep along the brushy edge of N.W. South Drive to go fishing.

As Zeigler let his dog loose, he saw a pair of legs sticking out from the underbrush. He called to his wife, "Oh, my God! There lays a woman's body!"

Police arrived at the scene within thirty minutes. They started gathering up evidence and irresponsibly placed it on the hood of a car. When the Dade homicide Criminal Bureau of Investigation arrived, they tried to put the stuff back where it was found for crime lab photography.

Next, wrong identification of the body was made, and it wasn't until 10:05 P.M. that night that Mary Meslener's husband, Frank Meslener, positively identified the body as that of his wife.

She had been shot once above the right temple on the right side. The projectile traversed down, coming out under the left eye.

Medical examiner, Dr. Ray Justi, expertly came to two firm conclusions: the canal bank couldn't have been the exact murder scene. Not enough blood was there. Secondly, from the condition of the body he calculated the time of death at twenty to forty hours earlier. There was no evidence of sexual assault.

Frank Meslener said his wife always wore sun glasses while driving. The glasses were missing. So were her pocketbook, bill-

---

*Dade County, Fla. Circuit Court #1951; State v. Joseph Franics Shea. (No appeal was involved). Miller, Gene: *The Miami Herald*, April 30, 1969.

fold and, oddly, her shoes. Most important, her car, a blue two-tone 1958 Nash Rambler, also was missing.

On Thursday, the 26th, an airman had found Mary Meslener's plastic billfold in his locker at a barracks a few miles from where her body was found. Homicide detectives questioned scores of airmen, to no avail. The police assumption, purely speculative, was that maybe the killer threw it away, somebody picked it up and put it in the locker.

An intensive search for the car began. A break came on April 3, 1959. Police in Tampa found the missing Nash Rambler parked in a warehouse district lot. It had been there some three weeks. Nine inches from the accelerator lay a mutilated .38 slug on the floor mat. Bone fragments and tissue still clung to the bullet.

An ID man went over the car and discovered one good latent palmprint on the horn ring button. It did not match that of the victim or her husband.

The investigation remained stymied until May 7, 1959. On that day, an eccentric airman third class at the West Palm Beach Air Force Base gave his sergeant a bloodied shirt and said he thought he had done something terrible. He couldn't remember what.

This was Joseph Francis Shea, AF 11313858, age 20, a loner with few close friends in the service.

The Air Force brought the bloodied shirt to the attention of the county solicitor of Palm Beach County. A routine query went to Dade. There, the homicide bureau decided to look into it.

In the meantime, the Air Force had shipped Shea to Elgin Air Force Base for hospitalization and psychiatric examination. So, a homicide sergeant, an assistant state attorney, and a fingerprint lab technician arrived at Elgin on Saturday, May 16. After talking with two OSI investigators, Shea was interrogated at length.

Subterfuge is an oft-used practice in some police interrogations. Some courts uphold such police methods in the belief that deceit is permissible in arriving at truth.*

---

*Miller, Gene: *The Miami Herald,* Is an Innocent Man in Prison, Section 4-F, June 13, 1965.

The police told Shea his fingerprints were in the victim's car, which was not true. They also told Shea that a witness placed him close to the car in Miami the night of the murder. They also told Shea the blood on his shirt was that of the victim's.

"Well, Shea?" the sergeant questioning him asked.

Hysterically, Shea confessed. "I did it."

"How did you do it?"

"I shot her."

"Why did you shoot her?"

"I was scared."

"Why were you afraid, Joe?"

"She was screaming and hollering and I thought I was going to be picked up by police."

The interrogation ended two hours later after Shea had regurgitated in a rest room.

In the first of five confessions, Shea graphically and vividly told of the murder:

"She was just about to get into the car. . . .I went over to her . . . .I hit her. . . .She woke up and started screaming. . . .I think she yelled rape a couple of times. . . .I put my hand over her mouth. She bit my finger. . . .All I heard was the gun go off. . . .I was frantic. . . ."

While incarcerated, awaiting trial, Shea confessed his guilt to a jailer, a priest and a police plant. He confessed to his parents and a psychiatrist.

He even confessed to court bailiffs while a twelve-man jury deliberated.

The prosecution had subpoenaed twenty-eight persons for the trial. Defense Attorney Mike Zarowny dramatically rested the defense without calling a single witness for his side. Thus, he had both opening and closing arguments.

When the jury recommended mercy with the verdict to Circuit Judge Ray Pearson, Zarowny felt "as if we'd won, almost. He didn't get the chair."

Shea's parents were grateful. There was no appeal. He was sentenced to life.

But, there were a lot of loose ends. The jury never heard a word from the possible never-called defense witness.

Nothing was said about a polygraph test given Shea by expert
Warren Holmes, then Chief Examiner for the Miami Police Poly-
graph Section. At that time Holmes told Dade homicide officers
Shea was innocent before the trial.

Detective Philip Thibedeau, in charge of the case, was never
satisfied with the pretrial investigation. His openly spoken remarks were shunted aside by his supervisors. He voluntarily re-
signed as a lieutenant in 1962. He was never even called to testify
at the trial.

Finally, Thibedeau went to the *Miami Herald* newspaper and
told his story. They listened intently, then commenced their own
investigation.

In June of 1965, from Apalachee Correctional Institution,
Shea wrote the newspaper:

"I was pretty desperate. I had a lot of faith in the polygraph
test and I told the sergeant (not the polygraph examiner, Holmes)
that I would give a confession if the lie detector said I was guilty
. . . . He told me (again meaning the sergeant) there was enough
on that test to send me to the chair. I agreed."

Thus Shea confessed, formally.

Now, six years later, he had no idea the polygraph test indicated innocence, not guilt.

Shea later said the blood-stained shirt was his own. He wanted
to show his sergeant something "physical" in his act to play crazy
to get out of the Air Force.

Initially, the prosecution wondered about the blood on Shea's
shirt, and asked Dr. A. S. Weiner of Brooklyn, New York, to test
the shirt. He did on October 2, 1959. He summarized his findings
in a letter:

"My tests indicate that the dried stains on the shirt submitted
are all human blood. . . .The grouping tests gave inconclusive results. . . .Since the reactions were indefinite, however, I would not
be willing to testify in a courtroom as to my opinion regarding
the group of these blood stains."

He was not asked to testify. He never appeared at the trial.

At the trial a psychiatrist testified that Shea had kept the shirt
as a "symbol of guilt."

For a killer calculating enough to successfully dispose of the murder weapon and the victim's possessions, it seemed logical that he would have simply gotten rid of the shirt the same way.

The prosecution didn't think so.

Warren Holmes later said, "It was obvious to me during my interview with Shea that he had been coerced into making his confession. The Dade County men decided to take Shea to their own polygraph man, John T. Bevan, who also tested him and declared him to be innocent. They suppressed his report."

With the help of Pulitzer prize winner Gene Miller of *The Miami Herald,* Holmes was able to convince the state attorney to reopen the case.

While Shea was in the state penitentiary at Raiford, Holmes polygraphed him several times. Each test indicated he was not involved in, or had knowledge of, the death of Mary Meslener.

On February 19, 1966, Shea, the malingering airman trying to get out of the service, was found innocent in a new trial, freed, and subsequently awarded $45,000 by the State of Florida for having been falsely imprisoned.

* * *

During December of 1959, spinster Ethel Little was murdered in Miami, Florida. The case went unsolved for three years.

Then the Miami Police Department received word from an inmate of the State Penitentiary, Monroe Spencer, that he knew something about the murder, and who did it.

He named Mary Katherin Hampton, his "child-woman," who accompanied him on a transcontinental crime spree in the late 1950's.

Spencer carefully detailed a spectacular but unsolved murder that had occurred on the outskirts of New Orleans during the New Year's holiday of 1959-60. A man and woman had been shot in separate locations, but within a few miles of each other, in circumstances that indicated the two cases were linked. The murders caused a sensational flurry of public notice through the South.

So clever was Spencer's story that Mary Kay, who had even born Spencer's son out of wedlock, confessed and was sentenced to double life in St. Gabriel Prison.

On a humid September afternoon, 1962, Warren Holmes emerged from a consultation room at the prison. He had just completed a two-hour interrogation of the young woman, concluding with a polygraph test.

He had a disturbing announcement for two Louisiana lawmen waiting in an adjoining office. Holmes told them:

"You have an innocent girl in prison."

The two officials nodded sadly. Although they were inclined to agree with Holmes, there was nothing they could do about it.

But Holmes felt a lot could be done about the plight of Mary Kay. He had already devoted much of his time and money to prove what he was certain was the truth at the conclusion of that interview at St. Gabriel Prison.

In his possession was documented evidence, in the form of a traffic ticket and record of cash bond posted in lieu of bail—both still on file in Florida—which showed that both Spencer and Mary Kay were four hundred miles from New Orleans area when the dual New Year's slayings took place.

These he had put in the capable hands of F. Lee Bailey of Boston, and his colleague, Attorney James Russ of Orlando.

Bailey meteorically rose to national prominence and criminal law stardom for his acquittal for Dr. Sam Sheppard in Cleveland. It was he who played a key role in the solution of the infamous Boston Strangler murder mystery, as well as the sensational Plymouth Mail Robbery in New England.

Through dogged investigation, Holmes also knew that Spencer, on Death Row at Raiford prison because of Mary Kay's testimony against him in 1960 for a Key West murder, hated her for that with a malevolence that knew no limits. Through the years, Spencer had fought by every means he could contrive to stave off execution. Most sensational of all his devices was a marathon series of "confessions" to some thirty-eight murders around the country. Virtually all of these turned out to be pure fabrications.

Without fee, Bailey went to work for Mary Kay. He was not alone. Among those working closely with him, in addition to Holmes and Russ, were Salvador Anzelmo of New Orleans and many others in the fields of law and related activities.

One of the two men at St. Gabriel to whom Holmes disclosed his certainty of Mary Kay's innocence that day in 1962 was Clyde Griffin, warden of the prison. The other was Captain John R. Thomas, head of the Louisiana State Police.

It was the latter's testimony at a subsequent court hearing that clinched freedom for the "child-woman from the hill country."

Bailey and his colleagues filed petition in U.S. District Court that Mary Kay be released on a Federal writ of habeas corpus while they could prepare their next move in her behalf.

The Federal Court ruled that the requested hearing must be held, but, in accordance with Louisiana law, it must be conducted first in a State court before the U.S. bench could take jurisdiction.

Bailey and Anzelmo accepted this compromise. The hearing was held in late October in the parish (county) court at Plaquemine, not far from Baton Rouge.

In questioning, Bailey drew forth testimony—never previously presented in an open court—that at no time had the slightest shred of physical evidence, other than the wild tale told by Spencer been brought to light in the investigation, that linked either Mary Kay or Spencer to the mysterious New Year's murders in New Orleans.

The ticket and bail bond evidence was admitted.

As an outgrowth of all this at Plaquemine, the state authorities unexpectedly offered Bailey another compromise. The prosecuting attorney presented it in a simple four-worded question: "Will you accept commutation?"

That meant state authorities were ready to toss in the towel, making Mary Kay eligible for release at long last on November 30, 1966.

Bailey, realizing that refusal of the offer undoubtedly would drag the matter on and on through still more court actions, accepted. At least, it meant immediate freedom for the frightened young woman.

Mary Kay agreed. Arrangements went forward for her release.

News of his one-time girl friend's impending freedom reached Spencer via prison grapevine on Florida's Death Row. So he played his final card of revenge.

Spencer sent word from his cell that he had a startling disclosure to make concerning Mary Kay. In this one, he accused her of killing a woman on April 11, 1960, during what Spencer described as a wild booze-and-sex orgy near Vero Beach, Florida.

The victim in this murder was Virginia Tomlinson, about 50, whose body had been found some weeks after death in a thicket near a woodland road.

Mary Kay's version of the Tomlinson crimes was entirely different. She told Holmes that Spencer had killed the Tomlinson woman with a knife, after he and a companion had raped her in the woods.

A polygraph test by Holmes verified Mary Kay's story as true.

But Spencer pressed a very convincing story to the extent that prison officials agreed to let him testify before a grand jury in Brevard County, Florida. The jurors heard Spencer's testimony in which he characterized Mary Kay as a "homicidal lesbian" and a "torture killer." As a result, the grand jury indicted Mary Kay for the Tomlinson murder. A warrant was issued for her arrest the moment she was to be released from St. Gabriel Prison.

However, Spencer again failed to reckon with the astuteness of Mary Kay's defense team. Attorney Russ went over the indictment meticulously and found a serious "legal mistake" in wording. He hurried to Titusville where the grand jury was sitting. His discovery technically voided the indictment. He asked the grand jury to reexamine the Tomlinson case and listen to testimony from eighteen top expert witnesses.

Fifteen minutes after listening to the sixth witness for Mary Kay, the grand jury squashed the first indictment and returned a no-true-bill in its place.

Ten days later, thin and drawn, wearing a twenty-dollar mail order suit, Mary Kay's six-year ordeal ended. She bade farewell to Warden Griffin, who believed in her innocence, then returned to her home in Sandy Hook, Kentucky. Christmas was only a few days away.*

---

*For further reference see Lowall, Gene: How Lee Bailey Freed the "Hillbilly" Lolita, *Argosy Magazine,* March 1967, p. 58.

For Warren Holmes, and his polygraph, the outcome of the Mary Kay affair was a gratifying triumph.

* * *

William Chain was convicted of armed robbery in a routine trial in Maryland's Upper Marlboro Circuit Court, on August 15, 1968, but he continued to protest his innocence with such vigor that the State authorized a polygraph test.

On Wednesday, October 30, 1968, Chain was freed.

Chain spent more than four months in jail before and after his trial, which was for the $1000 holdup of the State Loan Company in July of 1967.

"If you didn't do it (the robbery), Judge Ernest A. Loveless, Jr. told Chain the day of his release, "you were the victim of circumstances. If you did it, you're a lucky man. In any event, I hope the ends of justice have been served."

Chain was arrested by Prince George's County police in April as he completed a six-month jail term in Washington on narcotics charges. He was indicted and spent two months in jail until his bail was reduced from $5000 to $1000.

Chain's court-appointed attorney, John Connally, arranged on two separate occasions in August for polygraph tests to be administered. But Chain never appeared, claiming he had no way to get to Waldorf, Maryland where the tests were to be conducted.

Against the advice of Connelly, Chain requested a non-jury trial and was convicted on the basis of identification by a clerk at the loan company. Because of his failure to appear for the polygraph tests, Chain was sent to jail to await sentencing.

Apparently jarred by the prospect of what would probably be a long prison term, Chain wrote to Judge Loveless insisting he was innocent and requested that he be given another chance for the polygraph test.

The State's Attorney and Maryland State Police administered the test and submitted Chain to a battery of questions that, according to police, "only the perpetrator of the crime would be able to answer." The results were examined by the State and sent to an independent consultant in New York.

Chain had cleared his test. Results indicated that he could not have committed the holdup.

Connelly asked for and won a new trial. But the State had already agreed not to continue prosecution. The case, in effect, was dropped.

* * *

Right after World War II, in Chicago, about 4:00 P.M. one Friday, Negro Raymond Spotter (name fictitious) age 23, was delivering groceries house to house for his employer in one of the swanky residential sections of the city.

He was a little late on his schedule, so his foot bore heavy on the old panel truck's gas pedal.

Rolling into the triple driveway of a fashionable two-story mansion, where he had made deliveries regularly for two years, he drove in behind the house, turned around and parked by the back door.

If he did see the stripped-down roadster parked out on the street by the curb, he paid it no attention. There were many such roadsters in the area, operated by teenagers of wealthy parents.

Spotter opened the back door—he never had to knock or call out—and stepped into the kitchen. As he put three sacks of groceries on the kitchen table he kept thinking his boss would be angry because he was so far behind with his deliveries.

He left the bill on the table and bounced out the back door, hopped into his truck and pressed on the accelerator.

As the old panel truck shot out of the driveway, he recognized Mr. and Mrs. Harry Angerman (name fictitious) easing their big black Chrysler into the driveway. Ordinarily, he would have waved but he was too preoccupied.

Hitting the street, his foot mashed harder on the accelerator. As he drove off, he thought he heard something like a scream but figured it came from the old truck's worn-out generator brushes. He gave it no further thought.

Spotter had just completed his last delivery and was headed back to the grocery store when four police cars boxed him in at a stop light.

He had been careful. Were they after him?

Eight police officers with drawn guns surrounded the panel truck. A gun barrel was shoved under Spotter's nose. "Get your black ass out of there or I'll blow your goddamed head off!" yelled an officer.

Confused and frightened, Spotter opened the door, raised his hands, and started to get out. That's as far as he got on his own.

Two other officers grabbed him. A blackjack cracked across the top of his head. Blood cascaded down his forehead and the back of his neck. He fell to the ground. His eyes lost their ability to focus.

Vaguely, he felt his arms twisted behind his back, then the cold, tight pinch of handcuffs. A boot thudded into his side. The pain was excrutiating. "What have I done?" were his last thoughts, before he passed out.

Spotter regained consciousness in a cold, dark, solitary room. His body pulsated with pain. He shook with fear. He could only guess where he was.

They came for him in the afternoon. Again he was handcuffed, then taken into a darkened room and thrown into a hard wooden chair. An intensely bright light shot into his eyes. He closed them and dropped his head. A hand out of the darkness grabbed a handful of his hair and snapped his head back.

A voice growled, "Hold that head up, bastard. Open your eyes, and keep them open."

Spotter had no choice.

A fist slammed into his belly. He wanted to wretch, but there was nothing in his stomach.

"Easy," a voice said. "Let's not mark him up too much. We want him to talk."

"Oh, he'll talk," another voice said. "I promise you that."

"Okay, Spotter, let's have the truth. Why did you rape that Angerman girl?"

"Honest, Mistah," Spotter stammered, "I didn' rape no girl."

A fist smashed into his mouth. He felt the pain, and tasted blood.

"Lord no, Mistah," he cried, "I don' even know what you talkin' about. I don' never hurt nobody."

A rubber hose struck his rib cage. Spotter screamed.

"The girl says you raped her, Spotter," the voice from the dark boomed out. "The mother and the father say you raped her. The medical examiner says you raped her."

Spotter shook his head.

Another blow against the back of his neck, rendered Spotter unconscious.

For two days the brutal questioning and physical "persuasion" went on. Spotter was given two meals of bread and water.

After several hours of the same treatment on the third day, Spotter knew he could take no more. The pain in his kidneys was so severe he could no longer control his urine.

Although Spotter never finished the third grade in school, his instinct for self-preservation won out.

"Leave me be," he whispered through puffed lips. "Okay, I did it. I'll say anything y'all want. Please don' beat me no more."

"That's more like it," a voice sounded off exuberantly. "I told you the lousy bastard would break."

They took Spotter back to his cell. He cried and he prayed the best way he'd been taught. "God knows, Lord, I ain't hurt nobody."

He was fed some kind of greasy soup. They even gave him cold tea. The next morning a dim light imbedded behind a mesh screen in his cell went on. He felt unclean, having wallowed in his own waste.

They came for him again.

"Now, Spotter," the voice grated, "You're going to tell us the whole truth and nothing but the truth—you hear me?"

Spotter had made up his mind. He wanted to live. He nodded.

"Now, you motherfuckin' bastard, you did rape that little Angerman girl, didn't you?"

"Yessuh," Spotter whispered. "I done took advantage of her."

"You what! You sonofabitch, I'll cut your balls out! Now you tell the truth. You caught her alone and raped her. Ain't that right?"

"Yassuh. I reckon I raped her."

"We're gonna fix up a little confession for you to sign. Can you write?"

Spotter nodded his head. "I can write my name."

And so, Spotter crudely affixed his name to the prepared confession. His last reminder, before they took him back to his cell, was, "Nigger, when you go to court you better remember that it sure can get worse if you change your story."

He was transferred to regular cells and given a bath. Bail was denied.

One day, a well-dressed man came to his cell. "Spotter," he said, "I'm your court-appointed attorney. May we talk?"

Spotter sat erect. "Yassuh," he smiled. This was the first friendly voice he'd heard in a long tme. "Could you please help me?"

"Look, Spotter," the attorney said quite frankly, "I'm a busy man. I know I've been appointed by the court to represent you. That I shall do. But, I think you're guilty as hell."

Spotter slumped back on his bunk. Well, he surmised, a nigger shouldn't expect anything different.

"Actually," the attorney said, "in view of your signed and properly witnessed statement, your case appears hopeless. I think the most I can do is appeal for leniency, throw you on the mercy of the court. At least, it might save you from the death sentence."

Spotter recoiled inside himself. "Man, I don' wanna die."

"That I can understand. But, the State's case is too strong."

"They beat me an'made me sign," Spotter pleaded.

"Maybe so, but you signed. It'll be your word against theirs. All that little girl has to do is point a finger at you before a jury and you're a cooked goose."

"Please help me, Mistah lawyer."

"Seems the best thing for us to do is appear before the judge and plead guilty. I know him pretty well. Maybe I can convince him to go for a light sentence. "Otherwise . . . ."

Tears streamed down Spotter's face. "You d'lawyer. I don' wanna die."

A few weeks later, newspaper headlines blared:

RAPIST PLEADS GUILTY—GIVEN 20 YEARS

Spotter was taken to county jail pending his transfer to prison. And then, things began to take place.

An expensively-dressed woman in her late forties appeared at the offices of a Chicago polygraphist, Leonard Harrelson, recognized as one of the world's foremost experts, now President of the famed Keeler Polygraph Institute of polygraph training.

"I am Mrs. Angerman," she said. "May I talk with you?"

"Of course," Harrelson replied. "Do come in and be seated."

Obviously nervous, constantly wringing her hands, Mrs. Angerman began to unfold a strange story which contained sufficient substance to suggest to Harrelson that Raymond Spotter might be innocent.

After accidentally finding a blood-stained man's handkerchief bearing the initials C.R. in one corner of her daughter's bureau dresser drawer, she carefully unfolded it. She discovered a rubber contraceptive, of sorts, that men are supposed to use to keep girls from getting pregnant. She showed it to her husband.

When she brought this to her daughter's attention, Carroll (name fictitious) went into a fit of rage, screamed insults at her mother and stormed out of the house. The two hadn't spoken since.

"I know the C.R. initials on that handkerchief belong to Carroll's boy friend. I have no positive proof of anything but I certainly would hate to see an innocent man go to prison."

"How does your husband feel about this?" Harrelson asked.

"Sir, he is just as upset as I am. We are very fair-minded people—perhaps not the best parents. It was his idea I come to a man like you."

"I assure you, Mrs. Angerman, that I'll be into this matter tooth and toenail in a manner of minutes." He took her name and telephone number.

First, Harrelson got in touch with Spotter's defense attorney. After much harranging, they agreed to meet in the prosecuting attorney's office. There, a violent argument took place. But when Harrelson threatened to call in the newspapers, the two attorneys agreed to go before the sentencing judge and ask that Harrelson be permitted to polygraph Spotter before he was transferred to prison.

The request was reluctantly granted.

Two days later, Harrelson emerged from a bleak room in the County Building with seven polygraph charts draped over one arm.

"In my opinion," he said, "Raymond Spotter did not rape that girl. It is also very clear to me that his confession was beaten from him."

Stunned, the judge and both attorneys just looked at each other.

"I'd now like to polygraph Carroll Angerman," Harrelson said.

Spotter's transfer to prison was delayed.

Initially, Carroll Angerman refused to take the test. But her parents brought her to Harrelson's offices. Kindly, he talked her into agreeing to "just sit in the examining room chair and discuss the matter."

It was a slow process, gently going over the whole incident, step by step, probing and going through it again. It took three hours of soft interrogation, listening to differences in her account of the rape as she repeated them, then calling the discrepancies to her attention.

At last, Carroll Angerman broke. Her shoulders shook as she sobbed out the truth.

On the afternoon of the alleged rape, she and her boyfriend, C.R., were petting on the front room floor. They became inflamed with passion. It was her first affair. She bled quite freely. Through one of the big front windows, she saw Spotter drive in. She heard him leave the groceries. She noted his departure.

At the same time, right in the middle of the sex act, she saw her parents drive in and around to the rear of the house.

C.R. leaped up, handed her his handkerchief, pulled up his pants, ran out the front door and sped off in his roadster.

Carroll panicked when she saw blood on the carpeting. She tried to wipe it up with her panties. Then she fled into her room and hid C.R.'s handkerchief in her bureau dresser drawer.

But the blood stains were on the floor. Her parents would see them. Quickly, she rumpled up her hair and ripped the front of her blouse. She was lying on the front room floor moaning and crying when her parents entered.

Out of her mind with fear, she screamed rape and pointed the finger at Raymond Spotter.

In a nearby room, Mr. and Mrs. Angerman, Spotter's defense attorney, the prosecuting attorney, the trial judge, and one of the arresting officers, observed the whole proceeding through a one-way mirror, and listened to every tape-recorded word.

* * *

Since Erle Stanley Gardner so considerately opened the doors to this chapter, it seems only appropriate that his case brief should close it.

A young girl, Gardner relates, who had previously been in trouble, was convicted of a crime.

She vigorously protested her innocence.

The judge finally began to have some doubts. He had heard of the far-reaching reputation of C. B. Hanscom in Minneapolis.

He said to the girl's attorney, "If you will take her to C. B. Hanscom and if he certifies that she is telling the truth after a complete examination, I will grant a new trial."

Hanscom reported the girl was telling the truth.

The judge granted a new trial. The girl was acquitted.

Some weeks later, the true culprit was apprehended, and confessed.

* * *

A man was convicted of a sex crime, and was in county jail in Nebraska awaiting sentence.

Throughout the period of arrest and trial, he maintained his innocence.

But, due to the strong circumstantial evidence, the jury wouldn't believe him. Even his court-appointed attorney, though he put on a gallant defense "at law," quite frankly admitted, off the record, that he felt his client was guilty.

The day before sentencing, the subject pleaded with his attorney to get permission from the judge for a polygraph test. Despite some severe objections from the prosecuting attorney, the judge granted the request.

Alex Gregory was flown in from Michigan.

Gregory brought the first two charts out of the examining room and explained to waiting officials that each time he touched on questions concerning this crime, the subject's body produced responses containing "symptoms" indicative of guilt.

"We know he's guilty," an assistant prosecutor sneered. "This whole thing is just a farce as far as I'm concerned." One of the police officers who helped make the case vigorously nodded in agreement.

Gregory's unusually pleasant manner stiffened. His eyes turned cold. "I have to be fair and impartial to both sides," he said. "The test is not yet over." He went back into the examining room.

Initially, even Gregory thought the man might be guilty, but somehow the man's manner, his demeanor, everything about him, caused the polygraphist to keep probing.

Finally, it came out in the open.

The man had been mixed up in a somewhat similar sex crime, years ago and had never been apprehended. Whenever Gregory asked questions about a sex crime, the memory caused severe emotional disturbances on the charts.

Having gotten that off his chest, the subject ran a perfectly clear test.

Gregory reported that he was telling the truth—that he, in his professional opinion, was convinced the subject was innocent of the crime for which he had been convicted.

Despite the fact that police and the assistant prosecuting attorney were furious with Gregory, he stuck to his guns.

It was well he did, because a few months later the real criminal was apprehended and confessed.

V

FOR PROTECTION OF THE INNOCENT

In a central texas town some years ago, a middle-aged grocery store owner stood behind his counter on a dark Sunday night and watched a man buy a package of cigarettes, then pull a gun and shoot him.

Police thought the motive was robbery. But the bandit apparently had become frightened. The money in the cash register drawer was untouched.

From his hospital bed the next morning, the wounded store owner weakly whispered the name of the gunman to the county sheriff. "I know him," the grocer said. "He trades at my store."

Within hours, the suspect had been arrested and undergone a paraffin test as police searched for powder burn clues.

"He definitely has traces of nitrate on his hand," the chemist said.

Dee E. Wheeler, then employed by the Texas Department of Public Safety (now Chief Examiner with the Fort Worth Crime Lab) was called in to polygraph the accused.

After the test, Wheeler walked from the examining room and calmly told the sheriff, "The man's innocent."

"But what about the paraffin tests?" the lawman asked.

"He said he was fertilizing his front yard," Wheeler replied. "I believe him."

By the end of the next week, police had two more suspects in custody. One was a roving evangelist who had finished his sermon early on the night of the shooting and quickly caught a bus out of town. The second man was a drifter whom police arrested on an anonymous tip. They called him Big Spike (name fictitious).

Wheeler, recognized nationally for his competence and amazing case results, first tested the evangelist. "He didn't shoot the grocer, but he knows who did."

That afternoon, the evangelist rattled his jail doors and yelled, "I want to get out of here. I need to prepare my Sunday sermon.

"I saw the shooting."

He continued. "As I walked across the railroad tracks near the store this big fella ran up to me waving a gun. He said he'd just killed a man and would shoot me if I told on him. They call him Big Spike."

"Did you, or did you not actually see him shoot the grocer?" the sheriff asked.

"Well, no, I guess I didn't."

He didn't know that the man he named sat alone in a cell just a few steps down the hallway.

Wheeler polygraphed Big Spike, then waited while the suspect led police to the weedy spot where he had hid the pistol.

Later, the sheriff asked the victim why he had named the wrong man.

The grocer shook his head. "Sheriff," he said, "I don't even remember talking to you.

The doctor said the victim of the shooting had been in shock.

But his words almost sent an innocent man to prison, and might have had not "the Man called Wheeler" and his polygraph brought out the truth.

* * *

Texas Rangers walked into Wheeler's office one day with a pretty red-haired teen-aged girl who bragged about writing a string of hot checks.

"She's confessed to 37 forgeries," one of the Rangers said. "We'd like for you to put her on the box and see if we can clear up some others."

Twenty minutes later, Wheeler emerged from his examining room.

"Did you get any more?" the Ranger asked.

"No," Wheeler said. "She didn't even forge the ones she confessed to."

"Hell," the Ranger laughed, "we didn't bring her up here for you to ruin our case."

The girl's father was a constable—a strict disciplinarian. She wanted to strike back at his authority, she said. The teen-ager confessed to a crime because she wanted to shame his name. She was freed against her will.

Another redhead, identified by a handwriting expert, later confessed.

*   *   *

In August of 1956, on a misty Thursday morning, service station operator Elbert T. Wallace was murdered.

Investigating officers followed several sets of footprints leading away from the station to a shack where Sam Coleman, Calvin Coleman, and L. C. Franklin were sleeping.

After the three were "rudely" awakened, they readily admitted they had been at the station not long ago to buy a quart of oil.

They were booked on suspicion of murder.

It wasn't long before a group of citizens in Crosbyton County, Texas, gathered at a street corner. One held a rope in his hands.

The suspects were put in chains and hurried to safety in the Lubbock jail.

The investigation continued, turning up a 33-year-old ex-convict, Jesse Allen, and his 16-year-old companion, Willie Floyd Law.* They stated they had personally seen the Colemans and Franklin kill Wallace.

Police had a pretty good case. But to be certain, they decided to call in Dee Wheeler. The Coleman brothers and Franklin steadfastly maintained their innocence, and agreed to submit to polygraphy.

After Wheeler examined the suspects, he reported: "These fellows aren't the killers. Sure, they were in the station to buy a quart of oil but apparently this was before Wallace was killed. Maybe we ought to check the witnesses."

Willie Law cockily sat in the polygraph examining chair. Moments later, in whispered tones, he had confessed, telling how

---

*Potter County Prosecuting Attorney case Nos. 1240 and 1241. Case changed venue on May 27, 1957 on both parties because of possibility of getting impartial trial in Crosby Co., Texas, to Lubbock County, Texas. Cause #6228. Refer to, Law v. State, 309 SW 2d 443.

he slugged Wallace with a crow bar when the man turned his back to wrap 25 cents worth of sausage.

After the fatal blow, Allen robbed the register of $60.00.

As Franklin was set free, along with the Colemans, he knelt in a flower bed. "I'm so glad to be free, I'm gonna eat some of this free dirt."

And that he did.

* * *

During an argument in front of a Fort Worth, Texas, cafe on June 11, 1966, Fred Thaniel, 50, was shot and killed.

McKinley Powell, Jr. was charged with the murder.* He spent three days in jail while getting money to make his $3,000 bond.

Powell said he had gone to the cafe to visit with some friends, when a fight broke out.

"Someone started firing a pistol," Powell said, "so I ran outside and got behind my car for protection."

Moments later, Powell said he took a gun from the glove compartment of his car and fired it into the air in an effort to stop the affray.

However, Assistant District Attorney John Brady, assigned to the case, came up with an eye witness—a friend of Powell's—who emphatically pointed an accusing finger at Powell.

Obviously, he became the state's star witness.

But, when all of the witnesses stated that while they knew Powell had fired a pistol, they couldn't be positive that he shot Thaniel, Brady became suspicious.

He became more suspicious when informed that the slug taken from the body weighed less than each of the remaining five rounds in Powell's .22 pistol.

While Brady's investigation was in progress, Assistant District Attorney Truman Power was working on jury selection.

Shortly after the jury was impaneled to listen to the case in Criminal District Judge Byron Matthews' court, Brady went to Powell's attorney, Tim Curry, with a proposition.

I'm not sure we have the right guy," he said. "If your client

---

*State of Texas v. McKinley Powell, Jr., No. 72,739, Criminal District Court, Tarrant County, Texas. The case against Powell was dismissed upon motion of the District Attorney, Oct. 18, 1966.

will submit to polygraphy and clear the test, we'll drop the charges."

"Of course I'll agree," said Curry. "Powell has said all along he is innocent, and has been quite adamant about it."

The trial was scheduled to start at 10:00 A.M. on a day three months after Thaniel's death.

At 8:00 A.M., the same day, Powell faced polygraphy.

He was cleared.

Standing before Judge Matthews, Powell heard the charges dropped.

Brady next confronted his star witness, Henry Douglas. His story didn't quite coincide with the one he had previously told. Brady warned him of his rights.

Douglas confessed. He was taken before Peace Justice Jim Boorman, charged with murder and placed in county jail without bond.*

*   *   *

Shortly after midnight on December 7, 1961, in a residential district in Amarillo, Texas, a man stood in the doorway of a house with fear etched on his face. Police officers walked toward him.

"She's in the back bedroom," he cried.

Lying on her back and moaning was a voluptuous woman. Blood oozed from a wound in her head.

"Do something," the man yelled. "She's dying."

He identified himself as Jim Peterson (name fictitious), an oil-field roustabout. He said the bleeding woman was Mrs. Jewell Wilson, owner of the house. He told a fantastic story.

"We were asleep. I woke up all of a sudden. I heard something, like footsteps going away. I called to Jewell but she didn't answer. I reached over and shook her. I felt something very wet and sticky on her shoulder. I jumped up and turned on the overhead light. Then I saw the rifle lying across the foot of the bed."

Jim Peterson went on to say that he picked up the weapon,

---

*State of Texas v. Henry Douglas, No. 73,155, Criminal District Court, Tarrant County, Texas. Douglas was tried on Jan. 11, 1967, resulting in hung jury. The case was dismissed on motion of the District Attorney June 27, 1968, due to insufficient evidence.

and for some unexplained reason cocked it, then went into the kitchen and leaned the gun against a wall, before calling police.

Police conducted a minute search of the premises. They found a discharged bullet casing in the middle of the bed. The top sheet had been shot through twice. Powder burns were around the holes. Jewell Wilson's purse was found on the kitchen table. It contained $260 in $20 traveler's checks. In the woman's car, police found a box of .22 shells.

Detective Rex Cole faced Peterson. "Are you telling us everything you know about this?"

"Yes sir, I sure am," Peterson answered quickly. "I know it sounds weird, but I'm telling the truth."

"Okay," Detective Cole said, "let's go down to the station. We're holding you for investigation."

Detective Cole dispatched officer Needham to the hospital. With the doctor at his side, the officer asked the gravely wounded woman, "Did you shoot yourself?"

"No," came the whispered reply.

"Do you know who shot you?"

"No."

At 10:30 A.M. the next day, Jewell Wilson died.

Police Chief Wiley Alexander, a young FBI-trained lawman, called a conference. Under his administration, the Amarillo Police Department was reorganized completely in 1955 and brought up to date. In that modernization, one of the first steps taken was the training of a polygraph examiner. The job went to L. R. Waynne, a captain of that force.

Captain Wynne was present at the conference. The consensus of the officers at that meeting was that Jim Peterson was guilty of the shooting. All evidence pointed his way.

Early that afternoon, Peterson met Captain Wynne. The polygraph expert spent considerable time establishing rapport, seeking to relax the subject. After a smoke and a talk, he explained the mechanics of the polygraph, what it recorded and how and where the recordings originated from.

Oddly enough, the suspect, himself, Wynne noted, seemed convinced that the evidence against him was overwhelming. At one point, Peterson asked, Wynne, "What do you think I'll get —ten or fifteen years?"

Captain Wynne wondered whether the man couldn't bring himself to ask the question which must have been in his mind: "Or death?"

With such an attitude of being hopelessly ensnared, Peterson puzzled the lawmen in sticking so stubbornly to his story.

The test commenced.

"Do you actually know who shot Jewell Wilson?"

"No."

"Did you shoot Jewell Wilson?"

"No."

"Have you shot the rifle in the past month?"

"Yes."

"Have you fired the rifle in the past two days?"

"No."

"Were you present when Jewell Wilson was shot?"

"Yes."

"Had you ever planned to kill Jewell Wilson?"

"No."

"Have you deliberately lied to any question I've asked you on this test?"

"No."

And so it continued. Three polygrams were conducted, and the results were the same in each instance: Jim Peterson was telling the truth.

The polygraph procedure, much publicized for its criminal trappings, had cleared an innocent man about to be charged with a murder he didn't commit. He would have faced possible death in the electric chair.

No wonder, Wynne thought, Peterson had been a man with fear etched into his face.

On December 9, 1961, Walton Wheeler Wilson, an ex-husband of Jewell Wilson, after cracking under polygraphy and confessing, was formally charged with Jewell's murder.*

* * *

*On June 29, 1962, Walton Wheeler Wilson entered a plea of guilty, guilty without malice, 47th Judicial District Court, Amarillo, Texas. Docket #11,319. He received a 5-year suspended sentence. For further reference, see McNeil, B.G., *True Police Cases*, April, 1962.

Millie Miranda (name fictitious) walked her children to school on the morning of September 5, 1968 in Oxnard, California. She talked to a teacher at the school for a brief period, then started walking home.

About a half-block from the school, she crossed the street and suddenly noticed a green and white late-model car parked at the corner of an intersecting street. The car's motor was running. The door, on the driver's side was partially open.

Casually, she glanced at the car's occupant and noticed that he appeared to be playing with himself (masturbating).

Upon seeing this, she yelled to a woman standing on the sidewalk a few doors down the street. "Get that license number," Mrs. Miranda screamed.

While being questioned by police, Mrs. Miranda described the suspect as white, male, in his middle thirties, wearing brown pants with a tan, short-sleeved shirt, and hair-lipped. She told all she could remember, then signed a formal complaint.

Police traced the vehicle number and came up with its owner Jarret Ray (name fictitious), who also fit the description furnished by Mrs. Miranda. The reported color of the car also matched.

When contacted by police, Ray admitted that he drove by the school on his way to work each day at Hueneme Base.

He was not advised of his rights at this time.

Ray further admitted that he had experienced an itch in his crotch as he slowed for a yield sign, pulled around the corner and stopped. He said he unzipped his pants, opened the door and started to get out, but thought better of it. He said he was simply scratching his penis and scrotum when the complainant walked by, but he didn't even notice her until he heard her yell. Frightened, he drove off with tires screeching.

However, Ray denied masturbating or deliberately exposing himself to Mrs. Miranda.

He was formally charged, with trial scheduled for January 6, 1969, in the court of Municipal Judge Albert Blanford of Oxnard.

Ray obtained the representation of the very reputable law firm of Ferguson and Regnier. They began a detailed search of the facts and statements given by witnesses, and found many flaws, including conflicting descriptions of both Ray and the color of his car.

Attorney Richard A. Regnier presented his findings to the District Attorney's office. Aware of the questions concerning fact, the Deputy District Attorney stated that if Ray submitted to polygraphy and cleared the test, he would move that the charges be dropped. The case was bound over to January 20, 1969.

Regnier sought for one of the most competent polygraphists in California and came up with Alec E. Greene, now deceased, a former Executive Director of the American Polygraph Association, whose offices were in Hollywood.

The polygraph examination was set for January 10 at 10:30 A.M.

Greene's report at test conclusion read in part:

"The magnitude and lack of deception criteria on the charts clearly indicate that while subject Ray did expose his privates near the school at Evans Blvd. and B street on the day in question, and that he, in fact, was scratching these privates, there is no indication whatsoever that Ray deliberately did so to attract a female to his car."

Attorney Regnier wrote Greene on January 22, 1969: "You will no doubt be pleased to know that the prosecution decided to dismiss the charges against Mr. Ray. The motion was made on January 17th and granted by presiding Judge Donald Pollack.

"As you probably are aware, in misdemeanor cases, a dismissal is tantamount to a finding of not guilty in that the charges can never be renewed.

"The just result which has been achieved in this case is largely due to your polygraph assistance, for which I am most appreciative."

*   *   *

During early January, 1968, Peter Roser (name fictitious) heard pounding on the front door of his modest bachelor apartment in a metropolitan town in Minnesota.

When he opened the door, he was asked to identify himself.

After so doing, two burly police plainclothesmen pushed their way into his apartment.

"Roser, let me advise you of your Constitutional rights," one growled. He ended with, "You have been accused of the crime of rape."

"What!" Roser was visibly shaken. He sat on the edge of a chair, his mouth hanging open. "I'm charged with what?"

"I said you've been accused of rape," the officer grated. "No sense in denying it. The victim has positively identified you from your mug-shot at headquarters. Let's go downtown."

A block away, one of the officers cursed, twisted around in the front seat, and glared at Roser. "Where's the gun you threatened her with to force her to submit?"

Roser's face went blank. "Gun?"

"Yeah. You own one, don't you?"

"Well, as a matter of fact, I do. It's back in my apartment."

"Let's go get it." The unmarked police car spun around.

Roser was booked.

Because of the victim's identification and the gun Roser turned over to authorities, the judge at Roser's arraignment felt there was sufficient evidence to have him bound over to the District Court for trial.

On January 19, 1968, Roser, through his attorney, demanded polygraphy.

C. B. Hanscom, Director, Department of Police, University of Minnesota, was asked to conduct the test. Hanscom had worked on many famous cases, including some highly dramatic ones for the Court of Last Resort. To him, this case was routine.

Two hours and four polygrams later, Hanscom quietly reported: "There is no question about it—this man is innocent."

Roser was released on bond.

On February 2, 1968, Hanscom received a call from the County Attorney advising that an individual had been arrested for driving under influence of intoxicating liquor. In Minnesota, an "Open Bottle Statute" allows a police officer to search a person's automobile. During the search of this person's car, officers found an earring which was positively identified as belonging to the victim of the rape in question.

The victim appeared at police headquarters, matched the earring found in the suspect's car, and identified him as being the rapist.

The suspect confessed to the rape, giving details of the crime that would be known only to the perpetrator and the victim.

Hanscom thanked the County Attorney for the information, and cradled the telephone receiver. He smiled to himself and went about his business. It was just one of those routine cases—that made his heart feel real good.

*   *   *

At the peak of his career, Hanscom often muses about many cases. He told of one occurring two or three years ago when two detectives brought a juvenile to his office and requested polygraphy. The officers let it be known that they were thoroughly convinced the boy was guilty, and felt that a polygraph test was a waste of time.

A house had been burglarized and in the course thereof a woman's purse was rifled. All her money and her bank deposit book were missing.

Subject I, as we shall call him, was picked up for investigation mainly because of a prior record of house burglary where the method of operation was similar.

A police search of his high-school locker turned up the victim's bank book. Even in the face of this evidence, the accused continued to deny any knowledge or complicity.

Several polygrams were conducted. All indicated Subject I was telling the truth.

Both investigating officers frankly stated they were convinced Hanscom had failed.

Two weeks later, however, another boy was picked up for questioning and made a full confession of the burglary in issue.

Subject II was aware of Subject I's past record, and deliberately dropped the victim's bank book through the vent slots in the innocent boy's locker.

The chief of police stated he felt certain Subject I would have been convicted had it not been for C. B. Hanscom's polygraph proficiency.

John Dogger (name fictitious), an innocuous-appearing little man living in Los Angeles in 1963, brought a contempt proceeding against his second wife, twenty years his junior, for refusal to comply with the court's order giving him alternate visitation rights with their three-year-old daughter.

Dogger had a twenty-three-year-old daughter by his prior marriage and a granddaughter two and one-half years old.

Mrs. Dogger responded by saying that her refusal was based on her suspicions that he was sexually molesting their little daughter, who twice had returned home with the area around her genitals irritated. She also accused the father of breaking into her home when she was absent and destroying an oriental figurine on the television set.

All this, Mr. Dogger vehemently denied. Both attorneys thought it a good idea for him to submit to polygraphy, to which he most reluctantly agreed.

Lieutenant Warren King of the Burbank, California Police Department, was asked by the court to conduct the test.

Through extensive polygraphy, Mr. Dogger cleared himself concerning the charge of child molesting, but the test also indicated he was untruthful about breaking into his wife's home, and when so informed he admitted he had pried open a window and while crawling through he had knocked over the oriental figurine.

Lt. King reported that Mr. Dogger seemed not at all concerned about the charge of molesting his child, but that he was terribly embarrassed and upset over being found out on the house-breaking.

The polygraph test conclusion allayed the mother's fears and visitation rights were resumed. The contempt proceeding was dismissed.

* * *

On December 17, 1967, in Fort Worth, Texas, four men drove into a service station. One got out of the car holding a can and asked for 80 cents worth of gas.

The attendant complied, but while ringing up the 80 cents,

he noticed the customer putting more gas into the can. He ran out and demanded money to cover the additional gas.

The customer pulled a .22 revolver and fired a bullet into the attendant's stomach.

Several witnesses saw the shooting but in the excitement of the moment no one obtained the fleeing vehicle's license number.

Three men appeared the next day at police headquarters with their attorneys, and admitted they were the driver and occupants of the car connected with the crime. Asserting their innocence, they stated that while driving around the previous evening they came upon an old school mate, Lee Tillis, standing beside a stalled vehicle with a gas can in his hand.

Not having seen Lee for several years, they stopped and exchanged pleasantries, learned Lee had just been discharged from the military, and offered to drive him to a station.

All three steadfastly maintained they did not know Tillis had a gun or that he had any intention of using one. But after he did shoot the attendant, they panicked and fled, first taking Lee back to his car.

Through their attorneys, they agreed to submit to polygraphy.

All three produced truthful tests.

Lee Tillis was arrested, charged with murder, put in jail and subsequently indicted.

He violently insisted he was innocent, maintaining he was home with his wife at the time of the shooting.

He made no bones about demanding a polygraph test.

At the Fort Worth Crime Lab. Tillis underwent an exhaustive examination. The familiar words concluded it: "This man is telling the truth."

Investigating officers snorted in disgust. They just knew the polygraphist had missed the boat.

Backtracking, the state's three witnesses were again brought in for further interrogation. One thing kept cropping up—each witness repeated the story that the accused had recently been discharged from military service.

A check revealed that Lee Tillis had never been in any branch of the military. However, his brother, James Tillis, who so closely resembled Lee that he could be taken for his twin, actually served in the military and had just been discharged.

James Tillis was picked up. When asked if he would submit to poygraphy, he had no objection.

His test contained deception criteria.

He confessed to the shooting.

Subsequently, James Tillis was convicted and sentenced to fifty years in the Texas State Penitentiary.*

* * *

During the summer of 1967, in an Oklahoma town, two youths were observed stealing cigarettes from a delivery truck.

A witness said he saw the act, personally knew the boys, and gave their ages as 16 and 17 respectively.

With his parents' permission, the 16-year-old was polygraphed. Though he made no admissions, he did not "clear out." Because of a lengthy juvenile record, he was placed in detention.

Despite a severe respiratory ailment which complicated chart interpretation, the 17-year-old boy was declared innocent. He was released.

Within a few days, a vicious, yet cleverly worded, unsigned, typewritten letter (presumably from the eye witness) was received by the city council. Its contents amounted to a complete denunciation of local law enforcement and, in particular, polygraphy.

"How can a polygraph examiner," the letter read, "possibly arrive at such a conclusion when an eye witness not only saw the boys steal the cigarettes but also knew them personally?"

Soon, harsh words were being thrown back and forth between department heads of police and the city manager's office. This was delightfully exploited by newspaper reporters.

While this was going on, the 16-year-old in detention decided to confess. In so doing, he completely exonerated the accused 17-year-old, while implicating two other boys as accomplices at the time of the cigarette theft.

---

*State of Texas v. James Earl Tillis, Criminal District Court, Tarrant County, Texas, No. 74,578.

These two new suspects were brought in and admitted guilt, again exonerating the 17-year-old initially accused by an eye witness "who just couldn't be wrong."

*   *   *

During a dreary Friday night in the late 1950's in Austin, Texas, the body of Pedro Banda Sosa of Seguin, Texas, was found draped over the guard fence on the east side of the 600 block of Sabine Street.

Questioning by police of a dozen suspects brought out that several had seen Sosa in the company of one Julian Garcia (name fictitious) around 7:00 P.M. From that point on, none of the witnesses had seen either man.

Garcia was described by the witnesses as having a vicious temper. "He's just plain mean," they said.

Captain Ted C. Klaus led the investigating team. Sosa had been stabbed with a long-bladed thin knife which penetrated his lung, collapsing it, then cut his heart.

The big puzzle was, what happened between Sosa and Garcia, during the 7:00 to 7:30 period?

Garcia was found and picked up.

After lengthy interrogation, Garcia admitted being with Sosa up until about 30 minutes before his death. Further probing brought out Garcia's admission that he had beaten and robbed Sosa.

But he angrily denied killing Sosa.

Officers knew they had their man. So, they played their ace in the hole.

"Okay," they said, "we'll believe you if you consent to take and pass the polygraph test."

"Sure thing," Gargia replied. "I'm telling the truth. I'll be glad to."

They carried their "star" suspect to the Texas Department of Public Safety and polygraph examiner, H. A. Albert, subsequently appointed by the Governor to the Board of Polygraph Examiners which screens, examines and approves the license of every polygraph examiner in the State of Texas.

Within an hour, Albert verified that Garcia was telling the truth when he said he had gotten involved in an argument with Sosa over a girl, had beaten and robbed him.

Officers now were convinced, until Albert said:

"Garcia did not kill Sosa, and he doesn't know who did."

The weary detectives who had worked six days and nights on the baffling murder, returned to headquarters. They were at a dead end. Sosa's murder was within a frog's hair of going into the books as unsolved.

But, before the day was out, the case was wrapped up completely as far as the detectives were concerned. They had a statement from a man which sent them hustling to the court house to file murder charges.

"It must be St. Patrick's Day," was their only comment.

Joe G. Cruz, 32-year-old Austin laborer, was charged with the murder of Sosa in a complaint filed in Justice Travis Blakeslee's court by city Detectives K. R. Herbert and Woody Rampy and Lieutenant Beverly Laws.

The detectives, working on a tip, got a statement late Thursday afternoon from Cruz's wife. When he was presented with this statement in his cell, Cruz admitted the murder of Sosa.*

* * *

The case against a young porter who spent ten months in jail awaiting trial on a charge of armed robbery was dismissed in October 1968, after polygraph proved the prosecution had no case.

The proceedings involved one positive witness who finally decided he was not so positive, another who concluded he had had too many drinks to be positive about anything, an explanation that went unchecked, and a polygraph test.

Shortly before 2:00 A.M. on December 29, 1967, three men walked into Martin's Bar, 724 Avenue of the Americas, New York City, pulled guns, and took $600 from the cash registers, plus some $134 from customers.

One of the robbers fired his pistol a few times, ordered everybody to get down on the floor, then fired another shot and

*State v. Joe G. Cruz, Cause of Action #26904, County Courthouse, Austin, Texas.

warned: "I'd like to shoot me one." Then the three men ran off into the night.

About half an hour later, Patrolman Barry Williams of the 230 West 20th Street Station arrested Joseph Smiley, a Negro, who was walking along the Avenue near West 24th Street. He was taken to the bar, where a patron and the bartender identified him as one of the robbers. Smiley was booked on a robbery charge and taken to jail, protesting his innocence. He was unable to post $25,000 bail.

In the months that followed, a New York County Grand Jury indicted Smiley.

Lawyers for the Legal Aid Society decided to check out Smiley's story that he had gone to visit a friend, Bill Whitty, of 24 East Second Street, found him not home, then decided to walk back to his own room in an inexpensive West Side hotel.

Legal Aid investigators found there was a Bill Whitty, that he was not home that night, and that the police had not even bothered to verify his existence.

"Almost from the first we thought Smiley was innocent," said Anthony F. Marra, then the attorney-in-charge for the Legal Aid Society's Criminal Courts branch. "He had never been in trouble before. Here was a man who made only $60 a week and managed to send most of it to his grandparents in Alabama."

Legal Aid asked the District Attorney's office to consent to polygraphy for Smiley. There was hesitation. It was rather unusual to administer such a test when two persons had been positive in their identification, but consent was given.

Detective Nat Laurendi, an experienced polygraphist and professional police officer, conducted the test. He reported that he felt Smiley was telling the truth.

The district attorney's office pressed its investigation. It was found that one of the witnesses was no longer sure Smiley was the man. The other witness finally concluded he had had too much to drink that night to be sure about anything.

Assistant District Attorney Saverio J. Fierro stood before the Bench and recommended dismissal of the charges. Smiley was not in court but he was represented by a Legal Aid lawyer, Donald Tucker.

In granting the application for dismissal, Supreme Court Justice Irwin D. Davidson told Fierro: "I agree with your estimate that the probability of a conviction here is far from good and there would be great difficulty in proving the guilt of this defendant beyond a reasonable doubt. It may be that this man is completely innocent."

Smiley was freed.

* * *

Tuesday, February 18, 1969, Danny Chasteen, jailed for a year for a murder he did not commit, walked from a courtroom exonerated.*

The State of Florida readily acknowledged it had the wrong man for the murder of Isaac Macy, a socialite tennis pro who was killed January 7, 1968 during an exchange of gunfire with thieves who broke into his fashionable home in Miami.

Two other men, Frederick R. Yokom, 23, in prison for 99 years for robbery, and Peter Koulizos, 22, wanted by the FBI as a fugitive, were charged with the murder of Macy in a new indictment.

In the emotional upheaval of the murder, Ike Macy's wife, Mary Belle, herself critically wounded, said, "they just rammed and busted in the whole front door, feet shoulder high."

After the murder, a police informant mentioned that a "Danny" might be involved. Chasteen was known to be an acquaintance of Yokum and Koulizos.

The fact was that this acquaintanceship led to the faulty identification.

Chasteen had been in trouble before. Nine years previous he had a fight with a high-school principal. In 1966, detectives found some police uniforms stolen from a dry cleaner in a girl's apartment. Chasteen was there. They charged him with possesison of stolen property, then dismissed the charge.

On January 11, 1968, four days after the Macy killing, Detective James Michael Coon took five photographs to the intensive

---

*Fla., Circuit #2485; State's Attorney Case #2540. Danny Chasteen was never tried for the murder of Issac Macy. He was released after the polygraph test and the Grand Jury held a new hearing during which time they withdrew the indictment against him.

care unit of South Miami Hospital. They were photographs of Chasteen, Yokom, Koulizos, Charles Gibson and Ralph Goodman, now residents of Raiford Prison for other crimes.

Mrs. Macy selected Chasteen from a line-up in a closed-circuit television from her hospital bed, then twice again—at a jail behind a one-way mirror, and at a preliminary hearing.

"I could never forget that face, the longest day I live—never. I'll never forget that face," she testified at the hearing. She said she was absolutely positive.

Although Chasteen said he had several persons who could verify he was twenty-one miles away when the murder took place, Mrs. Macy's identification was overpowering.

Not a single alibi witness testified before the Dade Grand Jury that indicted Chasteen for murder in April of 1968.

Although police took the alibi statements Chasteen gave them to show where he was the day of Macy's murder (and these were turned over to assistant state attorneys David Goodhart and I. Richard Jacobs) the state took the position it was the responsibility of Chasteen's lawyer, Henry Carr, to bring in the witnesses. Carr took the position it was the state's responsibility.

Carr, sometimes called "the Grey Ghost," is a highly competent criminal lawyer. With detectives, he had allowed Chasteen to reenact his alibi route.

But he didn't want his client waiving immunity. For his labor, the Chasteen family in Miami, a mother, sister, and three brothers, paid a $300 fee.

Carr was quick to detect another flaw in the account of Mrs. Macy. She had Chasteen used as a battering ram at the door feet flying in shoulder high.

Six months earlier, June 16, 1967, scaffolding had collapsed under Chasteen while he worked as an iron worker for the Commercial Erectors Company. He fell and fractured his right heel. It was in a knee-to-toe cast for two weeks.

Chasteen still felt he couldn't work in January of 1968. He also realized the insurance company would soon make a settlement.

Said lawyer Carr, "We could get doctors to testify he was physically not capable of doing what the lady said he did."

While Chasteen was in jail, the insurance company settled. Chasteen's mother received a $4,700 check.

The Chasteens decided to change lawyers. They hired another attorney Philip Carlton, Jr., paying his $3,500 fee.

Carlton hired two ex-policemen investigators, Don DeLongchamps and David Hellman, who unequivocally substantiated Chasteen's alibi story, and tried to get the indictment squashed.

Attorney Carlson claimed the state wouldn't allow Chasteen to waive immunity. Prosecutors Goodhart and Jacobs said that wasn't true.

Nothing happened. Chasteen remained in cell 6C2 left. Trial was set for March 10, 1969.

Then Carlson, the shrewd fighting champion he is noted as being, brought in Warren Holmes, the polygraph-criminologist who already had psychophysiologically extracted some 1000 murder confessions over the years.

In the pretest interview, Holmes confirmed the investigations of DeLongchamps and Hellman. Then the polygraph test began.

Do you actually know who shot Isaac Hall Macy?"

"No."

"Did you shoot Isaac Hall Macy?"

"No."

"Have you ever been in the Macy home?"

"No."

"Have you ever been in a home located at 12055 S.W. 73rd Avenue?"

"No."

"Were you present when Isaac Hall Macy was shot?"

"No."

"Did you know on January 7, 1968 that the Macy home was going to be robbed?"

"No."

"Have you told the complete truth about your whereabouts between the hours of 6:00 P.M. and 10:00 P.M. on January 7, 1968?"

"Yes."

"Is Mrs. Macy correct in identifying you as one of the assailants?"

"No."

"Have you deliberately lied to any subject matter concerning this entire case?"

"No."

When Holmes concluded, he reported his findings to Philip Carlton, Jr.:

"There was no deception criteria present. It is my professional opinion that Daniel R. Chasteen is not guilty of being involved in, or having specific knowledge of, the murder of Isaac Hall Macy and the wounding of his wife."

In the meantime, *The Miami Herald* traced, found, and interviewed ten persons who, taken as a whole, strongly corroborated Chasteen's whereabouts and his assertions of innocence.

The prosecution dropped its charges.

Chasteen was freed.

Polygraphy had objectively cut another notch on the handle of protection for the innocent.

VI

A DAY OF RECKONING

Victor and Dorene Laird, who lived in the vicinity of Lake Arlington, Texas, disappeared September 1, 1966. Their car was found abandoned at one end of the lake. The Missing Persons Bureau of the local police and sheriff's departments began a search.

Immediately, their prime suspect became George W. Duke, a man with a lengthy criminal record.

Several years previous, the testimony of Dorene Laird helped the state obtain a long prison term for Duke. At the time of that sentencing, Duke publicly vowed he would surely get even with the Lairds.

He had not been out of prison very long when the couple disappeared.

When Duke was picked up for questioning, he had no objection to being polygraphed. Again, "the man called Wheeler," conducted the test.

After a lengthy session, Wheeler declared that in his opinion Duke was innocent.

His report thoroughly shook investigating officers who seemingly were positive of Duke's guilt.

Coincidentally, on the evening of September 22, traffic officers chased a speeding car through the hills west of Fort Worth. When finally cornered and stopped, a youthful driver by the name of Melvin Stuart Pittman, who would be 19 the next day, told officers that while the car was not his, he had permission of the owner to drive it.

He was held on suspicion of auto theft. The investigation began.

The vehicle was traced to a loan company in Houston. A

supervisor advised that the car had been assigned to one of their Fort Worth branch managers, Kenneth Eugene Jones.

Pursuing the matter further, officers located Jones' trailer home at Lake Arlington. A note on the front door read: "Gone fishing. Be back shortly. Go in and be seated."

Aware that the Laird's car had been found just over a mile from the Jones' trailer home, officers made a detailed report to homicide.

After being informed of all his rights, and flippantly waiving them, Pittman volunteered for polygraphy.

Following a lengthy pretest interview, the experienced interrogator had pretty well figured out what kind of a personality he was dealing with. So, he began polygraphy with a little game. He pulled a new deck of cards out of his desk drawer.

"Melvin," he said, "just to see what your insides look like before we start this test for real, let's you and me play a little game of pick-a-card. Is this all right with you?"

"Cool, man, groovy," Pittman laughed, "but let me pick the card just so we keep this thing on the up and up." He snickered.

"Fair enough," Wheeler said. "Pick out the 2-4-6-8-10 in any suit, shuffle them, pick out one card, look at it, then hide it under your leg. Put the rest back into the deck."

When Pittman was finished, Wheeler asked, "What suit did you pick?"

"Hearts."

Polygraph instrument components were attached to Pittman's body. "Okay," Wheeler said, "we're ready to play. You are to answer NO to every question. Since this is but a game, I think you'll find it rather interesting. Why don't you turn your head and watch yourself on this chart. Just sit still and don't move."

Pittman watched, an amused leer twisting his mouth.

"Did you pick the two of hearts?"

"No."

"Did you pick the four of hearts?"

"No."

"Did you pick the six of hearts?"

"No."

"Did you pick the eight of hearts?"

"No."

"Did you pick the ten of hearts?"

"No."

Wheeler deactivated the instrument and looked at Pittman's blanched face. The leer was no longer there. His eyes were downcast.

"Guess you could see it yourself," Wheeler said. "You picked the eight of hearts. Whatever gave you the notion you could beat the so-called lie detector test?"

With a deep sign, Pittman removed the card from under his leg and placed it face up on the desk. It was the eight of hearts.

That was the beginning of the end. Pittman admitted killing Jones as the man sat on a stump fishing, in order to steal his car. He said he hid the body in thick underbrush.

Then he casually admitted he had also shot and killed both the Lairds, stole their car, money and jewelry, also hiding their bodies in the thick lakeside underbrush.

Pittman showed no emotion as he related how he knocked both Lairds down with a single bullet from a .303 rifle as they walked along a pathway toward the shoreline.

After the Lairds were down, he said, he put more bullets in each body.

He used the same gun, the one he bought for $30 in a local pawn shop, to kill Jones.

Pittman signed a properly witnessed confession, then led officers to the bodies.

In Criminal District Court No. 3, March 7, 1967, Pittman was found guilty of the murder of Kenneth Eugene Jones and sentenced to death in the electric chair. Date of execution was held in abeyance pending Pittman's appeal to the Texas Court of Criminal Appeals.

This court upheld the death penalty assessed by a twelve-member jury.

Before formally setting the date of execution for February 28, 1969, Judge Lindsey asked Pittman if he wanted to say anything.

"Yes, I do," said Pittman, now 21. "My Constitutional rights were violated because I did not have a lawyer present when I was questioned at city hall."

Previously, several law officers had testified in Lindsey's court that Pittman never asked for a lawyer during the questioning.

After losing before the Criminal Court of Appeals, Pittman's court-appointed trial lawyers, Dawson Davis and Charles Dickens, filed an application for writ of habeas corpus before Federal District Judge Leo Brewster on Monday, February 24, 1969.

In their writ application, the attorneys claimed that:

1. Judge Charles Lindsey failed to instruct the jury members that unless they believed "beyond a reasonable doubt" that the confession was voluntary, they could not consider it as evidence against Pittman.
2. Twenty-three potential jurors were rejected because they said they had scruples against giving the death penalty, thus leading to selection of twelve "biased and prosecution-prone" persons.
3. State law leaves juries in capital cases with "unlimited, undirected and unreviewable discretion in determining whether the death penalty shall be imposed."
4. Pittman did not get a fair chance on the issue of punishment.
5. Because juries can impose a death sentence "wantonly, whimsically and without standards," the punishment is "harsh and unusual" and contrary to law.

Pittman was granted an indefinite stay of execution.*

Apparently it seems not important that this killer readily admitted, then voluntarily signed a statement detailing exactly how he deliberately killed Mr. and Mrs. Victor Laird and Kenneth Eugene Jones, and even led officers to where he had hidden their bodies.

* * *

The 23-year-old athlete shot his sweetheart to death in a jealous rage, faked amnesia in a strange town and thought he had gotten away with the crime.

---

*Pittman v. State, 434 SW 2d 352. Application for Writ of Habeas Corpus was filed February 24, 1969, CA-4-1177.

Even when he sat in the polygraph examining room chair and watched Dee Wheeler secure the instrument's attachments to his body, he joked and laughed, confident he would leave the room a free man.

But his smile faded when the instrument's slender recording pens spelled out the killer's escape route and pinpointed the spot where he buried the murder weapon.

"The boy was a respiratory reactor," Wheeler said. "We knew he was lying about the crime, but we had to find his gun."

The burly youth had waited in the darkness that night in 1950 for his girl friend and her date to return home. He sat alone in a parked truck, cradling the pistol in his hands.

He saw the car stop and the couple walk toward the door. They were laughing.

He aimed the gun through the open window of the truck and pulled the trigger. The girl staggered once, then fell dying in her front yard.

A second bullet tore into the boy's head as he stared at his mortally wounded date. He stumbled back to his car and drove to a hospital in Mexia before blacking out.

He was in surgery before police could question him.

The athlete was arrested at 4:00 A.M. the next day in Fairfield, Texas, wandering down the darkened streets, clutching his head and saying he couldn't remember who he was.

His stolen getaway truck was found abandoned at the forks in the road just outside the small town.

Wheeler first met the suspect in Austin. The polygraph man had spent all morning checking a road map, making mental notes of the landmarks along the 22 miles of highway that separated Fairfield from Mexia.

Wheeler knew the boy had thrown or hidden the gun some place, and he had to find it.

During the early questioning, the subject kept producing unusual physical manifestations when the interrogation centered around a small bridge stretching across the railroad tracks near Mexia.

"I thought he had planned to hide the gun there or possibly

had thrown it over the bridge, then gone back and picked it up," Wheeler said.

Then the polygraph instrument was activated. Wheeler began a search and disposition test.

1. Did you throw the gun in water?
2. Did you bury the gun in dirt?
3. Did you hide the gun under weeds or brush?

At question #2, the subject involuntarily experienced a respiratory block which lasted a full seven seconds.

Wheeler had his first clue.

1. Did you hide the gun in Fairfield?
2. Did you hide the gun near city hall?
3. Did you hide the gun near the courthouse?
4. Did you hide the gun near the funeral home?

Another involuntary respiratory block occurred following question #4.

For the youth, his game had ended.

Wheeler told the sheriff in Mexia, "You'll find the gun in Fairfield, buried near the funeral home."

The sheriff drove the youth to the small town and parked beside the mortuary. "We know it's here," he told the suspect. "You tell us where."

The boy gazed out the car window for a long minute, then softly said, "I'll go get it for you."

He dug up the gun in a vacant field only one hundred yards away.

But one thing kept worrying Wheeler. "Why did you squirm and react so when asked about the bridge?" he later asked the boy.

"Because after I killed her I was thinking about killing myself. I sat under the bridge and studied about it a long time."

Some attorneys in Texas had contended that polygraph testimony concerning tracing down a murder weapon might be admissible in court. Authorities thought this would be the test case. But it never got to trial.

While out on bond, the youth was caught burglarizing a building in East Texas. He decided he had nothing to lose. He tried to shoot it out with an officer, and was killed.

Fairly illustrated above is that polygraphy can be as valuable in tracing the "fruits of the crime" as in determining guilt or innocence.

* * *

In Amarillo, Texas, in the late 1950's, a 50-year-old man left his daughter at home one night and announced he was going to buy some hamburgers.

He returned in twenty-two and one-half minutes.

During that time, he had bought the sandwiches, drove to his estranged wife's apartment, bludgeoned her to death with a dull instrument, and gone home.

When he walked in the door, he glanced at his watch and remarked, "Well, that didn't take long."

His wife was found the next morning lying in a pool of blood on the floor. The murder weapon was missing.

Her husband was arrested when officers discovered his shoes were flecked with blood.

"He was a diminishing reactor," Wheeler said. "The first time I asked him about the crime, he reacted violently. Then his reactions would be normal.

"We put him on the polygraph twice a day for three days before we were able to determine where he had thrown the weapon.

"We decided it was a lead pipe, tossed away about one hundred yards from the murder scene in a southwesterly direction."

Officers found the lead pipe lying in a grassy field seventy-five yards southwest of the dead woman's apartment.

The weapon was flown to Austin. An officer walked into the room where the disgruntled suspect sat. He carried the pipe.

"The husband whirled around and threw his hands over his face," Wheeler said. "And for the first time he broke down, admitted the murder."

* * *

In Lubbock, Texas, Wheeler watched the pulse reaction of a young air cadet, as the polygraph's recording pens, through detailed question formulation, etched out the location of a shallow grave in a ditch near Reese Air Force Base where he had buried the body of his former sweetheart.

The young airman had promised to marry the girl, but he strangled her with the cord from a venetian blind, then put a bullet into her brain.

Wheeler told police they would find the gun in a pond near the forks of a road. The pond was drained. No gun was found.

Wheeler thought he had made a mistake until the man confessed and led officers to the pistol. About a half-mile farther down the road was a second small pool. In its water lay the rusty gun.

Police had drained the wrong pond.

*   *   *

After undergoing polygraphy on May 23, 1947, in Denver, Colorado, a 29-year-old armored truck driver confessed he had stolen a money bag containing $10,240.

Detective Sgt. Charles J. Burns said Edward K. Ambrose of Wheat Ridge signed a written confession admitting he took the money then became frightened and burned the bag and its contents without looking inside.

Burns said Ambrose had been under suspicion since May 15, the day he picked up the money at the Gano-Downs Company but did not deliver it to its destination, the Denver National Bank.

Burns said Ambrose, a former policeman and the father of four children, signed the statement in which he said that he became alarmed after taking the money and burned the bag at 3:00 A.M. the next day on a lonely road near Arvada.

Polygraph tests were conducted by polygraphist emeritus Alex L. Gregory, brought to Denver by Leonard DeLue, operator of the armored truck service.

Until he underwent polygraphy, Ambrose steadfastly maintained his innocence, saying he did not know what happened to the bag.

But when his brain and autonomic nervous system put deception criteria on the polygrams, Ambrose broke down and confessed. He said he was worried about debts and that when he saw the money at the store he took it to the truck and hid it in the sleeve of his jacket which was hanging in the money compartment.

*   *   *

On the morning of July 6, 1965, Sergeant Robert J. Roeske of Amarillo Air Force Base did not show up for duty and was put on report as absent without leave.

That same day, a terrible smell eminated from a locked dormitory locker in the 3320th Maintenance and Supply Group. OSI and the provost marshall's men opened the locker.

Peering inside, they viewed a badly decomposed and bloated body wearing Air Force pajamas. "There's a tie knotted around his neck," one agent observed.

The body was identified as that of Staff Sergeant Robert Roeske, 38, a veteran of seventeen years and nine months of military service.

The results of the autopsy were not surprising: the sergeant had been strangled to death with the tie found around his neck.

With a Herculean investigative task facing them, OSI men first focused their attention on the twenty-four men assigned to Dormitory 3419, where the slain sergeant had been quartered.

Interviews disclosed Sgt. Roeske last had been seen about 7:30 or 8 o'clock on the evening of July 1, seated on the dormitory steps. From another resident of Dormitory 3419, OSI sleuths gained their first information as to when Roeske might have met his violent end.

Around 9:30 or 10 P.M. on July 1, the airman recalled, he heard sounds of scuffling, apparently coming from Roeske's room or one nearby. Then he heard a man's voice cry out, "No, no, no!" followed by heavy running footsteps.

By the next day, the meticulous quizzing of base personnel turned up a possible motive for the brazen murder.

Recently Sgt. Roeske had mentioned—especially when drinking—that he had inherited about $16,000 following the death of his father. As a result of this story, a widely circulated rumor was that Roeske kept a large sum of money, in $100 bills, stashed in a drawer in his room.

Following up this lead, investigators learned that although Roeske's father had died, the sergeant had not fallen heir to a fortune. A careful search of the sergeant's personal effects was made. All missing items, including a watch with an unusual wrist band, were noted.

Meanwhile, the stories told by several airmen were checked and verified by OSI polygraph experts. Yet a week later the OSI agents were no nearer, seemingly, to a solution of the baffling homicide.

So, OSI enlisted the help of the Amarillo Police Department, specifically the detective division under the direction of Captain Paul Nickelson.

City police were asked to locate and question a former airman who only recently had become a civilian following his discharge from service at Amarillo Air Force Base. The man who had aroused OSI was identified as 20-year-old Robert Earl McIllwain, a former member of the 3320th M & S Group, and a known acquaintance of Sgt. Roeske's.

According to Air Force files, McIllwain had been given a general discharge, or in effect, a bad conduct discharge, on June 18, 1965, reportedly over such things as bad debts, theft and hot checks.

Meeting at police headquarters in Amarillo, the OSI men went over their file, including notes and photographs, with four members of the detective section: Captain Nickelson, Lieutenant Charles Hollis (in charge of homicide investigations) and homicide Detectives Jimmy Davis and Donald Prather. The briefing took four hours.

The next morning, Lieutenant Hollis assigned Detectives Prather and Davis to scour the city for McIllwain.

First, his name was checked against police files. This routine procedure bore fruit. McIllwain had figured in an accidental shooting in the city two weeks earlier. The young girl's parents told officers that she was accidentally shot while Robert McIllwain was cleaning a .25 automatic. McIllwain had also been wounded in the hand by the same bullet which struck their daughter in the hip. Since it had been an accident, the parents had not been interested in pressing charges.

Now, Detectives Prather and Davis drove to the section of town known as The Flats, where over a period of time they had established numerous friendly informants. They put out the word they wanted to talk to McIllwain about the accidental shooting.

Shortly, the sleuths learned that McIllwain was engaged to marry a girl employed by a firm specializing in wedding arrangements.

When they interviewed the nervous young woman, they learned she had known McIllwain about nine months, and confirmed they were engaged to be married. She was surprised to learn from officers he still was not in the Air Force.

"When did you last see him?" Davis asked.

The attractive girl thought a minute. "It must have been day before yesterday." The next information she volunteered startled detectives. She had noticed her spouse to be wearing a new watch, "a gold watch with what looked like slats on the sides and a stretchy thing in the middle."

Still using the accidental shooting as their reason for wanting to see McIllwain, Detectives Prather and Davis continued putting out the word. Eventually they located the suspect registered in a small hotel. He was not in. They left word for him to call them, and went back to the station.

Thirty minutes later, McIllwain telephoned and said he was at his hotel room.

"Stay put—we'll be by in a minute."

At headquarters, McIllwain learned that police wanted to discuss more than the accidental shooting with him. The talk started out that way but suddenly it switched to his whereabouts on July 1.

After lengthy interrogation, McIllwain still denied having seen Sgt. Roeske on the day of his death, and disclaimed any knowledge of his slaying, and he denied stealing Roeske's watch.

Lieutenant Hollis and Prather conferred with Nickelson and Davis. "His story is too pat," Hollis said. "He knows exactly where he was—what time and who he was with—all day on July 1st."

"Let's see if he'll agree to a polygraph test," Captain Nickelson said.

Captain L. R. Wynne was called in and quickly briefed on the details. McIllwain readily agreed to submit, and signed a consent-release form.

The first chart was over. "It shows he isn't telling the truth," Captain Wynne told the group waiting in an outer office. "But he is nervous and tense. He needs to relax before I run another one."

The suspect was given food, coffee and cigarettes. Then the second test commenced.

"Do you actually know who killed Sergeant Roeske?"

"No."

"Did you kill Sergeant Roeske?"

"No."

"Were you in Sergeant Roeske's room when he was murdered?"

"No."

"Did you strangle Sergeant Roeske to death with a tie?"

"No."

"Beyond a doubt, he is lying," Wynne said. He returned to the examining room and faced the suspect.

"Man," he said, "these charts indicate you are deeply involved."

McIllwain drew on his cigarette, mashed it out in a tray on the desk. He said he was ready to make a statement.

The confessed killer was booked into city jail. A formal complaint of murder with malice aforethought was filed against him the same day. He was ordered held without bond.

McIllwain was indicted for murder by the Potter Grand Jury on July 20, 1965.

Subsequently, he was convicted of murder in Potter County and sentenced to death in the electric chair. However, the Texas Supreme Court granted him a new trial, primarily because his attorneys alleged that Captain L. R. Wynne, in order to obtain a confession, asked McIllwain "how he wanted to die—gun, knife, or beaten to death."

He was re-tried on a change of venue to Childress County,

again found guilty of murder and sentenced to fifty years in the state penitentiary.*

* * *

In Minneapolis, Minnesota, November 19, 1960, at approximately 8:00 P.M., Mrs. Jane Black (name fictitious) was found lying on the floor of a combined restaurant and living quarters owned and operated by her husband and herself.

There were three wounds in her head, one on the right side of the forehead near the eyebrow, another on the left side directly above the left ear, and one in the front hairline slightly to the left of the nose.

She was dressed in pajamas over which she wore a wine-colored robe. A .25 caliber cartridge case was found between her outstretched legs. She was wearing socks and one shoe and, although her left shoe was found eighteen inches from her feet, there were no signs or evidence of a struggle.

The cash register, which was closed, contained $1.18 in coin. A .25 caliber bullet in good condition was found near the wall to the rear of the body.

The autopsy revealed that Mrs. Black had been shot twice in the head, and laboratory tests showed that a lodged fragment of metal therein proved to be a portion of the bullet.

The autopsy also indicated that one bullet, in piercing the head, had made an entrance wound on the right side and an exit wound on the left.

The time of death was established by the pathologist as between 11:00 A.M. and 7:00 P.M. on Saturday the 19th.

Investigating officers had only one possible suspect, John Doe (name fictitious), age 71, who for the past ten years had been a close personal friend of the victim and her husband. He had, on several occasions, loaned money to Jane Black and stated at the time of her death she still owed him $80.

He emphatically denied killing her and disclaimed knowledge of anyone else who might have committed the murder.

John Doe had an unbreakable alibi for the 19th, and he denied ownership or possession of a .25 caliber automatic.

---

*McIllwain v. State of Texas, 402 S.W. 2d 916.

On December 9, he submitted to polygraphy.

Eight charts conducted by C. B. Hanscom finally established that John Doe was guilty of the murder of Jane Black.

On Saturday, the 19th, he callously went about his customary routine business, thus unintentionally establishing a foolproof alibi which the autopsy report unbelievably and erroneously corroborated.

When C. B. Hanscom confronted John Doe with the polygraph charts, and pointed out the deception criteria, the suspect confessed. But he insisted he threw the murder weapon in the river.

Hanscom proceeded with a weapon search and disposition test.

"Did you throw the gun in the river?"

"Yes."

"Did you hide the gun on your property?"

"No."

Specific response appeared following the last question. Hanscom isolated his question formulation in one area.

John Doe eventually led officers to the gun, which was hidden in one of the outbuildings on his property.

It was recovered and tests proved it to be prima facie evidence.

John Doe was tried and convicted of manslaughter.

*   *   *

In August of 1962, the Hennepin County, Minnesota Sheriff's office held a 27-year-old man in custody on a charge of burglary.

While a background check was being run, the suspect summoned an investigator and stated he wished to make a deal for clemency on the burglary charge. For this he would give pertinent information regarding a murder which took place in July of 1962.

This was his story (all names are fictitious):

Jake Aaron said he was drinking in a bar one evening when he met an individual named Bill Green who showed him a revolver. Green bragged that he had used the gun July past to "blow the guts out of a no good bum" in a small town approximately seventy miles from the Twin Cities area.

Green offered to sell the gun to Aaron, and the suspect said he bought it.

At a later date, Aaron said he sold the weapon to a Dr.

William Smith. Investigation confirmed subject's sale of the gun as claimed, but because of an unsolved murder in the area to which he had alluded, he was asked if he would volunteer to verify the truthfulness of his story via polygraphy.

He agreed.

The examination was conducted at the University of Minnesota Department of Police laboratory.

The test began, initially probing only the critical areas involving Aaron's conversation with Bill Green, and the sale of the weapon.

Chart analysis indicated Aaron was truthful concerning his sale of the weapon to Dr. Smith.

However, his body produced specific response in two other areas: (a) his conversation with Bill Green, and (b) the method by which he obtained the weapon.

C. B. Hanscom bore down. His question formulation became exacting and precise.

Aaron's autonomic nervous system, in a manner of speaking, blew its control fuse. Hanscom backed off, then began a delicate and deliberate interrogation.

It wasn't long before Aaron had confessed not only to the burglary in question, but also to the murder.

Laboratory analysis of the weapon verified it was the one used in the murder in northern Minnesota.

Aaron was sentenced to fifty years and one day in the Minnesota State prison.

*　　*　　*

In February, 1968, a soft-spoken young farmer regarded as a pillar in his tiny community of Loco, Texas, not only upset but astonished the entire world after producing photographs and telling a weird story of his contact with alien spacemen.

Carroll Wayne Watts produced amazing photographs of a cylindrical type spacecraft and told of his meetings with small, grey, squatty men who came from the planet Mars.

Collingsworth County Sheriff John Rainey, normally an extremely cautious, analyzing man, said Watts had no possible motive, as far as the sheriff was concerned, in participating in a deception, and added that he felt as many as fifty other area residents would be willing to swear to Government investigators they had seen unexplainable lights or craft.

After examination of some of the pictures submitted for authoritative inspection, Dr. J. Allen Hynek, Chairman of the astronomy department at Northwestern University, and advisor to the Air Force Blue Book which handles sightings of unidentified flying objects (UFO's), said:

"If this is a hoax, it is a very, very clever one. In fact, it would be almost as interesting as what this farmer claimed has happened to him."

Then Dr. Hynek suggested Watts take a polygraph test.

Captain L. R. Wynne, at that time a member of the Texas State Polygraph Licensing Board, conducted the test.

After a four-hour session with Watts, Wynne reported:

"The whole story is just one big lie. I haven't found a word of truth in it from beginning to end."

Wynne added, "I've been in police work seventeen years and never saw a story as prefabricated as this one, or persons so eager and willing to undergo the polygraph challenge.

Later, Watts told reporters, "I didn't know how to stop the story once it got started. The whole thing just got out of hand."

*   *   *

On December 12, 1964, in Long Beach, California, Robert Cain (name fictitious) screamed into the telephone, "Get an ambulance out here quick to 1234 Atlantic Boulevard. My brother's been shot!"

Jones Ambulance Service was notified and rushed to the address. They found Junior Abel (name fictitious) lying on the front room floor. Blood oozed from a bullet hole in his side. He died before they could get him on a stretcher.

Police Sergeant W. R. Decker quickly arrived at the scene and began the initial investigation. Robert Cain said Junior Abel was his half-brother, some six years older, and that the two were very close. Tears streamed down his cheeks.

"How did it happen, son?" Sgt. Decker asked.

"I shot him! Oh, my God, I shot him!" He covered his face with his hands.

"Take your time, son," Sgt. Decker said gently. "Tell me about it."

"Lord, it was an accident. I didn't even know the gun was loaded."

He was referring to a .38 blue steel revolver found near a sofa across the room from the deceased.

Sgt. Decker fought back the tears in his own eyes. "Try to calm down, Robert. Easy does it. Just tell us what happened."

"Ma left about twenty minutes ago for the movies. Junior and me were watching TV. I decided to pull out some of my war souveniers. I went to my bedroom and got this old English-made .38 from a dresser drawer and went back in the front room and showed it to him.

"Junior looked at it and even tried to twirl it around on his finger. He couldn't. We just laughed about it. He gave the gun back to me.

"Then he got up and started toward the kitchen. I was just kidding. I said, 'I'm the Lone Ranger and I'm going to get you.' I pointed the gun and it went off."

Inspector McIntire and Technician Donnelley arrived and commenced their investigation. There was only one bullet entrance in the body. When they discovered a mashed bullet imbedded in a stucco wall, they became suspicious. Also, the position of the body on the floor where Cain said his half-brother was standing when the bullet struck him, and Cain's own position in the room, indicated something was not quite right.

On December 24, long after the funeral, Sgt. Robertson of the homicide detail again questioned Cain. He noted discrepancies from the boy's original story. He casually suggested polygraphy.

"Cain seemed unperturbed. "You betcha, sergeant," he said. "If there's any doubt, I sure want it cleared up."

The morning of December 26, Cain met polygraphist John A. Charney, a Keeler Institute graduate with several thousand criminal cases already under his belt. Part of the question formulation went thus:

"Did you know the gun was loaded before you pointed it at your brother?"

"No."

Deception criteria.

"Did you personally load the gun before you brought it into the front room?"

"No."

Deception criteria.

"Did you pull the trigger knowing the gun was loaded?"

"No."

Deception criteria.

"Did you and your half brother have an argument just before he was shot?"

"No."

Deception criteria.

"Did you deliberately shoot your brother?"

"No."

Deception criteria.

Charney deactivated the instrument and leaned back in his chair. "Robert," he said, "I don't think there's any need of going on. Why did you kill your brother?"

Robert Cain's head fell forward on his chest. He had difficulty clearing his throat. "He always bullied and ridiculed me about everything. We had a stupid argument. He told me he was going to kick the shit out of me. Then he said I was a chicken-livered sonofabitch. He said he was going to tell Ma I was a queer.

"I couldn't take no more. I just got the gun and shot him."

Case No. 648029, Long Beach Police Department was closed.

Robert Cain will be in a mental institution for many years to come.

*   *   *

This is the bloody, brutal, itinerary logged by Dennis Whitney, age 17, on his cross-country rob-and-kill rampage in which six persons died and another was left critically wounded.*

February 12, 1960: James Ryan, Victorville, California, filling

---

*Dade County, Fla., State Attorney Case No. 199. Legal case citations: 132 So. 2d 599; 152 So. 2d 272; 339 So. 2d 275. Appeal, Whitney v. State, 184 So. 2d 207.

station attendant, shot once in the back of the head when he argued with Whitney during a holdup. Ryan soon died. Whitney escaped with $30 taken from the cash register, stole a car and headed east.

February 20, 1960: Spencer Frazier, Negro chef, shot once fatally, through the head by Whitney at Frazier's shack in Phoenix, Arizona. Whitney said Frazier befriended him, later made homosexual advances. Whitney stole Frazier's 1950 convertible and drove it to Tucson.

February 21, 1960: Glen D. Smith, father of two and with a pergnant wife, shot and killed at a service station during a holdup which netted Whitney $85. Whitney then drove until he ran out of gas near Tombstone, Arizona, then hitched a ride with a Miami-bound truck.

February 28, 1960: Arthur Keeler, shot and killed in a service station holdup south of Perrine, Florida, on U.S. Highway 1. Whitney said Keeler "pulled something out of his pocket and I thought it was a gun. So, I shot him."

March 3, 1960: Jack L. Beecher, shot four times by Whitney during a holdup of a service station. Beecher survived.

March 4, 1960: Mrs. Virginia Selby, Hialeah housewife and grandmother, shot and killed by Whitney near Jupiter, Florida, after the killer kidnapped her because she refused to leave her car when he got in at a Miami parking lot and told her to get out.

James Buchanan, staff writer for *The Miami Herald* records the dramatic story of how a policeman, with the help of polygraphy, obtained a confession from Dennis Whitney.

In a small, quiet room at Miami Police Headquarters, in March of 1960, Whitney "told all" to polygraph authority Warren Holmes.

"Red, you've admitted one shooting at Peters and another at West Palm Beach but deny an earlier one here at Miami. Is that because it was your first murder? That's what usually bothers men most—the first one. It's the one they'll never readily admit. Now I feel you did this one in Miami and are holding back. Tell me, why did you do it?"

"I don't know why I did it."

"Was it the way the man (Ken Mazzarano) looked at you? Were you afraid to admit it because it was the first one?"

"I guess so."

In these simple words, and in a quiet conversation which led up to the admission, Holmes wrung from the youth not only the confession to the Mazzarano slaying, but to another murder in Victorville, California, a pair in Phoenix, Arizona, and still another in Tucson, Arizona, for a total of four newly admitted killings.

Whitney already had told Palm Beach County authorities that he was responsible for the fatal shooting of Arthur Keeler and Mrs. Virginia Selby, while escaping an ever-tightening police dragnet.

Oddly enough, Holmes turned the first trick without ever utilizing the polygraph instrument. He did it through a personal warmth which he developed with the boy, and with the background knowledge of technical details of the slayings provided by the City of Miami police department's homicide bureau detectives.

Only when Whitney insisted he knew nothing about the California and Arizona murders did Holmes resort to polygraphy, and then only to assure himself that the youth was withholding information.

The test lasted less than four minutes. The questions came at regular ten to fifteen second intervals, with irrelevant questions interspersed for the purpose of letting Whitney's autonomic nervous system return to its preestablished physiological "norm" following a relevant question.

"Do you actually know who shot the man in Tucson?"

"No."

Specific response.

"Did you tell the truth about the way the shootings occurred in Florida?"

"Yes."

No specific response.

"Did you commit any holdups in California?"

"No."

Specific response.

"Did you shoot the man in question in Tucson?"

"No."

Specific response.

"Do you know who shot the man in Tucson?"

"No."

Specific response.

It was at this point that Holmes, satisfied he was on the right track, discontinued polygraphy and began to query Whitney about the route he took from California to Florida.

"Red, the slugs from those California and Arizona killings are on their way here. You know our ballistics men can match them to your gun. What difference does it make to you to hold out the truth from us? Why don't you straighten yourself out all the way?"

"What happens then? I'd just have to go back to Arizona and California for trial, wouldn't I?"

"Not necessarily. Don't you want to go back?"

"I don't want to go back to California."

"All right then, you did the one in California and the one in Tucson, right?"

"Yeah."

"Now is there any more?"

"No."

"Why did you beat around the bush about these, Red?"

"Listen, I might as well tell you. . . . They'll find the guy anyway. I shot a queer in Phoenix."

"Did he die?"

"Yeah. The guy in Phoenix I'm not worried about because he was a queer."

It wasn't until later, when he again was questioned by Holmes that Whitney admitting shooting still another man in Phoenix, a Negro who offered him a place to sleep and whom Whitney also accused of being a homosexual.

The first Phoenix victim was elderly Ira Lee Hardison, whom Whitney described as a "bum who came into this old bus in which I was sleeping and started playing around."

It was the following day, after taking $10 and keys to the

Negro's old Oldsmobile, that Whitney started for Florida and abandoned the car on U.S. Highway 80.

He was picked up by Miami truck driver Howard Fraleigh, and brought to Miami.

Holmes' patient questioning also brought out more details on the abduction of Mrs. Selby. And Whitney told how, after his first Miami murder he left Mazzarano's filling station, returned to his hotel to do his laundry, and then went out again, bent on another holdup.

This was the time he picked Arthur Keeler's station, shot and killed Keeler.

He also detailed how, on the night following the Mazzarano and Keeler murders, he returned to the southwest section, picked up the same stolen car he had used in the slayings, and drove toward West Palm Beach looking for more holdup victims.

"How many more people were you going to kill?"

"I wasn't planning on killing any more if I could help it."

"Did you care if you got caught or not?"

"I guess I didn't."

"Did you feel sorry about the killings?"

"Yes."

"What happened when you were driving toward Palm Beach and back?"

"I was on A1A, and pulled into the first station. I had my gun and wanted money. But I just couldn't bring myself to hold the fellow up. Then I drove down the highway to another station and tried again. I planned to do it, but finally said, 'Aw, to hell with it,' and drove back to Miami."

Whitney also had a different description of his capture on a Palm Beach County canal bank than that offered by his captors. The youth said he was asleep at the time he was taken, "and not pointing a gun at anyone."

"I woke up with my own gun about two feet away and this fellow pointing his gun at my head. I wasn't going to reach for my gun, believe me. Then this fellow fired into the air and help came."

He described how he first tried to convince Mrs. Selby she should leave the car when he entered it.

"Did you take her with you at gunpoint?"

"Not at first. I tried to make her get out. Then I showed her the gun and told her to move over. Later she said she wanted to get out but I told her the cops were after me and I wouldn't let her out.

"Then, up north, around North Miami, I tried to put her out two or three times, but she said she was cold, couldn't walk, and that she was lost. I was heading for Jacksonville to look for a job and decided to take her along."

"Was she crying?"

"No, just sort of pleading. She got to arguing with me finally, and then found a hammer on the car floor. When she started hitting me I turned off the highway and shot her. I didn't beat her, just shot her."

Of all his murders, Whitney would admit there was no provocation only for the Mazzarano shooting.

"I was going to get gas (for the car he had stolen only minutes before), rob him, and let it go at that," Whitney said.

"Tell me what happened in the station, what took place?"

"I told him it was a stickup and got about $90 from the cash register and $10 from the wallet he handed me, and then walked him back to the rear of the station near a work bench. I was looking for something to tie him up. I couldn't find anything. Then I just turned around, looked at him, and shot him."

"What did you do then?"

"I went back to my hotel and took my laundry out to one of those coin places to do it. I came back and left the hotel again about 1:00 A.M., driving down Biscayne and found sometime later I was in Peters. I was thinking that since I'd pulled one robbery I might as well do a couple more."

In May of 1960, court-appointed attorney Charles Nugent, former county solicitor, filed notice in West Palm Beach that he would enter a plea of insanity for Whitney.

Dennis Whitney was sentenced to death in the electric chair. His counsel appealed.

The Florida Supreme Court upheld the death penalty on two

separate occasions, then granted a thirty-day stay two days before Whitney's execution was to be carried out.

On Thursday, October 19, 1967, the United States Supreme Court was asked to hear the Dennis Whitney case because, his attorney pleaded, publicity deprived Whitney of a fair trial.

Since then, Whitney has filed all kinds of appeals which have ended in failure. In March of 1969, the American Civil Liberties Union had secured a Federal Court order, in effect, blocking all executions of Death Row prisoners while a Federal Judge was trying to make up his mind whether or not capital punishment is cruel and unusual punishment.

We wonder if the Court will also consider whether or not Whitney's wholesale slaughter of so many innocent persons was not just a "little bit cruel and unusual."

*   *   *

Briefed forthwith are a few other cases of the legendary Warren Holmes, as his brilliant investigative brain and his polygraph techniques objectively explore both sides of the coin. These cases were solved only through polygraphy.

Mrs. Rebecca Nudel was murdered. Daniel Grant was one of seven people polygraphed as suspects.* He was a part-time employee of a home decorators and upholstery shop in Miami. The shop was owned by the murdered woman's husband.

There was no evidence or suspicion directed toward Grant. He was simply routinely tested along with others.

A "peak of tension" test concerning the placement of the victim's pocketbook revealed his guilt. He confessed after the polygraph test and led officers to evidence corroborating his confession.

He was convicted, and is now on Death Row in the penitentiary at Raiford, Florida.

*   *   *

A deaf mute, Harry M. Munson (name fictitious) was suspected of murdering a chambermaid in the Miami Colonial Hotel. There was no evidence linking Munson to this case, other than

---

*171, So. 2d, 361; State Attorney Case No. 2045, Fla.

the fact that he was a runaway boy of 16 and living at the hotel.

With the assistance of a Miami detective, who held up cards on which were printed the pertinent examination questions, Holmes conducted a unique polygraph test.

Deception criteria was present.

After the test, Munson confessed to Holmes that he had killed the chambermaid, stabbing her forty-seven times with a pair of scissors.

Munson was sent to a mental institution for life.

* * *

The case of George Milton was nothing unusual for Warren Holmes. During a routine polygraph examination of Milton, the subject admitted that he had murdered his wife by driving his car into a canal while she was sleeping on the back seat, and was involved in four other murders with his mother.

The mother took out insurance on various bums, then she and her son would kill them.

All of this came out following polygraphy, because a detective was interested in finding out whether or not Milton was drunk or fell asleep when he drove his car into the canal.

George Milton is now serving life in the Florida State Penitentiary.*

* * *

James Edward Brooks was given a polygraph test regarding the death of Miss Helen Louise Baier, a long-term employee of the Western Union office in Palm Beach, Florida.**

Brooks was a part-time porter and was tested only because he had access to the office.

Miss Baier was bludgeoned to death during a robbery of the office safe. There was no evidence linking Brooks to this crime.

Holmes watched Foster's body produce deception criteria on the charts.

During posttest interrogation, Foster confessed that he had, in fact, killed Miss Haskings.

---

*147 So. 2d 137; State Attorney Case No. 1904, Dade County, Fla.
**117 So. 2d 482; Palm Beach County Criminal Case, 1788, Fla.

Warren D. Holmes watched Foster die in the electric chair.

*   *   *

At 8:30 P.M., December 8, 1958, Whitney Abell was attending a business meeting at St. Thomas Catholic Church in the peaceful little town of St. Cloud, Florida.

Mr. Abell just happened to casually glance outdoors. To his shocked surprise, he saw a flicker or orange flame through the rear windows of a home owned by the widow, Laura Thompson.

The alert merchant grabbed a phone and called the headquarters of the local volunteer fire department.

Moments later, the serenity of St. Cloud was shattered by the shrill sounds of sirens. Firemen who arrived at the Thompson home found the doors and windows tightly locked.

Forcing their way inside, firefighters probed through thick smoke, tinted with the ominous glow of flame. Now, as they lugged hose lines through the front door, the volunteers discovered what appeared to be several separate fires throughout the premises.

With horrifying speed, the consuming flames spread rapidly, but the firefighters, attacking each blaze in turn, were able to put them all out.

Next, they opened doors and windows to let out the smoke. It was when some semblance of normalcy had been restored that the firemen made a gruesome discovery. Laura Thompson lay on the bathroom floor, obviously dead.

The widow was still attired in her street clothes, which had been partially burned from her body. The grim scene was made grotesque by the fact that the dead woman's head and shoulders were draped limply over the ledge of a shower stall.

From a quick survey of the scene, firefighters assumed that Laura Thomspon, discovering her house on fire, had, herself, tried to extinguish the flames, and in so doing had set her clothing on fire. Then, running to the bathroom to extinguish the flames, she had perhaps fainted and thus become the victim.

Since the conflagration had resulted in a fatality, the fire chief put through calls to the Osceola County Sheriff's office and to the state fire marshall, reporting the tragedy.

In due course, Deputies Fred Littlefield and Claude Tindall, who arrived from the sheriff's office, summoned a local doctor to perform a preliminary examination of the corpse.

From the very first, the physician was puzzled by what he found. "There are numerous bruises on the upper part of the woman's body," he reported. "In addition, her nose is broken, both wrists are fractured, as are several of her ribs."

When the doctor finished his report, the deputies asked his opinion as to the cause of the woman's death.

"I believe that while trying to fight the fire alone, Mrs. Thompson panicked and suffered several severe falls against furniture in the smoke-filled house," he theorized. "Then she ran into the bathroom to turn the shower on her burning clothing, but apparently lost consciousness and fell."

Deputy Littlefield looked up from the notes he'd been taking. "Then you believe the death was accidental?"

The physician frowned. "Well, the circumstances are rather unusual, but I see nothing to indicate otherwise."

Thus ended the life of a once-happy and highly respected woman—and commenced a fantastic investigation that was to set the whole state of Florida on its ear.

Early the next morning, Willard "Tommy" Knight, deputy state fire marshall, arrived in St. Cloud. At the same time, so also arrived the son of the deceased, Paul Johnson. With Deputy Littlefield, they went to inspect the fire-blackened premises.

Paul Johnson viewed the dwelling and shook his head in perplexity. "I simply don't see how my mother's death could have been an accident," he said. "If she'd come home and found the house on fire, she'd have called the fire department."

Investigator Knight asked Paul Johnson to try and determine if anything was missing from the house.

"She owned a rather expensive brooch which isn't in her jewelry box now, and I can't find her camera. Also, her handbag on the dresser contains only a little change. Mother usually carried at least $10 or $20 with her." A note of apprehension filled his voice. "I can't say for certain, but it looks like she was robbed."

Knight decided to make a thorough inspection. First, he discovered a dishrag, partially burnt, located under the wooden kitchen cabinet. It smelled of kerosene. There was no question but that the cloth had been placed in this spot and set ablaze in a deliberate attempt to fire the cabinet. He found other evidence which convinced him that arson and possibly murder had taken place.

When the grand jury convened, Knight was thunderstruck by its verdict: "We find that death was accidental and the fire was not of incendiary origin."

It was then Tommy Knight dedicated himself to finding the unknown person or persons whom he felt responsible for Laura Thompson's death.

For two years, Tommy Knight ran down hundreds of leads into dead ends. Then in late 1961, an informant in St. Cloud told him that two boys, Donald Ray Ball, 18, and his younger half-brother, Raymond Newell Jeffers, had been arrested there for an attack on an 80-year-old woman in her home. The motive had been robbery and they had beaten the old woman badly.

She had lived to identify the culprits and both were now serving sentences—Donald Ball in Apalachee Correctional Institution, and Raymond Jeffers at Okeechobee School for Boys.

It was not until March 1962 that Knight was able to interview Donald Ray Ball. When he was through, he was positive Ball knew quite a bit about Laura Thompson's death.

The determined Knight fixed the youth with a cold stare. "Would you be willing to take a polygraph test?"

"Sure. Why not?" was the reply.

Knight appealed for help from Warren Holmes in Miami.

Holmes was agreeable, and on March 27, 1962, he conducted the test on Donald Ray Ball in the reformatory. With the instrument activated and the chart moving at six inches per minute under the recording pens, Holmes began his question formulation:

"Do you actually know who killed Laura Thompson?"

"No."

Specific response.

"Did you kill Mrs. Laura Thompson?"

"No."

Specific response.

"Do you know for a fact who set fire to her house?"

"No."

Specific response.

"Did you set fire to Laura Thompson's house?"

"No."

Specific response.

"Have you ever stolen anything from Laura Thompson's home?"

"No."

Specific response.

"Do you know anyone who was involved in Laura Thompson's death?"

"No."

Specific response.

Warren Holmes broke off the questioning and joined Tommy Knight in another office. "You're on to something," the polygraph expert said. "That boy is lying for all he's worth, but he's not about to admit it."

The two got their heads together and decided to approach Raymond Jeffers.

On April 7, 1962, Holmes talked with Jeffers at the Okeechobee School for Boys. He had none of the bravado exhibited by his older half-brother. He consented to be polygraphed.

It didn't take long. Jeffers broke.

"My half brother and I were in the living room behind a curtain when Mrs. Thompson came home," Jeffers sobbed. "When she saw us, we grabbed her and dragged her into the bedroom."

"Why were you and Donald in the house?" Holmes interrupted gently.

"To kill her," Jeffers cried.

"Why did you want to kill her?"

"Because she didn't want to pay my brother the money she owed him for mowing the lawn."

"How did you get in the house?"

"Through the back door. We got a camera, some rings and jewelry and $30. Then we just waited. When she came in I held her mouth while my brother hit her several times with a big stick. From the bedroom we dragged her into the bathroom. My brother kept hitting her some more.

"We got a can of kerosene from the garage and started fires all over the house. We set her clothes on fire, too. We ran out the back door and locked it, then beat it down the alley and went home."

Warren Holmes patiently listened until the boy was finished then he conducted a simple truth verification test:

"Did you make up the story about you and your half-brother?"

"No."

"Did you make a truthful confession prior to this test?"

"Yes."

"Did you and Donald actually kill Mrs. Thompson?"

"Yes."

"Did you and your brother set the fires in Mrs. Thompson's home?"

"Yes."

"Was anyone besides Donald with you at the time of Mrs. Thompson's death?"

"No."

At test conclusion, Warren Holmes said to Tommy Knight, "The boy is telling the truth. He and Donald did kill Mrs. Thompson."

On May 19, 1962, an Osceola grand jury indicted the two young killers.

Strangely, Raymond Jeffers, who suffered genuine remorse, was the only one found guilty. Although his confession to Holmes was corroborated by specific physical evidence, neither the confession nor the evidence could be used to convict Donald Ray Ball.

It was Ball who actually bludgeoned Laura Thompson to death. However, the State could not introduce the Jeffers* confession because under that archaic law, as prescribed by the deci-

---

*Osceola County, 9th Judicial Circuit, Case No. 41-62: 174 So. 2d 552.

sion of the *U.S. v. Bruton* case, the confession of one defendant cannot be introduced as evidence to convict another defendant.

Because of this legal ruling, the main instigator of this brutal crime escaped punishment, while Raymond Jeffers was found guilty and sentenced to life.

Not only were the experts wrong in classifying Laura Thompson's death as accidental, but even when the case was solved through polygraphy, the "law" stepped in and prevented complete and final justice.

VII

THE POLYGRAPH IN PRIVATE INDUSTRY

SINCE LAW ENFORCEMENT seldom has the staff or jurisdiction to cope with the many dishonest and other internal operating problems which have plagued private industry for years, the polygraph again becomes an investigative tool to quickly verify the contents of a person's own employment application, and employment background.

If the polygraph test in preemployment were not beneficial, if it defamed, falsely accused, discouraged new applicants, if it were not exceedingly reliable, literally thousands of private industrial firms, law enforcement agencies, numerous Federal departments, could not afford to use it.

During 1968, 3,000 polygraph examiners throughout this country conducted in excess of 500,000 preemployment tests.

Part of the satisfaction many companies may have in using polygraphy is its relatively low cost, which varies from about $15.00 to $50.00 per test. This cost can be contrasted with the expense of a standard background check—primarily based on hearsay—which might take several days or weeks and involve many manhours.

Objective polygraphy can more easily be contrasted with the cost of many psychological tests, which are based on almost pure subjectivity, and have an accuracy rating of less than 60 percent.

In 1967 Dr. Elvis Stephens, Editor of Business Studies at North Texas State University, wrote a paper covering his studies of preemployment polygraphy.

In order to determine what kind of applicant information a polygraphist can provide a personnel manager, Dr. Stephens contacted a polygraph firm. Permission was secured to examine the reports which the firm sent to its clients. Proper care was taken to

130

protect the privacy of the individuals concerned. Below are some of his findings:

TABLE I

	Number	Percent
Total applicants polygraphed:	508	
Recommendations:		
Hire	277	55
Not recommended	205	40
No recommendation	26	5

In case the subheadings above are misleading, it should be made clear that the polygraphist only obtains certain facts which he forwards to the personnel manager.

The polygraphist does not make the final hiring or rejecting decisions.

Almost always, the polygraphist does indicate significant admissions that reflect upon the applicant's past and/or present ability to perform a job. In the vast majority of these cases, the applicant has admitted his past acts, such as felony arrests, to the polygraphist, during the pretest and postchart interviews.

Table II indicates the basic categories of information one polygraph firm reported to three client firms during a one year period.

TABLE II

Categories	Number	Percent
Arrests	82	16
Unstable work record	30	6
Wants only short-term job	10	2
Fired from previous jobs	15	3
Major employee thefts	64	13
Personal/domestic problems	11	2
Health defects	15	3
Mental problems	31	6
Use of "hard" narcotics	16	3
Other reasons	30	6

The last category, "Other reasons," includes several applicants who had major drinking problems but had never been arrested for public drunkenness.

One applicant admitted taking an average of twenty-four "bennies" each week. One truck driver applicant, who had claimed on his application he had never been involved in a truck accident, admitted to the polygraphist that he had been a driver in four major truck accidents. Another driver applicant admitted getting "bennied up" and leaving a refrigerated truck loaded with shrimp and frog legs stranded in the Arizona desert.

Every employer wants to ascertain six basic factors contained in the makeup of every prospective employee:

1. Are you who you say you are? ✔
2. Are you what you say you are? ✔
3. Will you fit in? ✔
4. Are you physically capable? ✔
5. Can you work in harmony with other employees? ✔
6. Can you treat customers (and/or equipment) the way they should be treated?

In order to obtain the many ingredients which make up the foregoing six basics, the polygraph examiner generally utilizes a specially prepared pretest data sheet (illustrated at the end of this chapter).

The reader will note that the front and back of this data sheet closely resemble the front and back of the average employment application. When an applicant enters the examining room for preemployment, the examiner merely asks the subject questions relative thereto. Then he turns the data sheet over and fills in the most current employment record, as the subject tells or relates it to the examiner.

But here, the actual similarity ends. Inside the data sheet are a series of specific relevant questions (in this case numbered from 39 to 95).

One preemployment procedure might go thus:

"Now, Mr. Smith, we are going to go through a series of simple questions which are designed to help present to X Company somewhat of a picture of you as a prospective employee. There are no personal or embarrassing questions. Answer the questions 'Yes' or 'No.' If you wish to explain your answer to any particular question let's do so as we go along to save time. If you do not understand a question, please ask me to clarify it, and I'll be happy to do so."

And so, it begins with Question #30.

Depending on the examinee's age, sex, education, and employment background, obviously not all of the questions listed will be presented to every subject.

From the daily files of preemployment fact-finding in polygraphy we list a few routine examples, and ask the reader "If you were an employer, would you put these people on your payroll?"

The admissions and dates are factual and of record, given by each subject as he or she answered data sheet questions during the pretest interview, prior to instrumentation.

Example I

Subject was W/F/21, never married, with two children. She was applying for a grocery checker's job with a nationally known company. She completed the ninth grade. Her application was dated 3-21-68.

To data sheet question #47, she admitted quitting one job without giving proper notice. At question #48, she admitted being fired from one previous job. To question #83, "Have you ever been arrested and placed in jail?" she answered in the affirmative. When asked, "how many times?" and for what reasons, subject related the following:

One time, 1964, for investigation of concealing stolen merchandise. Insufficient evidence—she was released. Three times, 1966, for prostitution, paying $100 fine each time. One time, 1966, for burglary, and says she is now on five years probation.

To data sheet question #89, subject admitted being an accomplice to forging and passing $2,000 worth of bad checks in 1966, for which she had never been caught. To question #92, she said the last time she smoked marihuana was six months ago.

Her employment background was listed as follows: One week at a small drive-in grocery, ending 3-20-68; one month at a furniture factory in 1968; from October 1965 to July 1966, as a mail clerk for the U.S. Post Office Department. She mentioned that she'd had two or three other part-time jobs out of state while in school. These were not listed.

After her admissions, the actual polygraph test was conducted. Question #47 was reworded: "Have you quit more jobs without giving notice than what you've told us?" Question #48: "Have you been fired from more jobs than what you've told us?" Question #83: "Have you been arrested for anything else besides what you've told us?" Question #89: "Have you been involved in more undetected crimes than what you've told us in the past three years?" The follow-up to question #82: "Have you used marihuana more recently than what you've told us?"

Needless to say, she had falsified her employment application and obviously had made no mention of the foregoing during her interview with the grocery concern's personnel manager.

Example II

Subject was W/M/18, single, sharing an apartment with a friend. He was applying for a delivery job with one of the largest auto parts store chains in the country. He quit school in the tenth grade. His application was dated 4-1-68.

To question #48, he admitted being fired from a hamburger drive-in job in 1967. To question #62, worded: "Have you received any moving traffic citations in the past three years?" he admitted to nineteen. To question #63, he answered 'Yes.' explaining a six-month's suspension in 1966 for receiving too many traffic tickets. To question #83, he stated he had been arrested numerous times for not paying traffic tickets, but had never been placed in jail.

He also said his parents had him confined to a juvenile home in 1964 for correctional purposes, and again in 1966 for taking his father's car without permission. To question #53, worded: "Have you ever suffered a nervous breakdown?" he said he entered a mental hospital for psychiatric observation in 1965 and remained there one month. To question #92, subject said he tried smoking marihuana one time in 1967.

Employment background as given by subject: 3-12-68 to 3-19-68, U.S. Air Force Exchange, terminated for being late to work. Cook at a hamburger drive-in from 12-67 to 1-68, stating he was terminated because he complained to the manager of being overworked. A cabinet shop in Maryland from 11-67 to 12-67, quitting to return to his home state. A marble and granite company for three days during 10-67. A punch press operator out of state from 9-67 to 10-67, terminated for falsification of age. Then he listed eight other different types of jobs, none of them lasting more than two weeks respectively, saying he had been terminated from three of those.

After the foregoing, subject was polygraphed.

Example III

Subject was N/M/32, single, living with his sister. He was applying for a job in a drug warehouse. He said he completed the seventh grade. His draft classification was 4-F because of a bad knee. He never had a driver's license, although he owned a car and drove it every day. His application was dated 1-31-68.

To data sheet question #47, he admitted two. To #48, he admitted one. To question #83 he stated: "about fifty times during my life, mostly for petty theft." He admitted serving four years in prison, starting in 1959, for burglary. In 1963 he was given life for another burglary, but had the sentence reduced. He was released from prison in July of 1967.

Employment background (since his release from prison): three weeks, 1967, as a laborer with a pipe and supply company, quiting after an argument with his supervisor. One week, 1967, helper on a construction job, terminated for being late to work. One month, 1967, painter's helper with a manufacturing company, terminated for missing work.

Following these pretest admissions, he was polygraphed.

Example IV

Subject was W/M/26, separated from his wife and one child for three years. He had a sixth grade education. He was draft classified 1-Y, for asthma, he said. His application was dated 5-21-68. He was applying for a warehouse job.

To data sheet question #33, he admitted two shots of whiskey just prior to his polygraph appointment. At question #47, he admitted three or four. To #48, he admitted five or six times. To #51, he said he suffered from acute asthma and hayfever. At #58, he said he received a minor back strain in 1961 while working for a butane company. At #62, he said he had received three traffic tickets in the past year. To question #63, he recalled a driver's license suspension in 1962 for not having liability auto insurance following an accident. At question #65, he admitted taking an occasional drink on several jobs. To question #77, he admitted theft of $15-20 merchandise from a service station job in April of 1968. He also admitted theft of about $100 worth of merchandise from a service station job at age 16. From the same service station in 1968, he admitted theft of $100 cash during a two-month period of employment. To question #80, he admitted selling stolen tires, radios and auto parts in 1960.

Following question #83, he listed his arrest record as: 1-1958, investigation of theft, released; 1-1958, accessory to burglary, receiving a three-year probated sentence; twelve times for drunk and disorderly conduct, the last time in 1965; one-destroying private property in 1967; eight or nine times for failing to pay traffic tickets, the last time in 1968.

At question #89, he said he had been involved in theft of hub caps and auto parts in 1967-68.

Employment background listed: two weeks during 5-68 as a retail milk route driver; 2-68 to 4-68, as an attendant for a service station; 1-66 to 1-68, as a floor hand for a well service company; one year in 1965 as a laborer for a roofing company; one year in 1964 as a driver for a lumber company, terminated, he said, for "goofing off."

After these pretest admissions, he was polygraphed.

Example V

Subject was W/M/25, married, the father of one child. He had one previous marriage. He was applying for a drive-in grocery job. His draft classification was 1-Y, for "emotional" reasons, he said. He completed the eleventh grade. He served from 4-60 to 7-60 in the U.S. Navy, receiving a general discharge. His application was dated 8-15-68.

To data sheet question #47, he admitted three times. To #48, he said three times. Since age 18, he had ben involved in six minor automobile accidents. He had received one moving traffic citation in the past year. At question #53, he answered in the affirmative, saying he spent one month in a naval hospital in 1960 under psychiatric observation. To question #77, he admitted theft of $50 merchandise from a service station job where he worked part time while in school. From that same job he admitted theft of $150 cash. At question #80, he said he's sold stolen auto tires and wheels in 1960.

At question #83, he advised: arrested 1961 for petty theft, and fined; 1-1965, for delinquent traffc tickets; 1-1967, for delinquent traffic tickets. To question #80, he admitted forging and passing two checks in San Antonio, Texas in 1962.

He listed his employment background as: 2-68 through 8-68 as an assembler for an aircraft factory; nine motnhs for a service station in California; one month for another service station in California; two years as self-employer owner of a service station; part-time attendant for a service station while in school.

After his admissions, he was polygraphed.

Example VI

Subject was N/M/18, single, living with his grandparents. He had received no draft classification. He completed the tenth grade. He said he never attempted to get a driver's license. He was applying for a grocery warehouse job. His application was dated 9-9-68.

To question #47, he admitted one. From his last job, he admitted $10 worth of merchandise. To question #80, he admitted selling stolen hub caps, a camera, and various items of clothing within the past year.

He gave his arrest record as follows: 1-1965, burglary, spending eight months in a state reformatory; 1-1966, assault, put on six month's probation; 1-1966, burglary, put on one year's probation.

At question #89, undetected crimes in the past three years, he listed: one burglary of a Bar-B-Q place, 1966, stealing food and candy; one theft of a payroll check amounting to $120 which he forged and cashed; one burglary of a clothing store, stealing bows and arrows, footballs, basketballs, and tennis equipment.

To question #91, he admitted taking a shot of "speed" on two

separate occasions in 1966, and at question #92, he said he smok-
ed his last marihuana cigarette three days ago.

He listed only one job, from 2-68 to 6-68, as a machine operator for a door manufacturing plant.

On completion of the data sheet questions, subject was polygraphed.

Example VII

Subject was W/M/24, married with three stepchildren. He
completed the eleventh grade. He had a 4-F draft classification
following a general discharge from the U.S. Navy in 1963. He said
he was $2,000 in debt and behind in his payments. He was ap-
plying for a clerk's job in a liquor store. His application was dated
1-15-69.

To data sheet question #38, he said he'd had some ten to fifteen jobs besides those listed on his application. To question #47,
he said three. To qestion #48, he said five times. At #60, he told
of two minor auto accidents wihle he was driving. At #61, he said
one minor commercial vehicle accident, not chargeable to him.
To question #63, he said he had his driver's license suspended in
1965 for receiving too many tickets.

At question #77, he admitted theft of $200 worth of merchan-
dise from two large grocery chains where he worked three months,
respectively, in 1967. From a service station job not listed on his
employment application, he admitted theft of $50 in merchandise
and $75 in cash while employed for two months in 1967. To
question #80, he admitted selling stolen watches, tires and auto
parts consistently between the ages of 18 and 22.

He listed his arrest record as: five times for forging and passing a large number of worthless checks during 1966 and 1967. As a
result, he was convicted and served time in a state penitentiary
from 4-68 to 1-12-69. Additionally, he said he had previously been
picked up by police for "investigation of" some ten times, being
released each time.

To question #89, he admitted three separate thefts of auto
parts and one burglary of a service station in 1967 for which he
was never caught.

Although he had falsified his application with respect to arrest record and employment background, he listed with the polygraphist the following: Texas Deaprtment of Prisons, 4-68 to 1-69; one week, 1968, for a delivery service, getting fired for obtaining his driver's license under an assumed name; several service station jobs; three months with a grocery chain; three months with another grocery chain. He couldn't remember names of some places of previous employment, or the dates when so employed.

After the foregoing admissions, he was polygraphed.

Example VIII

Subject was W/M/26, married, no children. He said he had a 1-A draft classification. He was applying for a driver's job with a statewide pipe and supply company. His application was dated 1-15-69. He admitted drinking one beer prior to coming in for his test.

To question #47, he said three or four. To #48, he said once. To question #60, he said two minor, one chargeable. At question #62, he said two in the past year. At #65, he admitted taking an occasional drink on some previous jobs. To question #78, he admitted theft of $215 cash from a service station job in Mesa, Arizona in 1965. This job was not listed on his application. At question #80, he admitted selling a stolen stereo in 1968.

At question #83, he listed the following arrest record: one—age 14, six months in reformatory for theft; two—Mesa, Arizona, 1964, once for loitering and once for petty theft; one—1962, Davis, Oklahoma, burglary, serving two years in a reformatory; one—1959, Shawnee, Oklahoma, burglary, sent to orphanage for 14 months; two—1957, theft of money and accessory to auto theft; one—1960, burglary, receiving a two-year suspended sentence.

To question #89, undetected crimes in the past three years, he admitted: one—1968, house burglary, stealing a color TV set; one—1968, apartment burglary, stealing a stereo; one—1968, theft of television and record player set; one—1969, theft of two guitars in house burglary.

At question #90, he admitted forging one check for $7.50 when he was 16 years old. To question #92, he said the last time he smoked marihuana was late in 1968.

He listed his employment background thus: 9-68 to 1-69, as a driver for a delivery service; 6-68 to 9-68 as a driver for a lumber company; three years as a driver for a produce firm in Arizona; eight months as a hand for an Arizona farmer in 1963, where he was fired following a disagreement with his supervisor.

After the pretest admissions aforementioned, he was polygraphed.

Example IX

Subject was N/M/21, married with one child, but separated from his wife. He completed the eleventh grade. He was applying for a stocker's job in a large department store. His application was dated 7-3-67.

To data sheet question #48, he said three or four times. At #62, he said one in the past year. To question #77, he admitted in pretest: $50 merchandise or materials from his last job; $25.00 merchandise and $75 cash from a job in 1965. To question #80, he admitted receiving and selling about $300 worth of "hot" merchandise in 1966-67.

He said he had been arrested in 1964 for fighting, in 1965 for delinquent traffic tickets, and in 1967 for failure to pay child support.

He listed his employment background as: two days, ending 6-67 for a steel company; six months in 1967 for a cement mixer company; seven or eight months in 1966 for an auto supply store, terminated for missing work; eight months in 1965 as a laborer for a construction company, again let go for missing work.

Subject was polygraphed.

Example X

Subject was N/M/32, married, and the father of three children. He was applying for a job as a refrigeration mechanic trainee. His application was dated 6-29-67. He smelled strongly of alcohol. His speech was thick.

To question #48, he said he had been fired from a railroad company two years ago following an on-the-job argument. To question #58, he said he hurt his back on a construction job in

1966, was off two weeks, drew workman's compensation insurance, received four chiropractic treatments, was medically released but did not go back to work. Through an attorney, he filed suit and settled out of court for $3800, his lawyer receiving 40 percent.

He became rather vague about dates of arrests, but volunteered the following:

Theft of a watch in 1950, receiving six months in jail. Arrested for investigation of murder, 1960, held twenty-four hours and released; assault with a deadly weapon, 1961, which involved the wounding of two teenagers—held thirteen days and released; investigation of theft of a lawn mower in 1962, released; three times for delinquent traffic tickets in 1964, paying fines amounting to a total of $685; attempted robbery in 1966, paying a $65 fine, and released.

Due to some unknown amount of alcohol in his blood stream, he had difficulty remembering dates of employment, but he thick-tongued as follows: three months, 1967, driver for a freight line; three months, 1965, for a railroad; nine months as a driver for a lumber company, but he couldn't remember what year.

Subject was not polygraphed.

Example XI

Subject was W/F/36, divorced three times, no children. She was applying for a grocery store job. Her application was dated 6-28-67. Though employed at the time of her polygraph interview, she was merely seeking to change jobs.

At question #77, subject admitted theft of about $100 worth of merchandise, and at #78, about $100 worth of cash monies on an average per year from her current job where she had been employed four years. To question #89, she stated she and her 13-year-old daughter had jointly shoplifted an estimated $500 worth of clothing from local stores in the past year. To question #88, she said she had four INSF checks out totaling some $93.

She listed her employment background thus: four years at a grocery store; three years at an electrical fixture company, and two years at the Post Exchange in Camp Pendleton.

After pretest admissions, subject was polygraphed.

At the conclusion of polygraphy, the administering examiner writes a test report on the back of his data sheet, then advises the employer concerned.

Generally, a polygaphist will never know if a person is hired or rejected.

Invariably, the uninformed and misinformed ask an oft-repeated question: Why has government and private industry so avidly turned to polygraphy for preemployment screening of applicants?

The most practical answer, which speaks for itself, is because while most people are good and most people are basically honest, some are not.

Some people are not even "who" they say they are. A lot of people are not quite "what" they say they are. Stolen credit card users, swindlers, narcotics users, child molestors, and those involved in undetected crimes are but minor examples.

Law enforcement seemingly attracts two types of applicants— outstanding, and misfits. There are few in between.

Why does an undesirable apply for police work?

By becoming a policeman, the candidate—who has up until then been a misfit—proves to his parents, wife, friends, and most importantly to himself, that he is not the failure they thought him to be.

Supposedly only those who are the elite among society—as far as honesty, moral standards, and personal habits are concerned— are permitted to become police officers. This very well might be the first time these men have been considered on the right side of law and order.

Who can argue with them, for they are correct. The outstanding candidates who want to become policemen, apply for the job because of the job itself and its challenges and responsibilities which offer more satisfaction than material possessions, comfort, and safety.

This is all reflected in the pretest interview. Because of their attitudes, they are reconciled to a low salary and are prepared to get along on that salary without having to resort to taking bribes, shaking down people, or stealing.

On the other hand, the undesirables not only are a risk because of their previous activities, such as committing undetected crimes, but often they have been dissatisfied with every job they have ever held, and find no type of work rewarding. They work only because they have to work, and they regard a police job as one from which they can't be fired.

In addition, many want to become policemen only because of the power and authority the job offers. Once on the force, this type, which includes the sadist, is not only a potential scandal to the entire force and its reputation, but he will probably be inefficient, unhappy, and only good at "goofing off."*

Dr. G. H. Lawrence, Assistant Professor, Neuropsychiatric Department, St. Louis University School of Medicine, wrote of his first contact with polygraphy in the March 1966 issue of *Security World* magazine:

> I believe there is some uniqueness in my experience with polygraphy in that I have been seeing police applicants after the test, and have had a chance to evaluate the polygraph report with psychiatric orientation and, in addition, have had the opportunity to see the reaction of many people to the polygraph. I do very vividly remember my initial astonishment at the type of material gained by the polygraph technique.
>
> It became immediately apparent then, and still is, that polygraphy obtains information that cannot be obtained from any other source, such as the employment application, background investigation, psychometric testing or psychiatric examination.
>
> My knowledge of the use of polygraphy is quite limited and for the most part of an academic sort, but I believe I know enough about its use in criminal investigation to say that there are some very marked differences as it is presently being used in selection. I feel that the real value in selection is when polygraphy is so done that positive admissions are obtained.
>
> I think it should be stressed that no one can detect a good and clever liar, although there are some psychiatrists among my acquaintances who believe they have this most unusual gift. Most people, including psychiatrists, will detect the clumsy and obvious lie, and will be successfully lied to by a good liar. The way most people lie

*Arther, Richard O.: Polygraph Picks Potential Policemen, *The Journal of Polygraph Studies,* Vol. II, No. 2, Sept.-Oct., 1967.

is not outright denial but by an evasive process where they do not tell materially what they know is of significance.

It is probably well to spell out that the psychiatric exam is an evaluation procedure, whereas polygraphy is an information-getting procedure, although, in fact, there is some overlap.

Psychiatric examination brings in many clarifying and frequently mitigating circumstances about information discovered through polygraphy.

I have been seeing the borderline cases in that it was felt that people who clearly passed the polygraph examination did not have to undergo psychiatric evaluation, and that if very damaging information was discovered by the polygraph, it was pointless to have psychiatric examination.

I have even had doctor friends ask whether the polygraph ever makes a mistake, and from this source I must confess the question has been one of some annoyance in that I feel a doctor ought to know better. He ought to know better because nearly every procedure in medicine carries with it a percentage of errors. Many things "slip through" in medicine.

If it can be accepted that there is real value in medical science, even though it is not free of error, then the same courtesy should be extended to polygraphy.

Psychometric testing by the psychologist and psychiatric examination by the psychiatrist do not obtain the same information, and such esoteric procedures as intravenous pentathol, or the like, would find even chillier moral and political climate than polygraphy (also impractical and ineffective compared with polygraphy).

The polygraph, despite its hostile critics, is playing its part in law enforcement by objectively helping to select police applicants of satisfactory character, and with a higher degree of reliability.

*   *   *

Of every three accepted police applicants who have successfully passed the mental tests, physical examination, and background investigation necessary to become policemen, one should not be a police officer.

Why?

Because he does not meet the minimum qualifications.

This was not discovered or actually realized until the polygraph was utilized in the selection of police applicants.

There is no paper and pencil test that can uncover the great majority of those mentally ill persons wanting to be policemen. Even IQ tests have a large margin of error.

Let's look at some examples of what has been admitted during preemployment polygraph examination of police candidates.

Hit-and-run death of a pedestrain, severe beating of a captain while in the military, undetected embezzlement of some $3,000 from his present employer, exposing himself on at least four occasions to unknown females, beating and armed robbery after having engaged in homosexual acts with an estimated twenty victims.

A young 21-year-old police applicant acknowledged during his polygraph test that he previously had committed eleven armed robberies. He labored under the impression that since he had never been caught, he should not be held accountable.

The prospect of having such persons become police officers is frightening. The field investigator could not possibly have learned any of this disqualifying information. Since not one of the victims knew the applicant's identities, no arrests were ever made. In fact, there was no one to learn this from but the applicant himself.

Some people claim that the polygraph is not necessary—that a good background investigation will uncover the unfit. Such distractors have just ridiculously assumed that 100 percent of all crimes are cleared by arrest.

Before World War II, a field investigator could interview many neighbors who really knew the candidate, not only as a boy but also as a youth and young man. Today, with the high rates of population shift and population density, in-depth knowledge of one's neighbors is unknown in many parts of our country.

This is the main reason why—with the advent of a very fluid mobile, and unstable society—more and more law enforcement agencies, as well as business firms, are utilizing the skills of polygraphists.

About ten years ago, Commissioner Leo J. Mulcahy of the Connecticut State Police instituted their preemployment polygraph program after having two men trained under Richard O. Arther, Director of the National Training Center of Lie Detection, New York City. In June of 1964, Commissioner Mulcahy wrote:

The use of the polygraph by properly qualified examiners in the preemployment selection of the police candidate is one of the most valuable tools we have for eliminating the unfit.

The Polygraph Unit of the Connecticut State Police has identified sexual deviates, embezzlers, burglars, thieves. Since these persons had never been apprehended for their criminal acts, it was only by their own admissions that this was learned. Even the most careful background investigation would not have uncovered this information.

Yet, there are those who would attempt to deny the police service the use of polygraphy. This would allow such persons as criminals, sexual deviates, and sadists to enter the police service and be turned loose upon the public.

That certain people are against the polygraph is hard to believe; however, I can only attribute it to a lack of knowledge on the part of these people who propose laws stopping the use of polygraphy in preemployment selection.

I feel very strongly about this. My position on the matter is taken only because I am acutely aware of the types of persons the polygraph examiner has exposed. These persons otherwise would have been accepted as Connecticut State Police Troopers.

Ours is a position of trust. I must demand that every Connecticut Trooper be a person who can be trusted.

If I were not to avail myself of the polygraph—knowing what I know about its qualities—I would consider myself derelict in my duty and unfaithful to the trust confided in me by my Governor and the people whom my department serves.*

In one particular series of preemployment tests on police applicants conducted by John E. Reid & Associates, Chicago, Illinois, 57 percent were turned down because of their admissions to undetected burglaries, robberies, auto thefts, and rapes.

Had it not been for polygraph, these otherwise personable and pleasant-appearing persons might have been hired to "protect the public."

The fact that the efficacy of polygraphy in preemployment has proven itself beyond all doubt comes through the words of Robert E. Williams, Assistant Vice-President and Personnel Director of the Zale Corporation, the world's largest jewelry concern.*

---

*Personal letter to Richard O. Arther, June, 1964, pub. in *The Journal of Polygraph Studies*, Vol. II, No. 2, Sept.-Oct., 1967.

*Holmes, Sam F., Jr.: The Polygraph: Should Banks Use It In Selecting Personnel?, a thesis presented to The Faculty of the Southwestern Graduate School of Banking, Dallas, Texas, July, 1968, pp. 20, cir. 12.

Williams says, "Zale's has used the polygraph about ten years, but greatly expanded its use about four years ago. Now, all applicants for sensitive positions—those involving the handling of jewelry as salesmen, warehousemen, artists, designers, photographers, are screened by polygraphy."

Zale's has ten highly trained, full-time polygraph examiners on its staff (something an averaged sized or small, firm would not find practical). The examination of an applicant takes no more than an hour and confirms or reveals what would otherwise take weeks to find out through normal investigative means.

Williams continues. "Too often a reference simply won't give you the complete story on an applicant, and one can never be absolutely sure about reference comments. We feel the best place to go to find out the background of a person is to the person himself, and the polygraph is the best way to do this. We know we can trust the results.

"Using the polygraph in preemployment has prevented the hiring of many individuals who were thieves or whose background otherwise made them undesirable applicants.

"Most importantly, perhaps, and surprisingly, has been the relationship with the employees since the start of polygraphy. An amazing morale change, for the better, has resulted. Now, we know a store manager or other employee is honest, and he knows we know it—and that is very good for morale."

The reason for the employee's attitude toward polygraphy, and that of applicants, too, undoubtedly is due to the way Zale's personnel staff and polygraph examiners "sell" the reasons for using it.

"We explain," Williams says, "very carefully to the employee that the best way we know how to make sure the persons working around him are honest, and not stealing, is through polygraphy. The employee is told that if he ever should be suspected or accused of any wrong doing, the polygraph is instantly available as a means of clearing himself.

"Ten percent of our profits, before taxes, goes into an employee profit-sharing plan. It isn't hard to convince the employee that dishonesty costs him personally. Our employees don't want dishonest co-workers around.

"Zale's runs thousands and thousands of polygraph tests," adds Williams. "We are completely satisfied with the results. It helps us have a better shop, and the employees are better satisfied, and they work in a better atmosphere than ever before."

In 1968, the Personnel Director of the Lake Shore National Bank in Chicago, which has deposits in excess of $120 million, said, "We give a polygraph examination to every applicant if we are seriously interested in him. Very seldom is an applicant resentful of the polygraph when its use is properly explained to him. We have found the polygraph to be of great help in selection, and we will continue to use it for that purpose."*

John Murren, Personal Director of the huge dairy-drug firm, Foremost-McKesson, appeared before the Connecticut House of Representatives Labor Committee, March 10, 1967, and stated:

"We're using the polygraph merely to verify statements made by applicants. The fact is. . .there is no invasion of privacy, no more so than a physical examination prior to employment. This is no more an insult, or degrading thing, than a credit check when you go in and apply for a mortgage."**

An executive of a retail food corporation, which operates thousands of drive-in grocery stores throughout most of the nation, emphatically states: "We have successfully and beneficially utilized the many advantages contained in polygraphy nearly every hour of the working day since 1957. It has saved us literally hundreds of thousands of dollars. We wouldn't be without it."

The number three grocery chain in the nation, Kroger-Wyatt, Inc., has within its security staff polygraph examiners stationed in numerous regions for the purpose of preemployment, and to handle problems as they arise.

The most obvious advantage of polygraph preemployment is the basic verification of an applicant's claims on the job application form. However, there are several important advantages that are not so obvious.

---

*Pompian, Lillian: Business Turns to the Lie Detector, *Kiwanis Magazine,* Vol. 44, Dec. 1962-Jan. 1963, 55-60: Holmes, Sam F., Jr., First Nat'l Bank, Dallas, Texas. A thesis presented to The Faculty of the Southwestern Graduate School of Banking, July 1968, in a personal interview with Suzanne, Gillogly, personnel dicetor Lake Shore National Bank of Chicago, January 1968.

**Connecticut State Library, transcript of public hearings, March 10, 1967.

Although there is no absolute guarantee of the future, generally a person who has been an honest employee will continue to be an honest employee.

Through polygraphy, an insight is gained into this person's general attitude toward employers, pay, willingness to work, duties, fellow workers. For example, if he has thought very poorly of most or all of his previous employers, it is highly doubtful if he will now suddenly become a "company man."

Likewise, a man who believes he has been grossly underpaid at his previous job will hardly be satisfied if this new one is offering him only $19 more a week.

The person's attitude toward strangers is often noticed. For example, a person who is very antagonistic toward the polygraphist will probably be antagonistic toward clients/customers.

We are reminded of one applicant who was extremely hostile towards a certain polygraphist. Although he admitted being arrested several times for barroom fighting, the client hired him because he considered this to be "extracurricular" activity and had nothing to do with employment.

Within three weeks, after being hired, the new employee broke the jaw of a customer who had complained about the service. The company settled out of court for more than double the cost of the entire polygraph program for four years.*

Turnover is greatly reduced by spotting the person who is only seeking a short-term position. Not only does this greatly reduce the amount of money spent on hiring, but it also greatly lessens the direct and indirect costs of having to pay a beginner while he is being trained to perform his duties.

Finally, the polygraph in preemployment ferrets out those who go from job to job alleging phoney back injuries and filing insurance claims, at the same time revealing those persons who are accident prone and potential workman's compensation claims cases.

In 1965 a study released by Dale Systems, a security consulting firm, indicated the consequences of lax preemployment investigation. Research involving 4,000 admitted thieves, revealed that 68

---

*Arther, Richard O., in *The Journal of Polygraph Studies,* Vol. III, No. 4, Jan.- Feb., 1969.

percent of them were repeaters in major thefts. To the consulting firm's astonishment, 98 percent of the employers of these dishonest employees did not know of their past histories.

That same year, the Council of Polygraph Examiners, in a report on preemployment screening, indicated that while 70 percent of all persons tested for positions of trust pass their polygraphy test and get the job, a critical 30 percent were rejected. Out of this 30 percent, 90 percent are rejected on their own admissions of serious criminal behavior and use of narcotics.

The widespread use of narcotics almost staggers the imagination. Of 823 young persons between the ages of 17 and 22, tested and interviewed by this writer from October 1, 1968 through October 1, 1969, 618 readily admitting smoking marihuana from once to a thousand times. Of this 618, some 362 further admitted experimenting with LSD from once to 100 times. Two hundred and ten of these young people also admitted main-lining speed and "joy popping" with heroin. Twenty-six admitted smoking opium at least one time. Thirty-two stated they had started with marihuana and ended up "hooked" on the heavy stuff. As a result, they committed crimes to support their habits.

Yet, there are individuals and various groups about the country clamoring for legalization of marihuana.

A man who has been on the front line against the narcotics traffic for many years, John Storer, Chief of the California State Bureau of Narcotic Enforcement, stated in late October, 1969, that in no place in the world are penalties against possession and use of marihuana being removed.

In an interview with Arthur Ribbel, Sacramento Bureau, Copely News Service, Storer said that bulletins from the United Nations show that the trend is for stiffening narcotics penalties, including marihuana, rather than easing them.

Storer, who has spent most of his life fighting the drug traffic, does not agree that marihuana is a mild, harmless smoke, as some persons with title have suggested. "It may not be in the sense of physical addiction, per se," Storer said, "but it creates a psychological dependence and addiction. It also generates a curiosity about other drugs and leads to use of heroin and other harder narcotics."

Storer also remarked that he had seen enough "weed-heads" to be convinced that use of marihuana causes loss of ambition and restraint; the abandonment of ideals and ambitions; breakdown of reserves, and disturbance to memory; initiative and drive. A weak addict loses interest in his health and well-being, he indicated.

What is the reaction of a personnel director, or business owner, when he is advised, following a preemployment interview and polygraph test, that his new applicant admits being a periodic or frequent user of various types of narcotics?

Obviously it is somewhat negative. Many are simply not hired.

Has subject previous file? Yes_____ No_____   FILE NO. _____

							BUSINESS	
ACCOUNT NAME			CITY:				PHONE	
APP'T BY				REPORT TO				
APPT'T DATE		TIME		TEST GIVE: DATE			TIME	
TYPE OF TEST:	PE		PC	S	PT/FT	POSITION		
SUBJECT	FIRST		MIDDLE		LAST		MAIDEN	
ADDRESS						PHONE		
RACE	SEX	AGE	HT.	WT.	DOB	Place of Birth		
WHERE REARED				TIME HERE		Location Before		
DRIVERS LICENSE	STATE	NUMBER	EXPIRES	Social Security No.			Draft Class.	
EDUCATION				COLLEGE:				
MARITAL STATUS: M	(GRADE COMPLETED)			OTHER MARRIAGES	DIV.			SEP.
CHILDREN	DATE	PLACE		Spouse Employed	DATE	PLACE	INCOME	DATE
CHILDREN BY PREV. MARRIAGE	NUMBER	AGE		CHILD SUPPORT				
		NUMBER	AGE			AMOUNT	PAST DUE	
MILITARY RECORD BRANCH:		DATE OF ENTRY		DATE OF DISCHARGE		RATING RANK		
TYPE OF DISCHARGE				COURT MARTIALS			DISAB. COMP.	
FINANCIAL STATUS: HOME:				AUTO				
TOTAL OWED	RENT	BUY	PAYMENT	STATUS OF ACCOUNTS	MAKE	MODEL	OWE	
CREDITOR'S JUDGMENTS			BANK REFERENCE			CHECKING	CURRENT, BEHIND, ETC. SAVINGS LOAN	
FAVORITE HOBBIES								
INDEX DATA: TIME OUT:		TOTAL TIME		REPORT TO			BY	
RESULTS:	IND 1000-200-500	NG	G&PC	CA/WSM	NA GOE	TESTED BY:		

SPECIAL INSTRUCTIONS:

Figure 1A.

NORM QUESTIONS:

	Yes	No
1. IS TODAY _____ (DAY OF WEEK)? 2. IS THIS THE MONTH OF _____?		
3. DO YOU LIVE IN THE STATE OF TEXAS? 4. ARE YOU SITTING DOWN?		
5. HAVE YOU EVER SMOKED A CIGARETTE? 6. DO YOU EVER DRINK WATER?		
7. IS YOUR LAST NAME _____? 8. HAVE YOU EVER RIDDEN IN A CAR?		
9. ARE YOU WEARING A RING? A-WATCH? B-TIE? C-SHIRT? D-GLASSES? E-EARRINGS?		
10. DID YOU EVER DRINK COFFEE?		

GENERAL QUESTIONS:

	Yes	No
30. HAVE YOU GIVEN US YOUR TRUE AND CORRECT NAME?		
31. HAVE YOU EVER TAKEN A POLYGRAPH TEST BEFORE?		
32. HAVE YOU TAKEN ANY PILLS OR MEDICINES TODAY?		
33. HAVE YOU DRANK ANY ALCOHOL TODAY?		
34. DO YOU FEEL WELL TODAY?		
35. HAVE YOU EVER BEEN EMPLOYED BY THIS COMPANY BEFORE?		
36. HAVE YOU EVER BEEN EMPLOYED BY A SIMILAR COMPANY BEFORE?		
37. DID YOU TELL THE COMPLETE TRUTH ON YOUR EMPLOYMENT APPLICATION?		
38. DID YOU LEAVE A FORMER EMPLOYER OFF YOUR APPLICATION? (HOW MANY?)		

JOB RESPONSIBILITY QUESTIONS:

	Yes	No
39. HAVE YOU GIVEN US YOUR TRUE AND CORRECT AGE?		
40. HAVE YOU TOLD THE TRUTH ABOUT YOUR EMPLOYMENT BACKGROUND?		
41. DID YOU TELL THE COMPLETE TRUTH TO THE PERSON WHO INTERVIEWED YOU FOR THIS JOB?		
42. DO YOU KNOW WHAT JOB YOU ARE APPLYING FOR?		
43. DO YOU FEEL QUALIFIED TO DO THIS TYPE OF WORK?		
44. DO YOU NEED TRAINING FOR THIS JOB?		
45. WILL YOU BE SATISFIED WITH THE STARTING SALARY? (WHAT IS IT?)		
46. ARE YOU SEEKING LONG TERM (TEMPORARY) EMPLOYMENT WITH THIS COMPANY?		
47. HAVE YOU EVER QUIT A JOB WITHOUT GIVING REQUIRED NOTICE? (HOW MANY?)		
48. HAVE YOU EVER BEEN FIRED FROM A JOB FOR ANY REASON? (HOW MANY?)		
49. HAVE YOU EVER BEEN ASKED TO RESIGN FROM A JOB?		

ACCIDENT PRONE QUESTIONS

	Yes	No
50. HAVE YOU HAD ANY MAJOR OPERATIONS WITHIN THE PAST TEN YEARS?		

SECURITY QUESTIONS:

	Yes	No
70. ARE YOU APPLYING FOR THIS JOB FOR ANY REASON OTHER THAN EMPLOYMENT?		
71. ARE YOU BEING PLANTED ON THIS JOB FOR ANY PURPOSE?		
72. COULD YOUR EMPLOYMENT BE HARMFUL TO THIS COMPANY IN ANY PLANNED WAY?		
73. ARE YOU AWARE OF ANY ACTIVITY WITHIN THIS COMPANY WHICH IS DESIGNED TO CHANGE ITS PRESENT POLICIES AND PROCEDURES?		
74. DO YOU BELONG TO ANY GROUP WHICH ADVOCATES OVERTHROW OF THE AMERICAN SYSTEM OF GOVERNMENT?		
75. ARE YOU NOW OR HAVE YOU EVER BEEN A COMMUNIST SYMPATHIZER?		
76. DO YOU ACTUALLY KNOW ANYONE WHO HAS EVER WRITTEN A THREATENING LETTER TO THE PRESIDENT OR VICE-PRESIDENT OF THE UNITED STATES?		
77. HAVE YOU EVER STOLEN MERCHANDISE OR MATERIALS FROM A PLACE WHERE YOU HAVE WORKED?		
78. HAVE YOU EVER STOLEN MONEY FROM A PLACE WHERE YOU HAVE WORKED?		
79. COULD YOU BE WANTED BY THE POLICE ANYWHERE FOR ANY KIND OF A CRIME?		
80. HAVE YOU EVER KNOWINGLY SOLD STOLEN MERCHANDISE?		
81. HAVE YOU EVER CHEATED A CUSTOMER FOR PERSONAL GAIN?		
82. HAVE YOU EVER BEEN INVOLVED WITH A THEFT RING?		
83. HAVE YOU EVER BEEN ARRESTED AND PLACED IN JAIL?		
84. HAVE YOU EVER SERVED TIME IN A REFORMATORY OR PENITENTIARY?		
85. DO YOU KNOW ANY EMPLOYEE PRESENTLY WORKING FOR THIS COMPANY WHO HAS BEEN STEALING MONEY OR MERCHANDISE?		
86. HAVE YOU EVER BEEN TURNED DOWN BY A BONDING COMPANY?		
87. HAVE YOU EVER PAID A DEFAULT TO A BONDING COMPANY?		

Figure 1B.

51. ARE YOU IN GOOD HEALTH NOW?
52. HAVE YOU EVER BEEN TREATED BY A DOCTOR FOR DIZZY SPELLS?
53. HAVE YOU EVER SUFFERED A NERVOUS BREAKDOWN?

54. HAS A DOCTOR ADVISED THAT YOU MIGHT NEED AN OPERATION WITHIN THE NEXT YEAR?
55. HAVE YOU EVER HAD A BACK INJURY, OR STRAIN?
56. HAVE YOU EVER HAD A RUPTURE OR HERNIA OPERATION? (REPAIR?)

57. ARE YOU ATTEMPTING TO CONCEAL THE EXISTENCE OF ANY PRESENT PHYSICAL DISABILITY OR HEALTH PROBLEM?

58. HAVE YOU EVER BEEN INJURED ON ANY JOB WHERE YOU LOST TIME?

59. HAVE YOU EVER FILED FOR OR COLLECTED WORKMEN'S COMPENSATION INSURANCE FROM AN ON THE JOB INJURY?

60. HAVE YOU EVER HAD AN AUTOMOBILE ACCIDENT WHILE YOU WERE DRIVING? (HOW MANY TIMES?)

61. HAVE YOU EVER HAD A COMMERCIAL VEHICLE ACCIDENT WHILE YOU WERE DRIVING? (HOW MANY TIMES?)

62. HAVE YOU RECEIVED ANY MOVING TRAFFIC CITATIONS IN THE PAST YEAR? (3 YEARS?)
63. HAVE YOU EVER HAD A DRIVER'S LICENSE REVOKED OR SUSPENDED?

64. HAS DRINKING EVER INTERFERRED WITH YOUR WORK?
65. DID YOU EVER DRINK BEER, WINE OR WHISKEY ON THE JOB?

66. HAVE YOU EVER BEEN ARRESTED FOR DRIVING WHILE INTOXICATED?

67. HAVE YOU EVER HAD STOMACH ULCERS?
68. HAVE YOU EVER TAKEN THE CURE FOR ALCOHOLISM?
69. HAVE YOU EVER SOUGHT PSYCHIATRIC CONSULTATION FOR ANY REASON?

88. HAVE YOU WRITTEN ANY BAD CHECKS IN THE PAST YEAR? (ANY OUT NOW?)
89. HAVE YOU BEEN INVOLVED IN ANY UNDETECTED CRIMES IN THE PAST THREE YEARS?

90. HAVE YOU EVER FORGED ANOTHER PERSON'S NAME TO A CHECK?
91. HAVE YOU EVER USED OR SOLD NARCOTICS ILLEGALLY?
92. DID YOU EVER TRY SMOKING MARIHUANA?
93. DID YOU FALSIFY YOUR EMPLOYMENT APPLICATION IN ANY MANNER?
94. DO YOU LIKE TO GAMBLE AT CARDS, WITH DICE, OR AT HORSE RACES? (PREFER WHICH?)
95. HAVE YOU EVER FOUND IT NECESSARY TO SUE A FORMER EMPLOYER FOR ANY REASON?

INFORMATION: SUBJECT'S EXPLANATION TO DATA SHEET QUESTIONS

Figure 1C.

EXPERIENCE RECORD	COMPANIES WORKED FOR? LIST LAST EMPLOYMENT FIRST	INCOME AND JOB	GIVE IN DETAIL THE REASONS YOU LEFT EACH COMPANY
FROM			
	NAME		
TO	ADDRESS		
	TELEPHONE		
FROM			
	NAME		
TO	ADDRESS		
	TELEPHONE		
FROM			
	NAME		
TO	ADDRESS		
	TELEPHONE		
FROM			
	NAME		
TO	ADDRESS		
	TELEPHONE		

EXAMINER'S REPORT SECTION:

Figure 1D.

VIII

PROBLEM TESTING IN PRIVATE INDUSTRY

Every business can efficiently conduct its affairs only to the degree that its employees are both capable and reliable. There is a significant difference in these two terms.

Capable connotes expertise, the ability to perform well those duties and responsibilities assigned.

Reliable connotes dependability, integrity, good character— all of those characteristics so traditionally attributed to honesty.

Capability can be tested before an applicant is hired; it can be taught.

Reliability is brought to the job. An employer expects an individual to be reliable. But it is a quality much harder to determine in an individual (and applicants are usually strangers) than is capability.*

Rare is the individual employer who can size up another person and accurately judge or assess a person's quality of reliability. The employer, then, often is hard put to determine the ingredients of this factor.

A Chicago representative of Lloyd's of London, the worldwide insurance firm, outlines a case in which a southern bank, not otherwise identified, hired a female employee from a first-rate employment agency, assuming she had properly been checked out by the agency.**

Actually, the agency had checked the references given by the girl, but nothing more.

After $10,000 mysteriously disappeared from the bank, poly-

---

*Holmes, Jr., Sam F., First National Bank, Dallas, Texas. The Polygraph: Should Banks use it in Selecting Personnel? A Thesis presented to The Faculty of the Southwestern Graduate School of Banking, July 1968.

**Pompian, Lillian: Business Turns to the Lie Detector. *Kiwanis Magazine,* Vol. 44, Dec. 1962-Jan., 1963, pp. 55-60.

graphy was brought in. The girl admitted serving a prison term and to being on probation for the embezzlement of a similar sum from a previous bank employer.

Said the insurance representative: "This girl could have been saved from committing the second embezzlement if she had been given the preemployment test."

The results some banks have had with the polygraph are startling, if not reassuring. One midwestern bank, reported *Business Week Magazine,* June 18, 1960, got 80 percent of its workers to admit thefts averaging $2.00 or more per week. A Chicago bank says it found that, although certain employees were not stealing, they were borrowing sums to "tide them over" until payday. A bank official pointed out that sometimes these funds were slow in being replaced, and said such practices easily led to the next step —embezzlement.

After several tellers had been fired from a Chicago bank for constant shortages, the bank president became suspicious and requested all employees be privately polygraphed.

The tests indicated the innocence of everybody except an auditor who admitted he had stolen $22,000, and then fired tellers to cover the thefts.

*　　*　　*

Several years ago, a bank in Massachusetts discovered a $3,000 cash shortage. The bank president, Elias Broderick (name fictitious), called in Lincoln M. Zonn, 2 Park Avenue, New York, head of the world's largest private polygraph and security control consulting firm.

Thirty employees were polygraphed and every one of them checked out innocent concerning the $3,000 in question. However, one of the senior investment counseling staff members produced specific response when routinely asked, "Have you ever embezzled any monies from this bank?"

In the interim, an honest customer who had come in to pick up his payroll money reported that he had been given $3,000 over and above what he had ordered.

The initial problem had resolved itself.

But Lincoln Zonn was not pleased with the specific response

on the charts of one George Pleasington (name fictitious). He suggested to the bank president that Pleasington be retested.

Elias Broderick bristled. "Why, he is one of our oldest and most trusted employees. Our problem has been resolved. Even you said he was innocent of that, and now we all know it. I rather resent the inference contained in your suggestion."

Zonn, known in national interrogative circles as "the old master," bit his tongue. A thought so common to experienced polygraphists flitted through his mind: You want and need help more than you'll ever know and yet you don't know how to broaden your own security.

He casually spread his hands and smiled. "Sir, most people are basically honest and most people are good. Unfortunately, some are not."

Broderick literally snorted. "You're sounding very unprofessional, I must say."

"I beg your pardon sir," Lincoln Zonn replied softly, his eyes narrowing ever so slightly. "Still, I would like to retest Pleasington, of course with your permission."

Broderick began to boil. "We have never had any serious shortages in this bank and, hopefully, we never shall. Tell me your fee and we shall be done with this madness."

The old master presented the bank president his bill. A phone call was made and the check ordered written.

"I'm almost sorry I called you into this," Broderick said somewhat caustically. "Obviously there was no need."

"Out of simple curiosity," Lincoln Zonn queried, "how long has it been since this bank was audited?"

Broderick's answer snapped back. "Thirty days ago and we balanced out perfectly, as usual."

Linclon Zonn leaned back in his chair. "As I understand, under the present banking regulations and the laws of this state dormant accounts or those inactive for five years are not required to be audited for a minimum of twenty years. Is this not correct? And doesn't George Pleasington work in this area?"

"Well yes, I suppose so." The palor of the bank president's face slowly began to turn from grey-white to bright red.

Pursuing the issue, "Again, with your permission, I should like to retest this man."

"You just want more money."

"I'll do it for free if you agree. No results, no fee. Results, and you pay the standard fee."

"And if Pleasington refuses?"

"He won't," Zonn said confidently.

"What makes you think that?"

"Because he thinks he's gotten by with something."

"What?"

"Who knows. I feel that it is something of importance."

"This may destroy the whole morale of my staff. It's almost like forceful coercion. In banks we just don't do this."

"You already have, and not one person seriously objected."

"But this is different."

"How different?" Zonn asked.

"The issue is closed."

"Is it, really?"

"What are you after?"

"Just the truth, all of it."

"This is almost degrading." The bank president sighed and pressed on the intercom. "George will you please come in for a moment?"

George Pleasington entered the room. He was a tall man, ruggedly handsome, greying at the temples, with the demeanor of a movie star combined with a diplomat. "Yes, Mr. Broderick?" He smiled at Lincoln Zonn.

"George," Broderick said reluctantly, "As you know, everybody cleared the polygraph test with respect to the missing $3,000 which has now turned up. However, Mr. Zonn here is of the impression that some portion of your test was not quite satisfactory. He wants to retest you. Personally, I'm against it. Therefore, such will have to be strictly on a voluntary basis."

Other than momentary flaring at the nose, the countenance of George Pleasington remained totally impassive. There was a long silence. "Of course, Mr. Broderick. I will be most happy to straighten out any question." With a tight purse of his lips and the hint of a bow, he formally said to Lincoln Zonn, "I am at your service, sir. Shall we begin?"

During the pretest interview, Lincoln Zonn specifically explored every area of the bank's dormant accounts. Although he made no admissions, George Pleasington's suave demeanor began to slowly deteriorate.

Zonn decided to start right off with "an amount" peak of tension search test. Instrument attachments were applied to Pleasington's body. The test was underway.

"Have you ever embezzled any monies from this bank?"

"No."

Deception criteria appears.

"Have you embezzled as much as $5,000 from this bank?"

"No."

Deception criteria.

"Have you embezzled as much as $20,000 from this bank?"

"No."

Deception criteria.

"Have you embezzled as much as $40,000 from this bank?"

"No."

Deception criteria.

"Have you embezzled as much as $60,000 from this bank?"

"No."

Deception criteria.

"Have you embezzled as much as $80,000 from this bank?"

"No."

Deception criteria.

"Have you embezzled as much as $100,000 from this bank?"

"No."

Deception criteria continues. Heart rate increases to one hundred beats per minute. Apnea (blocking) appears in the respiratory recordings. The galvanometer pen records a triple bounce.

"Have you embezzled as much as $120,000 from this bank?"

"No."

Relief sets in. Suddenly, pulse pressure drops back to 80. Respiration returns to a three to five inspiration-expiration ratio.

The galvanometer tracing flattens out and becomes inactively fluid.

Now, Lincoln Zonn was positive. He conducted another identical chart with the same results. He deactivated the instrument, removed the charts and laid them in front of the subject.

"George, you can see it on these charts just as clearly as I can. How close to $100,000 have you embezzled?"

Pleasington's stiff facade crumpled. Tears streamed down his rudy cheeks, disappearing into a carefully trimmed Victorian beard. His chin dropped forward on his chest.

"How much, George?" The deep golden tones of Zonn's voice danced throughout the room.

"I—I guess about—well, just about $100,000," came the soft reply.

"What did you do with it, George?"

"I invested it just as I would with any other monies of the bank that I've handled for years."

"And did those investments pay off?"

George Pleasington nodded. "Yes. I have run that money up to $463,000. It is all secure and intact."

"Are you willing to return it to the bank?"

"My God, yes. No matter what happens, maybe now I can at least live with myself."

Lincoln Zonn took a detailed signed statement from Pleasington, then called in Elias Broderick. The bank president read, then reread the statement, turned purple, acted as though he was suffocating, and bolted from the room without uttering a word.

Zonn packed up his instrument and quietly departed, leaving Pleasington still slumped in his chair.

Ironically, a whimsical O'Henry twist enters this case. Some weeks later Lincoln Zonn learned that Pleasington had made full restitution to the bank, including his profits. Instead of being prosecuted, George Pleasington found himself promoted to department head of all investment counseling.

As far as we know, he still holds that same position.

However, banking laws and regulations with respect to auditing of dormant accounts have since been changed.

*   *   *

No employer knowingly accepts for employment an unreliable person.* But, many are hired. That banks have not been consistently successful in keeping unreliable persons off their staffs is evident. The table below shows that incidents of known embezzlement among bank employees increased at least 50 percent between 1960 and 1967.**

TABLE III
VIOLATIONS OF THE NATIONAL BANK ACT
FEDERAL RESERVE ACT

Year	No. of Cases	$ Involved
1960	1,771	7,400,000
1961	1,909	10,937,000
1962	1,959	10,704,000
1963	2,172	12,192,000
1964	2,404	13,369,000
1965	2,426	18,801,000
1966	2,537	14,920,000
1967	2,676	18,072,000

In 1967, Arthur Charles Bolls, Vice President with the First National Bank of Dallas, Texas, one of the largest in the Southwest, acknowledged that his bank had used polygraphy for more than seven years to screen applicants for all positions involving money handling.†

Said Bolls, "Some employers may feel uneasy about using the polygraph, as a matter of principle, but there is no question that it has been highly useful and effective, and has prevented our hiring of some individuals who unquestionably would have jeopardized the reputation of this bank for honesty and integrity.

"Applicants do not seem to resent a polygraph screening if the purpose is clearly explained; not one applicant in seven years objected to taking a polygraph test as a matter of principle; a few, but very few, applicants did not show up for the examination."

A polygraphist was requested to conduct tests on all employees

---

*The Wall Street Journal, Jan. 22, 1968, p. 1, col. 1.

**Holmes, Jr., Sam F., The Polygraph: Should Banks use it in Selecting Personnel; A thesis presented to the Faculty of the Southwestern Graduate School of Banking, July, 1968.

†Holmes, Jr., Sam F., The Polygraph: Should Banks use it in Selection of Personnel? A Thesis presented to The Facutlty of the Southwestern Graduate School of Banking, July, 1968.

of a North Dakota bank where a substantial shortage had occurred. The first subject tested was an assistant cashier of the bank who had been employed there for twenty years.

While he produced very dramatic responses to all critical questions, he emphatically denied ever taking any money from the bank. He was told he would be recalled for further examination after other employees had completed their tests.

In subsequent tests, one of the tellers confessed to theft of the money in question. The assistant cashier was then recalled. Again, he produced violent response to all pertinent questions. During interrogation, he broke down and started to cry.

Subject then said that although he had never stolen any money, he had been planning for some time to embezzle bank monies and had even made plans how to do so, and how he would falsify the books. He thanked the examiner for preventing him from becoming a thief.

As of March 1968, subject was still employed by the bank.

Let us face more realistic facts.

A large number of retailing firms are currently caught in the dilemma of rising costs on the one hand and resistance against price increases on the other hand. Inventory losses, alone, are estimated to vary from 1.6 to 3 percent of sales.

In 1968 the American Management Association set losses from employee theft at $3 billion annually, and only about a fifth of this loss was covered by insurance.

Although shoplifting has increased about 20 percent per year, employees are out-stealing shoplifters by a 15 to 1 ratio, and professional thieves by a 5 to 1 ratio.

Norman Jaspan, a nationwide security consultant, estimates that each working day employees steal approximately $5 million worth of company property. Jaspan's records show that executives and supervisory personnel account for more than 62 percent of this pilferage.

As a result, it is estimated that from 3 to 7 percent of United States bankruptcies are attributed to employee dishonesty.

It is no wonder that business has turned to polygraphy.

A recent survey of business firms in Texas indicates that 13.3

percent of them presently use the polygraph for some purpose: three fourths using it for both preemployment and problem situations.

Among firms not using it, 25 percent indicated they had considered, or presently were considering using polygraphy. The survey also brought out that wholesale and retail trade firms use polygraphy much more than other types of businesses; only 8.6 percent of financial firms (which includes insurance and banking) use it.*

Reasons given by most firms using polygraphy were:

1. Results in better and/or more honest employees.
2. Acts as a constant deterrent to employee dishonesty.
3. Protects innocent employees from false accusation or suspicion.
4. Determines who is guilty when thefts arise.
5. Eliminates the narcotic addict, job jumper, chronic alcoholic, accident prone, and the habitual thieves.
6. Eliminates poor security risks.
7. Permits basically honest employees to work in harmony with their counterparts.

A southwestern grocery chain, with over one hundred stores in operation, hired its own polygraphist to test all applicants considered for full time employment. His first yearly report contained the following figures, which are a matter of record:

1. Present employee admissions when inventory and cash shortages developed.
   a. Theft of cash $23,162.68
   b. Theft of merchandise $49,361.00
2. Applicant admissions of theft from previous employers.
   a. Theft of cash $76,145.00
   b. Theft of merchandise $98,216.50

An employee of a gasoline service station reported he was the victim of an armed robbery involving some $3,000. Three weeks later, when cash shortages continued to appear, the owner asked

---

*Stephens, Dr. Elvis C.: The Use of Polygraphs by Business Firms in Texas. *Business Studies,* North Texas State University, Fall 1967, p. 65.

the subject if he would volunteer for polygraphy. He readily agreed.

During the pretest interview, subject denied that he would be able to identify the holdup man if seen again. His first chart contained specific response to some of the critical questions, and after between-chart interrogation subject admitted he had taken $40 in cash which was left behind by the holdup man.

Another chart still revealed specific responses. This time, interrogation brought forth an admission that prior to the holdup this subject had actually stolen $800. Therefore, the holdup man did not get $3,000 as subject initially reported.

A third chart did not clear the employee. Again interrogation brought forth an admission that subject had stolen $1,900 prior to the holdup, and the bandit had actually gotten $1,350.

The fourth chart was no better. Subject finally admitted he knew the holdup man and had made a deal with him to rob the station of $1,350. They later met in subject's home and split the money.

Both were tried and convicted.

*   *   *

In 1966 in Chicago, Illinois, the assistant manager of a large drug chain opened his store and then immediately reported the store safe had been burglarized of $7,000. Investigating officers examined the well-type safe. The top lid had been opened with a spare key taken from the store's office. Both the top lid and the key were on the floor. Empty money bags were found on the floor at a rear delivery door which appeared to have been pried open.

The burglar alarm was still intact.

Further investigation revealed that the inner safe compartment, which also had to be opened with a key, was empty but had been relocked. Officers theorized that only an employee who regularly opened and locked the bottom safe well, as a matter of habit, could be involved. If the burglary had occurred before opening time, the alarm should have been ringing when the assistant manager arrived. He said it wasn't.

Though he reluctantly agreed to submit to polygraphy, he

acted chagrined and stated he would sit mute throughout the entire test. This he did.

Three relevant-irrelevant charts were conducted. Each contained deception criteria. Then, a "search and disposition" test was conducted.

Specific chart responses led officers to a hole in a block wall in the store's stock room where two bags of the missing money were found. A search of subject's person revealed $1000 in hundred dollar bills concealed in his shoes.

What the startled subject did not realize is that verbally answering a polygraph test question is of little consequence, other than to facilitate chart marking. The function of his brain and its command of his autonomic nervous system involuntarily answered the questions for him, in deviations from physiological norm which his body produced on the charts.

*   *   *

In late June, 1968, an attorney called and requested this writer's presence in Dallas, Texas for the purpose of probing the amount of theft by the office manager of what we shall call C Wholesale Electric Supply.

A company auditor had already discovered several discrepancies involving suppliers' rebate and discount checks. The CPA's investigation also uncovered the fact that subject and his wife had opened a florist shop in a fashionable district some six months previous.

After being confronted with irrefutable proof of the foregoing, the office manager, a handsome man of 30 years with a master's degree in business administration and active as a Sunday School superintendent, admitted theft of $2500, and volunteered to submit to polygraphy.

As a precautionary measure, he was advised of his rights. He also read and signed a test-consent form.

With the first relevant-irrelevant chart underway, subject responded violently to the question: "Have you knowingly taken more money than what you've told me from C. Wholesale Electric Supply?"

Following deactivation of the instrument, the physiological responses his body had produced were called to his attention. Beads of perspiration broke out on his forehead. He slumped in his chair.

Slowly and gently, the probing continued. Finally, the subject admitted that he might have stolen as much as $5,000 from his employer.

An "amount" chart was conducted, the questions commencing with $5,000 and graduating up to $40,000. He failed to "clear" on even the largest amount. A thirty-minute recess was called.

Questioning turned into a form of decisive interrogation.

All at once, the subject broke into tears and admitted he had embezzled $52,600, almost half of which he used to open a floral shop which was operated by his innocent and unknowing wife.

He signed a properly witnessed statement.

*   *   *

In November 1965 a young man was accused of taking $10 from a hardware store's hunting and fishing license sales box. All circumstantial evidence pointed his way.

Facing discharge, subject maintained his innocence and asked for polygraphy.

The test conclusively cleared him.

Later the same day, another employee who worked part-time on hardware lunch relief was tested. After he was confronted with the deception criteria his body produced on the polygraph charts, he admitted theft of the $10 in question.

He also admitted theft of a sizable amount of merchandise during a relatively short period of employment.

While the foregoing is a small example, it must be remembered that $10 and a job reputation were very important to the falsely accused.

Within an hour, the innocent had cleared himself by the truthfulness of his answers which, in turn, eliminated physiological deception criteria from his charts.

The guilty person "caught himself" because he failed to answer the issue questions truthfully. As a result, his body produced the physiological deviations which entrapped him.

An applicant for a liquor distributing firm made admissions during his preemployment test of theft of over $20,000 worth of merchandise from his previous employer within a four-year period. The information relating to this theft could only have been determined through polygraphy, because his previous employer had absolutely no knowledge that subject was a thief.

* * *

A supermarket operator discovered that 90 percent of his employees were taking home one or two dollars a week in cash and merchandise, for a grand total of more than $1½ million per year. Reexamination, periodically, with the polygraph indicated that only 3 percent of the employees continued their pilferage.

Employee dishonesty finds polygraphy a devastating adversary. In such applications it has proven invaluable in pinpointing areas of suspicion and circumventing thousands of hours of investigative time.

A periodic audit disclosed a $30,000 inventory shortage in the warehouse of a large retail dealer in household items. The missing items were of a compact and expensive nature such as radios, mixers, blenders, can openers, and irons.

Only certain management personnel and the warehouse staff had access to this merchandise and as there was no evidence of break-in, these people were placed under suspect.

Polygraph tests showed that the management people were not involved. However, the warehouse superintendent, as a result of polygraphy, admitted he knew that the chief culprit was the shipping clerk, who had taken large quantities of merchandise to support his escapades with a married woman.

The manager of a dairy store reported to the police that he had found the back door of the establishment opened and $700 removed from the safe. However, when the police examined the evidence, it was determined that the door's lock had not been picked and that the safe had not been broken into.

Upon further investigation, it was found the manager had $300 on his person which he could not account for, other than a vague reference made to a poker game. The police felt they had found the thief until the owner of the store stepped in—because of his faith in the manager—and demanded a polygraph examination.

Much to the surprise of the police, the polygraphist found the manager innocent and, upon further investigation, the examiner produced the real criminal, a trusted clerk, who was subsequently tried and convicted.

A book author, while expressing his ideas of what he considered mass invasion of privacy, wrote: "I would never take a lie detector test unless my minister, lawyer, and doctor were present."

In 1967 a minister was polygraphed on suspicion of murdering his wife for insurance money. He failed his test, and formal charges followed.

A lawyer was tested for procurring, and attempted bribery of a witness. He failed his test, and subsequently was disbarred.

A doctor requested polygraphy on himself in an effort to support his medical and hospitalization claim against an insurance company following what appeared to be his attempted suicide. He also failed his test, and the claim was denied.

Again in 1967 a minister pleaded with a Texas licensed polygraphist to conduct a test on his son after the boy was formally charged with rape of a police officer's wife.

Plaintiff's attorney studied the depositions of defense witnesses in a paternity suit, then sought and obtained stipulation for them to be polygraphed.

Following their tests, both admitted they never had intercourse with plaintiff and further that they didn't even know her. As a favor to the defendant, they had perjured themselves in an effort to discredit plaintiff.

A doctor asked his entire staff to volunteer for polygraphy when silver extracted from exposed x-ray film mysteriously disappeared.

Two employees admitted the theft.

A psychiatrist spent a frustrating week with a patient. Then he brought his patient to a polygraphist with a set of prepared questions. Not only was he amazed, but expressed his profuse thanks when specific physiological chart tracings opened previously closed doors to the immediate exploration for getting to the roots of his patient's problem.

On January 24, 1969, executives of a nationally-known soft drink company came to this writer's offices with a problem.

They suspected one of their route supervisors, who had been with them ten years, of falsifying his "load sheet asked for," and altering the figures on his "load sheet received."

The subject agreed to verify his "honesty with the company" via polygraphy.

Following the pretest interview and two polygrams, subject's signed statement read:

> My name is Louis Fairchild (name fictitious). I am 39 years old. I have been employed by Sparkle Serene Bottling Company (name fictitious) as a route salesman and supervisor for some ten years. During the first part of December, 1968, I found myself in a financial bind and started stealing cases of merchandise. I admit stealing as many as twenty cases of merchandise at one single time on at least fifteen separate occasions, which amounts to $675. I admit stealing as many as ten cases of merchandise at one single time on at least nine separate occasions, which amounts to $225. I admit stealing one case of merchandise at one single time on at least ten separate occasions, which amounts to $23. Prior to becoming a supervisor, I admit stealing about $10 worth of Sparkle Serene beverage.

Thus, facts prove that polygraphy is an effective management tool.

A tremendous role polygraphy secretely plays behind the scenes is in industrial sabotoge. Corporation secrets, new ideas, inventions, proposed mergers, discrediting of competitors—they can be worth millions to rival companies.

Large and small corporations alike thus are often forced to turn to polygraphy to discover those responsible for information leaks and sabotage.

In 1967, in Houston, Texas, a large dairy firm was plagued with complaints and threats of suit about foreign matters found in hundreds of cottage cheese containers.

Polygraphy was called in. The fourth testee, a supervisor who had been passed over for promotion, admitted he had made "a deal" with a competitor to contaminate the product.

*   *   *

Long Beach, California Police Case No. 552647, dated January 15, 1962, began with a call from Sam Smith (all names in this case, excepting those of police officers, are fictitious) owner of Sam's Meat Market, located at 2665 Boles Avenue.

He reported that $387, in cash and checks, wrapped in meat paper, had been stolen from his store safe sometime after 5:45 p.m. on the 14th.

Sgt. D. M. Tubbs of the Bunco Detail began the investigation. He first asked three employees on duty, when the money was deposited in the safe, if they would submit to polygraphy. They had no objection.

Polygraphist John A. Charney conducted the tests, and reported all three suspects innocent of being involved or having knowledge thereof.

Sergeant Tubbs went over the list of employees working on both days. He noted one adult, who had called in sick on the 15th. His eyes also caught the name of a 16-year-old who worked in the market on a part-time basis. The name rang a bell.

He turned to Sam. "What time did Kenneth Morely punch out on the 14th?"

Smith pulled the time cards. "At 6:01 P.M. But that kid wouldn't even think of getting involved in something like this. Besides, look at the time element. I know he wasn't back in the store after he punched out, and he certainly doesn't have a key."

"No doubt you're right," Sgt. Tubbs said. "Well, for the moment, we'll have ID dust for fingerprints. The chances are slim, but maybe we'll be lucky. I'll check back with you later."

At police headquarters, Sgt. Tubbs sent the name of Kenneth Morely through the Juvenile Division. It came back, attached with a record of petty thefts. He asked Juvenile to follow it up.

The next Tuesday, Sgt. Cowan of the Juvenile Division brought Kenneth Morely, accompanied by his father, to John Charney's offices. A polygraph consent form was signed. Kenneth's father then waited in one of the Bunco Division's interrogation rooms.

The test commenced:

"Do you actually know who stole the $387 from the safe where you work?"

"No."

"Did you take the missing $387 from the safe?"

"No."

"Do you know where any of the missing money is now?"

"No."

Morely's respiratory pattern became so ragged, nearly to the point of hyperventilation, that Charney deactivated the instrument.

"Son," he softly said, "now you know, and I know, and you know I know. Let's just quit playing games and clear up this whole mess once and for all."

Sgt. Tubbs and Sgt. Cowan were called in. Kenneth Morely confessed.

Within two minutes after Sam Smith put the money in the safe, subject removed it and hid it behind machinery in the refrigeration room. He had burned the checks. All but $60 in cash, which he spent for a set of new hub caps for his car, was under some undershirts in his dresser drawer at home.

That money was recovered.

Because of Kenneth Morely's past record, he was sent to a correctional institution.

Polygraphist John Charney fed a fresh roll of chart paper over the kymograph sprocket of his instrument, and waited for his next test.

He hoped it wouldn't be another juvenile ghost-riding toward the "plains of no return."

*   *   *

During the last part of May, into June of 1967, Tucson, Arizona, radio stations frantically broadcasted reports that a pyromaniac was on the loose.

The primary target of numerous fires was the Super Discount store (name fictitious) located on East Speedway. Local area residents maintained a wary night-watch lest they also fell victim.

When police and fire department investigators ran into a stone wall, management of Super Discount immediately called the New York headquarters of Lincoln Zonn, Inc., explaining the problem and requesting assistance.

Two of the country's top polygraph-investigators, Charles Jones and LeRoy Lussier were aboard a jet within two hours. Outwardly calm and relaxed, both felt the import as well as the tenseness of the situation they faced. Informed that six separate fires had already been started at various locations within the Super Discount store during a three-day period, both these experienced examiners instinctively began concentrating on various question formulation approaches.

On June 2, 1967, Jones and Lussier arrived. By 4:00 P.M. they were in serious conference with local officials and store management. Police and fire investigative reports pointed toward the possibility that the pyromaniac might be a Super Discount employee. While management was reluctant to agree, they did submit names of twenty employees who were on duty each time the fires were discovered.

The final decision was to ask these twenty employees to voluntarily submit to polygraphy. All of them readily consented.

Charles Jones, for many years a West Virginia police officer and crack interrogator prior to joining the Lincoln Zonn worldwide operation in private industry, interviewed and polygraphed four Super Discount employees. Each had no problem clearing the test.

The hour was growing late. Jones took a quick coffee break and chatted with LeRoy Lussier, retired CID and Interpol agent. Neither was dismayed. To them, this was little different from other cases which each ordinarily conducted somewhere every working day. If the answer did rest with Super Discount employees, they were confident they would find it.

Wearily, Jones finished his coffee and signaled the store manager to send in his last test for the night. He was making up his preliminary work sheet when Pamela Rosemead (name fictitious) walked into the room.

Walked? Hardly. She floated in upon a haze of moonbeams, literally gliding upon galaxy dust with a sensuous flow that left Charles Jones feeling like he'd been kicked in the solar plexus. He stood, noting that she almost reached his six-four height.

Searching for words that would permit his vocal cords to activate the sound of a simple hello or howdy-doo, he could only motion for her to be seated. Beauty incarnate moulded her curvacious figure into the chair.

It was then he caught her eyes. Charles Jones came back to harsh reality. There was a gorgeous figure, fine featured face with high cheek bones, and long blond hair which nestled graciously on her shoulders. A full, red mouth invited only the kisses of ancient Roman gods. But, there were the eyes.

Open, blue as Mediterranean waters, her eyes saw, but did not see. They appeared dead, lifeless as the biblical cities of Sodom and Gomorrah.

Jones collected his wits. Once again he was the experienced interrogator. He queried, "Miss Rosemead, do you know why you are here?"

She slowly turned her head. Jones had the feeling she was looking through and beyond him. "Yes, I think so," she said. The tone of her voice contained an aura of childlike wistfulness.

"Do you have any objection to taking a polygraph test?"

"I guess not." Jones detected a faint lisp.

"You have heard about the fires in the store?"

She nodded. "Oh, yes. I know I didn't set them. Fires are bad."

A furrow of wrinkles creased Jones' forehead. "Miss Rosemead, let me get just a little information for my file and then we'll go right into the test."

Out of a clear blue sky she asked, "Do you ever get lonesome?"

"All people do at one time or another," he answered carefully.

"My daddy is gone all the time," Pamela Rosemead said rather sadly. "And sometimes my mother goes away for a while and I have to work here and work in the house and take care of my little brother. I get so tired." Tears flooded her eyes. She sniffed them back.

Jones gently questioned her about her full name, address, schooling, relevant medical history, and length of employment. He couldn't believe she was only 19.

"Do you mind if I call you Pamela instead of Miss Rosemead?"

A whisp of a smile tugged at the corners of her mouth. "I like it fine. I used to love to hear my daddy say my first name. You have a pretty voice like his."

Jones dropped his voice a full octave and softly probed. "Pamela, do you know anything about the fires which have been set in this store?"

"Yes I do. I helped put out one or two of them. It's really a terrible thing."

"Did you see anyone around when you helped put them out? I mean any other employees?"

"When I found a fire, or when one of the other girls did, we yelled and everybody came to help." She seemed perplexed about the fires.

"Pamela," he said, "do you know the most important thing you can do during our interview and your polygraph test?"

She looked up, and through him. He wondered what she was thinking.

"Simply tell the complete truth, Pamela," Jones finished.

"I know I can tell the truth. I was in the restroom when one of them started. A girl saw me there."

Jones considered that she was not so child-like or mentally deficient as not to be able to hold a job, run a cash register, and wait on customers to the satisfaction of her employer. Yet, her personality projection, the vagueness in her answers, intrigued him. The way she said certain sentences, the disjointed context, her signature on the test consent form which revealed every other letter to slant first from right to left, then vice versa, produced a big red light in Jones' mind that perhaps Pamela Rosemead was suffering from some psychological maladjustment. He proceeded cautiously.

At the end of the first relevant-irrelevant chart, he noted the effects of an emotional disturbance which presented itself consistently throughout her entire respiratory tracings. And, her cardio-vascular pattern contained specific response at the issue questions.

He conducted the second chart, inserting two guilt complex questions. Again the deception criteria appeared. He deactivated the instrument.

"Miss Rosemead, would you like some coffee, a sandwich, or a trip to the restroom to relax for awhile?"

The first sign of real emotion took place in her eyes. They popped wide open. "No thank you." Her voice carried a quality of flat monotony. "I know you understand now that I did not set the fires."

"Didn't you, Miss Rosemead? Suppose I told you this test clearly indicates you certainly might have set them?"

Her eyes narrowed to mere slits. A single stream of tears poured down one cheek. She spread her hands. "Well, I—I guess if the test says I set the fires, then I guess I did."

There was a long silence, broken when Pamela Rosemead suddenly realized what she had said. She quickly snapped, "But, I didn't do it." Her shoulders shook. "Even if I did, I couldn't tell the truth."

Jones rose. "Miss Rosemead, I know you are tired. Go on home for now and get some rest. Think it over and come back at ten in the morning. Truth is a strange thing, Pamela. To tell the truth sets one free of all cares and worry. Give it some thought, Pamela, and we'll have a friendly chat tomorrow."

Lussier and Jones conferred at length that evening. They decided that a personality change might provide the key to an admission.

At noon the next day Lussier left the examining room. "I get the same responses as you," he said as he laid his charts before Jones. "She just won't come across and admit it."

Jones scratched behind his ear. "Let's finish up all the others and then softly double-team her."

The final interrogative session began some twenty-four hours later. Lussier led off. "Miss Rosemead, do you know the meaning of the word *truth?*"

"Doesn't everyone?"

"But, do you?"

"Of course I do. Why shouldn't I?"

"Do you enjoy telling a lie?"

"No. A lie is bad. My parents used to tell me never to tell a lie or they would punish me. Maybe some day they'll both come home."

Jones took over. "Pamela, would you want us to tell your mother and father you set the fires?"

"No! Please don't!" She leaped to her feet. "They might never come home together!" Her arms crossed over high tilted breasts, fingers clawing at opposite shoulders. She uttered a tiny groan.

"Pamela," Jones urged, "if I promise that neither myself or Mr. Lussier will say even one word to your parents, do you think you could reach the truthful goodness I know rests deep in your heart and tell us the truth about the fires?"

"You won't tell anyone? Promise?"

"We can't promise you anything, Pamela, except that neither of us will personally tell your parents." Jones added, "Where is your father, Pamela?"

"In the army in Panama."

"And your mother?"

"She just up and left a week ago. She said she'd be back soon."

Lussier cut in, more directly. "Miss Rosemead, do you like fires?"

Her eyes brightened. She hummed strains of a nursery tune. "Fires are very pretty. Don't you think fires are pretty? But, they are also bad."

"Yes, they are pretty," Lussier soothed. The flames have such pretty colors."

Then Pamela asked simply, "Would you really like me to tell you about the fires in the store?"

"As long as you're completely truthful," Jones interjected.

She laughed, like a delighted child. "You promise you won't tell my parents or anyone else in this store? The people here musn't know. It's my secret."

Jones put his finger to his lips and nodded. "Promise, cross my heart. We must, however, tell the fire department investigators so they can quit worrying about the fires. Surely you want to help them?"

She seemed to have difficulty reaching a decision. Finally, her head rocked to one side and she giggled. "They must be awfully worried. I feel sorry for them."

"Pamela," Jones urged, "here is a blank piece of paper and a pen. Write us a story and tell us just how it all happened."

Her story, in the form of a statement, reads as follows, using her exact words (she was aided only in remembering dates and days) :

June 4, 1967

My name is Pamela Rosemead and I have been employed here in the Super Discount for some three months. This past Wednesday at about 1:30 for some reason I can't explain I obtained a book of matches from the ladies wear office and stuck them in my pocket and had thoughts of setting a secluded spot on fire. I then kept thinking, 'no' that's a stupid thing to do," then after a while I seen no one was around and I lit a match and held it against a ladies duster hanging on the rack. I then got scared and sort of got my senses back and tried to shake the fire out. By that time the flames rose so I hurried away and then I heard a lady yell "fire," and I felt awful so I hurried back and tried to put it out. Then everyone was all excited so it was too late to hide the fact. I was afraid someone had seen me near the fire when it started so I set another one and hurried away, trying to put all suspicion away from myself. I kept getting more scared and it just seemed I was getting more and more involved. I set another fire while the firemen were there about 7:30, as I know they had seen me where they were, so I figured if I got away from their vicinity and set the fire and then hurried back to where they were all suspicion of me would be cleared and I could forget about the whole thing. I set these three fires on May 31, 1967. On June 1 about 1:30 I was plenty scared so I again tried hiding the fact I'd set the first 3 by setting a rack of ladies lingerie on fire and hurrying 5 or 6 aisles away. On my supper hour I called the office of the ladies department and tried disguising my voice like a man and said, "Fire," and I hoped this would completely clean all suspicion of me. I made this call from my home. The person I spoke to on all 4 phone calls was Letty Yates (name fictitious) . I returned to work and thought that I'd set one more and make sure I was completely in the clear, so I set fire to some children's clothing and then hurried off to the restroom, knowing another employee was also in the restroom and could verify I was in the restroom at the time of the fire. The other employee in the restroom was Agnes (name fictitious) , a cashier. June 2nd at about 2:30 I was trying to find another way to clear all doubt about me being guilty when the man who had put the 5th fire out, Barry Zolta, (name fictitious) had said he was on the phone talking and had seen the fire start so I was scared he'd seen me there at the time, so I lit a match and dropped it in the wastebasket and hurried out of the restroom. I put the wastebasket inside the cubicle where the toilet is so no one would get burned when they walked in the restroom and discovered the fire.

I started all 6 fires with paperbook matches. I did not light any more fires after Mr. Jones and Mr. Lussier arrived as I thought that I was already a suspect and was in too deep already. I make the above statement freely and without threat or promise because it is true. I wish to add that during this interview I was well treated and I was told in the beginning that I was free to conclude the interview at any time.

s/Pamela Rosemead

Witnessed:
s/ Charles Jones
s/ LeRoy Lussier

Fire and police department investigators were called in. A police matron led the girl away. On June 9, 1967, Lincoln M. Zonn received the following letter:

CITY OF TUCSON

Department Of Police

P.O. Box 1071

In reply please refer to our: D.FU. #403328 RA

9 June, 1967

Lincoln Zonn, Inc.
2 Park Avenue,
New York City, New York.

Gentlemen:

We refer to our arson case which involved the Super Discount Store (name fictitious) here in Tucson on 4 June 1967.

During your interview with Pamela Rosemead, which was conducted by your investigators Jones and Lussier, Miss Rosemead signed a confession attesting to her activities in this matter.

Miss Rosemead is now claiming that a 3½-hour interview with your investigators resulted in her signing a confession under adverse circumstances, i.e., duress and coercion.

Our County Attorney, Mr. Dubar, has requested that you forward to us a complete resume of this interview and to include a transcript of the conversation which took place between Miss Rosemead and your investigators.

In order that we may continue our study of this allegation, we would appreciate your prompt attention to this matter.

Sincerely,

s/ Bernard L. Garmire,
Chief of Police.

BLG: RA:da

Jones and Lussier were called to testify at Pamela Rosemead's trial. She was found guilty, but sentence was deferred pending confinement and treatment in a mental institution.

A psychiatrist testified that in his opinion the girl only wanted to create attention to bring her mother and father home.

Neither appeared at, during, or after the trial. Pamela Rosemead stood alone, bewildered and further confused.

* * *

When company auditors pulled a surprise inspection of the books at Fairmont Furniture (name fictitious) in San Antonio, Texas, August 16, 1968, they discovered a large defalcation.

The chief CPA confronted Elliott Kelly (name fictitious), store manager, and abruptly said, "Will you take a polygraph test?"

Kelly's face blanched. The inside of his mouth suddenly turned to cotton. His struggle for self-composure was quite evident. He finally blurted, "Well, I—uh—I suppose so. Certainly. What for?"

"There is a big shortage. How much, as yet, we don't know. Mr. Fairmont will be back in town next Wednesday. I think it would be a good idea for him to know exactly where you stand when he gets back."

Kelly nodded. "Of course, of course. Oh, my! I just can't believe it!"

"You better believe it," the CPA's words clipped out "Kelly, I'm not accusing you or anyone else of anything, at least until the audit is finished. But if I were you, I'd put myself in the clear now."

"Yes. Yes, you're right. Oh, my goodness!"

"Shall I make an appointment for you in Dallas?"

"Huh? Yes, to be sure." Kelly sank into a chair.

The telephone rang in the offices of Wallace Rash, president of Truth Verification, Inc., Dallas, Texas. The Keeler Institute graduate and former police detective, tape-recorded the information and facts relayed to him. He confirmed a 3:00 P.M. appointment the next day. Yes, he would have a man at the airport to drive Kelly to his offices.

At noon, the following day, Kelly boarded a plane in San Antonio and found a seat in the tail section. He was oblivious to the takeoff.

His thoughts ran rampant. He had a good job and a good community and church standing. While his wife was rather plain, and indifferent, she came from a wealthy, quite socially conscious family. He could afford to send his two children to the best private school. . . .

Six months ago, was it? How did it start? So simply, so innocently. Yes, it was at the usual staff cocktail party every Friday evening. Mr. Fairmont had introduced him to the newly hired cashier, Sandra Miller (name fictitious). He had welcomed her with a click of champagne glasses.

Their eyes met and locked with a magnetisim he had never experienced in his whole life. She was beautiful. When she smiled, he felt a whole new surge of manhood flood his entire being. He drove her to her apartment that night. She asked him in for a nightcap.

For two or three months, Elliott Kelly was a new man. He was happy, alive. He had the whole world by the tail. Even his family, friends, co-workers, and business associates complimented him on his exuberance.

Then, he sensed a coolness in Sandy, as he called her. She broke several dates, because of "sudden headaches." Her aloofness became more pronounced.

He didn't want to do it. He knew better. But, he did take some money, just for a little gift. Sandy responded. So, he took a little more. Was it for the car or the diamond necklace? He couldn't remember. It was only right that he should have paid her apartment rent. The mink jacket had really brightened her eyes. How she had loved him that night!

And then, one day, Sandy didn't show for work. At noon he had hurried to her apartment. It was empty. "She just packed up and left," said the building manager. No, she didn't leave any forwarding address."

The plane touched down at Dallas Love Field. Kelly came back to harsh reality. His knees were rubbery as he stepped down the ramp.

An hour later he entered the plush offices of Truth Verification, Inc., and was escorted to Rash's examining room.

As he sat in the testee's chair, Elliott Kelly saw his whole world crumbling. His eyes blurred. His breathing became ragged. He had trouble correlating his thoughts. He felt nauseated.

Wallace Rash observed Kelly closely and silently. Then he gently said, "Mr. Kelly, would you like a drink of water?"

"Please. Do you have a restroom? I feel sick."

"Of course. Right this way."

Rash requested a pot of coffee and two cups be sent to his room.

When Kelly returned, he was still pale and drawn, but seemed more settled down. He appreciated the coffee. Rash broke the ice with inconsequential chitchat. When he had the "feel" of his subject, he opened the first door.

"Elliott, do you know why you're here?"

"Yes. The auditors say they've found a large shortage in my store."

"Do you know whether it is in cash or inventory?"

"It is in cash."

"Did they tell you how much?" Rash asked.

"No. They hadn't finished when I left. I gathered it was pretty large."

Rash doodled some shorthand notes on a pad. "Why did they ask you to come here?"

"To clear myself and prove my innocence before Mr. Fairmont comes back to town."

Rash made his first move. "Are you innocent?"

Kelly sat erect. "Innocent? Of course I am! Why do you think I'm here!" His voice squeezed into a high pitch. "If I was guilty, do you think I would come here?"

"Of course not," Rash soothed. "But some guilty ones do, you know."

"This is terrible," Kelly cried. "Why, I'll be ruined! How could they possibly think I took money to buy that girl—" His mouth snapped shut. He glanced at the ceiling and groaned.

"What girl?" Rash probed.

"Sandy—uh, a cashier that used to work for us. She just disappeared one day."

"Maybe she took the money."

Kelly's eyes flared angrily. "Not Sandy. She wouldn't never do a thing like that!"

Rash sensed the abrupt temperment change.

"Did the auditors tell you the shortage was actually in cash?"

"Well no, not really."

"They didn't tell me either, because at the time they called and made an appointment here for you, they weren't sure."

"So?" Kelly said, his eyes narrowing.

"You're the only one who says positively the shortage is cash. How come you are so positive?"

"Well—" he spread his hands in futile gesture.

"Isn't it because," Rash continued, "you are the only one who really knows? The auditor did not say one word to me about the girl you called Sandy. Shall we go any further?"

Kelly's hands shook violently as he tried to light a cigarette.

Now, Rash followed up more sternly. "It's better to face me and the facts, rather than the police."

"But my family! Oh, Lord, what have I got myself into!"

"What's done is done," Rash softly led him along. "It can't be brought back, but you can start correcting it now."

"Correcting it? How?"

"Very simply. Let's you and me get our heads together here, man to man, and try to figure out just how much money you have taken. If we work it out to a figure that comes close to the final auditor's tally, you're on the first step to softening the future consequences. By being truthful, you might avoid prosecution."

"Do you really think so?" Kelly asked.

"I've seen it happen many times," Rash replied.

Together they started listing the individual types of gifts, and the approximate cost of each, Kelly had bought for his Sandy. Then they figured in her apartment rent, plus various other odds and ends.

When Kelly could recall nothing more, Rash would conduct a test centered around the question: "Have you knowingly bought more presents for Sandy than what you've told me?"

Three times Kelly remembered something else. On the fourth chart, he "cleared out" fairly well. His admissions totaled $23,600.

Two days later, the auditors in San Antonio called Rash and gave their final total as $24,150.

Since Kelly had never kept a record of his individual embezzlement sums, Rash was more than satisfied. So was the owner of Fairmont Furniture, who became a regular client thereafter.

Polygraphy had psychophysiologically searched a man's memory, and had come pretty close.

*   *   *

Conversely, it should be pointed out that in many instances the polygraph presents a last resort for the individual to prove his innocence when factual evidence is missing. Few people object to the use of polygraphy for this purpose.

Perhaps the most rewarding phase of polygraph utilization, especially for the examiner, is the large number of people exonerated entirely of guilt—a 3 to 1 ratio—in circumstances where the polygraph was the only means of proving their innocence.

We have seen specific evidence that polygraphy can be an important business tool for screening of applicants and as a deterrent to employee dishonesty. Since so many private industrial firms are successfully reaping polygraph's dual benefits, five guidelines are now set forth for new concerns who decide to follow suit.

1. Polygraphy should be used only as an adjunct to other management control procedures.
2. The prospective user should carefully choose a reputable, licensed (or well-known, established) examiner or firm.
3. The polygraph firm (examiner) and management should institute a public relations program to indoctrinate em-

ployees on the instrument, purposes, and benefits to all
concerned.

4. Polygraph test results should be evaluated as an "investigative aid," and, except when conclusive, per se, not as an
   infallible mandate of innocence or deception.

5. Under no circumstances should polygraphy be sprung upon
   employees without warning; under no circumstances should
   force or coercion be used to gain employee cooperation.

Such an indoctrination program can be well worth the small
effort. If these guidelines are followed, there is no reason why
polygraphy will not eventually become invaluable to every business in the nation.

IX

THE POLYGRAPH IN GOVERNMENT

In 1964, in response to a subcommittee questionnaire, nineteen Federal agencies reported that their policies permitted the use of polygraphy in carrying out Government business.

Cited by fourteen of the nineteen agencies, the most frequently reported purpose for the Government's use involved security matters. In this context, security ranged from investigation of security leaks to operational uses in intelligence and counter-intelligence activities.

The number of defense organizations included among the nineteen users underlines the important role polygraphy plays in the many-sided efforts to safeguard the nation's security.

Each of the military services was accounted for, with the Intelligence Corps and the military police both reporting polygraph use within the Army, and the Marine Corps and Naval intelligence answering the roll within the Navy Department. The Office of Special Investigations was the sole reported Air Force user. Civilian components of the Defense Establishment were also represented. The Central Intelligence Agency reported extensive polygraph use, as did the National Security Agency. Also within the Defense Department, the Defense Atomic Support Agency and the Defense Supply Agency acknowledged use of polygraphy. Several nondefense agencies also indicated that their activities in the security field involved use of polygraphy.

Investigation of criminal law infractions was listed by ten agencies as an area in which polygraphy was employed. Private citizens as well as federal employees came within the scope of such investigations.

The Agriculture Department, for instance, has considered the results of polygraph tests conducted outside the government in investigating cases of alleged fraudulent transactions with the Agriculture Marketing Service.

Investigation of employee misconduct was a reason given by eight agencies for utilizing polygraphy. This category included offenses not considered to be criminal violations.

The Central Intelligence Agency and the National Security Agency indicated that polygraph testing is included as a routine part of preemployment personnel screening. The armed forces also reported a similar use during fiscal 1963 in connection with the program of enlisting Cuban refugees. This was a unique situation, however, since the military normally does not employ polygraphy in recruitment or induction proceessing.

The Health, Education, and Welfare Department reported that three of its bureaus—the National Institutes of Health, the Public Health Service, and St. Elizabeth's Hospital in the District of Columbia—used polygraphs for medical purposes.

As an instrument which measures pulse rates, respiration rates, and blood pressures, along with electrical energy changes affecting body temperature and sweat gland activity, the polygraph has been used to record the reactions of patients under anesthesia. The instrument has also found use in cases involving patients with mental or neurological disorders.

More frequently, it has been used on animals undergoing experiment.

Except for the personnel screening category, user agencies declared that polygraphs were not used in every case. The Atomic Energy Commission, for instance, said that polygraphy was involved in only one of 23,300 security clearances processed during fiscal 1963. Similarly, the polygraph technique was employed in 0.14 percent of the FBI investigative matters handled in fiscal 1962.

The frequency of polygraph use in Air Force investigations varied from once every forty-three cases in 1959 to once every eighteen cases in 1962. The Internal Revenue Service, which restricts polygraph tests to employees who request them, reported such tests were used in fewer than ten cases in the last ten years.

Other agencies indicated that investigative techniques affected the extent of polygraph use. The Defense Atomic Support Agency said that polygraphy is used normally to "gain information not otherwise attainable by other investigative techniques."

The Coast Guard said that polygraph tests are administered when "there is conflicting evidence, or the subject requests an examination, or it appears that polygraphy would materially aid the investigation."

The Post Office Department limits the use of polygraphy to "cases of more than average importance where the investigation is at a standstill because the inspector cannot prove a suspect guilty or eliminate him from suspicion even though he has exhausted all normal investigative techniques."

In the area of personnel screening, the two agencies concerned —the CIA and the National Security Agency—flatly stated that "all applicants and employees are afforded polygraph examinations as a part of security screening procedures" while also implying a less-than-mandatory practice by saying that a refusal to take a test would be "considered along with other information developed in processing an applicant."

The NSA said that polygraph interviews are a required part of preemployment processing for all civilian applicants. After becoming a NSA employee, however, a person is subjected to such a test only in connection with matters "extensively investigated but difficult to resolve."

The Federal Government conducted 19,122 polygraph tests in 1963. And this amount did not include the thousands of tests which the CIA and NSA gave to "all applicants and employees."

That same year, the Army conducted roughly 12,500 tests, and the FBI utilized polygraphy 2,314 times.

Since not all Government units using polygraphy maintain their own specialized staffs and facilities to carry out the tests, many are "farmed out" to private sources or local law enforcement agencies.

Again, in 1963, these nineteen Government agencies owned 512 polygraph instruments at a cost of more than $425,000. Some 639 examiners were hired and trained to operate the instruments, and operating costs were estimated at $4.5 million.

In 1967, the Department of Defense allocated $240,000 for polygraph research.

Many of the criminal cases in which polygraphy has played a major role are highly dramatic. One of these involved U.S. Army Col. Jack Durant and his wife who, while on occupation duty after World War II, stole the crown jewels of the Duchy of Hesse.

The Army Criminal Investigation Division used the polygraph on the Durants, detected deception, and subsequently secured a confession from them.

Leonard Keeler, who refined the instrument while a member of the Berkeley, California Police Department in the 1920's used polygraphy to put his hands on eight Nazi POWs who had beaten a fellow prisoner to death.*

During the late evening hours of a winter day on a U.S. Army post in the Eastern part of the United States, a military policeman observed a car with headlights off moving at a suspiciously slow pace through a security area.

The MP turned on his red light and signaled the car to stop. Instead, it sped up as though it was trying to get away. The MP radioed his headquarters, and in a manner of minutes the suspicious car had been boxed in and halted.

When the MP walked up to the car and opened the driver's door, Mrs. Mabel Bryant (name fictitious), a handsome woman of 35 and mother of two children, cried, "Oh, thank God you've finally stopped us. He's already raped me twice!"

"She's nuts," said Cpl. Jeffry Walker (name fictitious), age 24, dressed in civilian clothes, and sitting beside Mrs. Bryant.

"Watch him," Mrs. Bryant sobbed. "He's got a big knife."

Another MP pointed a .45 automatic at Walker. "Okay, buddy, get out of the car until we find out what's going on here."

"Sure," Walker said pleasantly. "I've done nothing wrong. We been together all evening. I don't know why she's suddenly hollering rape."

When the MPs found a hunting knife with an eight-inch blade, and a pair of work gloves under the seat where Mrs.

---

*Christie, Robert: Do Lie Detectors Lie? *Popular Science,* Vol. 183, Sept. 1963.

Bryant was sitting, they decided they'd better take both suspects to the Provost Marshal's Office.

CID was called in and Benjamin Malinowski, Chief Warrant Officer, now retired, was assigned the case.

During his interview with Mrs. Bryant, Malinowski heard the following story:

"I had picked up my children at the theater about 6:00 P.M., took them home and was on my way to work at the drive-in restaurant. When I stopped for the red light at Montgomery and Pilsen Blvd., this man jumped into the car.

"I noticed he was wearing a pair of gloves. He put a big knife at my throat and made me drive into a heavily wooded park area. Then he ordered me to get in the back seat and take off my clothes or else he'd cut my throat.

"Then he raped me.

"We sat there talking for a while. He kept the knife at my throat. I did most of the talking. I remembered what my husband once told me if anything like this ever happened. He's a sergeant here in the Motor Pool. He said to just keep talking and tell the man all about myself, my husband and the children, and try to talk him out of it. So I just kept talking.

"After about an hour—he wouldn't let me dress—he started playing around with me again, and made me have sex with him the second time. Then he let me dress, and ordered me to drive back here to the post. I was praying some MP would see the car lights were off and stop us."

Malinowski interrupted. "How come the gloves and knife were under your side of the seat?"

"He ordered me to try and get away from the MPs," the woman said. "But after we were stopped and one of the MPs started towards the car, this guy laughed and put the knife and gloves under my side of the seat."

While Mrs. Bryant was being examined by an Army doctor, who confirmed she had been involved in a recent sexual act, Malinowski interviewed Cpl. Walker. This was his story:

"Heck, I been going with Mabel for six months. Sure she's married to Sgt. Bryant of the Motor Pool. And, she's got two boys ages 8 and 6. She's been working at that drive-in restaurant for about eight months.

"There's no question that I screwed her twice tonight. Hell, we've bedded many times. We just had an argument tonight and all of a sudden she pulls a stunt like this and calls me a rapist."

"What was the argument about?" Malinowski asked.

"She wanted some more nooky but I was petered out. I called her a nymph and it made her mad."

"What about the knife and gloves?"

"They're mine. I always take them along when we go to the park at night. You never know when these thugs are gonna attack you in those out-of-the-way places."

That was his story and it sounded even more convincing than the one told by Mrs. Bryant. It simply was one person's word against another.

Malinowski, a veteran polygraphist and former polygraph instructor at the Army's Fort Gordon School of Polygraphy, suggested both be tested.

Neither objected, and both signed test-consent forms required by the military. Walker volunteered to go first.

In the pretest interview, Walker stuck with his original story.

However, when the first chart had been completed, Malinowski knew Walker was lying. Deception criteria were all over the chart.

He pushed it under the suspect's nose and flatly stated "Walker, look at this. See it for yourself. I don't know what kind of a man you are, but it's damn well obvious you're lying up a storm about this matter."

Walker broke. He admitted that Mrs. Bryant's story was true —that he had raped her at knifepoint.

After a properly witnessed confession was obtained, Malinowski asked, "How come you knew so much about her and her family?"

"She told me while we were in the car. I just remembered it."

A second chart—a verification chart—was conducted. One of the questions Malinowski asked went thus: "During the past six months have you raped any other woman?"

A violent cardiovascular response developed.

Then Walker admitted that one month previous, in a nearby town, he had pulled the same act on an 18-year-old girl. He described the incident.

A check with police authorities in that town confirmed Walker was telling the truth. The 18-year-old girl positively identified Walker as her attacker.

Subsequently, Walker was convicted by courts-martial. He will be in prison for many years to come.

Had it not been for polygraphy, Mrs. Bryant's original complaint would have been closed out because of insufficient evidence, and would have marked the victim as a "loose woman," and would have allowed a rapist to escape.

* * *

In the military, there are three types of courts-martial, summary, special, and general, for enlisted men.

But for officers who get in trouble, there is only one—the general. Found guilty in a general courts-martial, an officer is dishonorably removed from the service.

A slight misunderstanding between a young lieutenant and a post commander at a West Coast Army post in 1960 almost ruined a young officer's career.

Lt. George Adams (name fictitious) went to the officers' club one Friday evening and consumed more alcohol than he was generally accustomed to. He was in civilian clothes.

In the process of leaving the club, he mistakenly attempted to push open the entrance door, thinking it was the exit door. Obviously it would not budge.

Drunkenly aggravated, Lt. Adams removed a heavy marking pen from his shirt pocket and proceeded to switch the IN and OUT signs on the doors which were adjacent to each other.

While doing this, he was approached by an elderly man, also in civilian clothes. "Just what do you think you're doing, young fellow?" the older man asked.

"I reckon I'm straightening these damn doors out. Too much confusion aroun' here."

"What is your name?" the older man asked.

"None of your business, grandpa," Lt. Adams muttered thickly. "Beat it"

The older man bristled. "I'm the post commander here!"

"Yeah, and I'm the president of Egypt. Get lost."

At this point, Lt. Adams saw his battalion commander approaching, in uniform. Before thinking, he snapped to attention and saluted.

"Good evening general," the battalion commander said to the elderly man in civilian clothes. Is there a problem?" He turned to the lieutenant. "I see you're getting acquainted with the post commander, General Archer" (name fictitious).

Lt. Adams started to sober up. He clicked his heels and saluted. "My most sincere apologies, General Archer. I guess I had too much to drink."

"Your apology is not accepted, lieutenant," the general barked. "We don't need men like you for officers in this army. You may expect charges to be filed against you tomorrow. In the meantime, you are confined to your quarters."

True to his word, General Archer filed charges the next day for insubordination and disrespect.

Fortunately, the military authorities responsible for approving the courts-martial proceedings, were curious as to "the intent" behind Lt. Adams' conduct. Through his defense counsel, Lt. Adams was asked if he would submit to polygraphy. He readily agreed.

Again, Ben Malinowski conducted the examination. He reported Lt. Adams to be telling the truth, that the incident would never have occurred had he not been drinking, and that certainly he would never have spoken in such a manner to General Archer if he had known who he was.

The courts-martial proceedings were dropped three days before Lt. Adams was to go on trial.

He did receive some minor reprimand and punishment, but nothing like what could have resulted had polygraphy not prevented the courts-martial from taking place.

* * *

In 1964, a sensitive Federal agency found through clues uncovered during polygraphy that seven job applicants who had successfully passed all other security tests, were former Communist Party members.

But even in Government, there arose opponents attempting to outlaw this highly effective scientific informer. However, as noted below, their efforts became incongruously pathetic.

In late 1963, Congressman Cornelius E. Gallagher, New Jersey, member of the Committee on Government Operations, William L. Dawson, Illinois, Chairman, by letter to Dawson, instigated the appointment of an investigative subcommittee with John E. Moss, California, Chairman, to study and report on the use of polygraphs, the economy and the efficiency thereof, by the Federal Government.

The hearings took place with much political fanfare. The newspapers gleefully jumped on the bandwagon.

On Tuesday, April 7, 1964, the subcommittee met at 10:00 A.M., John E. Moss presiding.*

Present: Representatives John E. Moss, Porter Hardy, Jr., Henry S. Reuss, John S. Monagan, George Meader, and Robert P. Griffin.

Also present: Representative Cornelius E. Gallagher.

Mr. Moss: Our witnesses today are Mr. Fred E. Inbau, Northwestern University School of Law; Mr. Cleve Backster, School of Lie Detection, New York; Mr. John E. Reid, John E. Reid & Associates, Chicago; and Mr. George Lindberg, John E. Reid & Associates, Chicago.

Before swearing in the witnesses, Chairman Moss asked, "Do any of the subcommittee members wish to make statements?"

Mr. Gallagher: Mr. Chairman.

Mr. Moss: We have a very distinguished member of Congress, not a member of this subcommittee, Congressman Gallagher.

Mr. Gallagher: Thank you, Mr. Chairman.

I wish to take this opportunity to thank Mr. Dawson for forwarding the letter I sent to him requesting this investigation. . . .

---

*Hearings before a Subcommittee of The Committee on Government Operations, House of Representatives, Eighty-Eighth Congress, Second Session, April 7, 8, and 9, 1964, Use of Polygraphs as "Lie Detectors" by The Federal Government, Part 1—Panel Discussion with Private Polygraph Practitioners.

I am concerned with some of the basic rights which people sought when they came to this new land in the face of grave danger and hardship, seeking to be free of the oppressive tyrants who ruled elsewhere at those times. I am specifically concerned with the Fourth Amendment of whether a person can take the Fourth and not be denied his basic right to employment.

Taking the "Fifth" has become a familiar practice, but we should be mindful that our Founding Fathers considered the Fourth Amendment to have greater priority than the Fifth in the Constitutional Bill of Rights. . . .If we are concerned with an increasing tendency to invade the privacy of our homes through wire tap and other types of scientific and electronic instruments, let us be doubly concerned with the widespread use of these techniques that we speak of here today and these instruments that may be used, and perhaps are being used, to invade the privacy of a man's mind, which after all, is the most private of all sanctuaries. . . .

So, the hearing goes on. John E. Reid, Fred E. Inbau, and George Lindberg were called to testify jointly.

Professionally sincere, though they were, they inadvertently projected the impression that only they—and absolutely no one else—were the "great authorities" on polygraphy.

In effect, their testimony appeared so shallow that they not only caused serious questions, based totally on misinformation, personal concern, and curiosity, to be put by Mr. Kass, Mr. Moss, Mr. Hardy, and finally Mr. Galagher, but also brought reflection on their own images as national polygraph leaders.

After a portion of John Reid's testimony, Congressman Gallagher interrupted.

Mr. Gallagher: Mr. Chairman, may I interrupt before we get off on another tangent?

Mr. Moss: Mr. Gallagher, the Chair regrets—he is very pleased to have you sit with the committee and will afford the maximum opportunity within the rules for you to participate—he cannot recognize you for questions.

Mr. Gallagher: It was my understanding, Mr. Chairman, that as a member of the Government Operations Committee that I would be allowed to sit with this committee and participate as a member. I was in the process of following up a question by Mr. Hardy.

Mr. Moss: It would have to be by unanimous consent. The Chair is not attempting to restrict the gentleman.

Mr. Gallagher: I ask unanimous consent.

Mr. Hardy: I am pleased that Mr. Gallagher is participating . . . .In fact I am ready to yield the floor.

Mr. Moss: There is a unanimous consent request.

Mr. Hardy: Mr. Chairman, I would have to object to that. . . . There is nothing personal about it at all, but I think from a procedural standpoint, it would not be desirable.

Mr. Gallagher: Mr. Chairman, may I make a statement? I am a member of the Foreign Affairs Committee. . . . It was as a result of my interest that this committee is meeting here today.

Mr. Moss: The Chair is going to have to terminate any discussion. . . . The Chair did not write the rules under which this committee operates. The Chair is bound to enforce those rules, and those rules are very specific. . . .

Mr. Hardy: I regret to object, but I think in the interest of protecting the committee against further problems, it is the only thing to do. I have no objection at all to Mr. Gallagher pursuing any subject he wants to pursue, but I think if we start that we will be in trouble from now on.

Mr. Gallagher: I did ask unanimous consent.

Mr. Hardy: I understand you did, and I objected because I think every member of the committee ought to object.

Mr. Moss: The subcommittee will continue in regular order.

Questioning of the witnesses proceeded.

Some time later, when the politicians—some really sincere, others seeking personal publicity and could care less—issued their final report and recommendations, intelligent lawmakers took a long look at it.

An American-minded and security-conscious answer to the unsubstantiated testimony before the Moss Subcommittee, particularly that of several "educated" and thoroughly uninformed psychologists, who never conducted a "live" polygraphy test in their entire lives, came from Congressman Donald Rumsfeld, Illinois:

"This report," Rumsfeld wrote, "apparently concludes that because of questions raised concerning the use of the polygraph, the proper course of action is, for all practical purposes, to suspend its use by agencies of the Federal Government. I disagree.

"Polygraph examinations are voluntarily taken. There is lack of evidence citing specific instances of harm to the individual within the Federal Government. It is my conclusion that while the research and study concerning the polygraph is necessary, and desirable, the agencies of the Federal Government should not be denied use of the polygraph as an investigative tool.

"Throughout the history of this country, the pendulum of Government action, whether executive, legislative, or judicial, has moved between the two equally undesirable extremes of excessive protection of rights of the individual at the expense of society as a whole, and the excessive protection of society at the expense of the rights of the individual.

"Each is equally important. A delicate balance between the two is desirable, but difficult to maintain. As society changes, we must be alert to see that the pendulum does not move to either extreme.

"At this point in history, it is my conviction that the pendulum has moved off the balance. Today we are witnessing an ever-increasing series of circumstances which hamper efforts to detect, prevent and curtail crime. Each year the rate of crime increases while the rate of conviction declines. Similarly, at a time when the United States is engaged in hot wars and cold wars to halt Communist expansion and subversion, we see growing restrictions on these efforts. The rights of the individual must be protected. But, we must not unnecessarily restrict the ability of the Government to protect society as a whole by hampering its ability to detect and punish criminal behavior and breaches of security to a degree which jeopardizes the rights of all its citizens.

"The directives by the Department of Defense, its supporting agencies, and the military services establishing uniform standards and control over the use and operation of polygraphs are reasonable and desirable steps toward the goal of avoiding any possible misuse of polygraphy.

"To go beyond these conclusions or recommendations at this time, however, is both unwarranted and unwise. The subcommittee presently lacks the evidence to do so. By so doing, it may be jeopardizing the ability of Government to exercise its responsibilities in protecting the Nation's freedom, and the freedom of its citizens."*

Support of the foregoing opinion also came from Congressmen William Dickeson and Jack Edwards, Alabama; John N. Erlenborn, Illinois; and Robert Dole, Kansas, as follows:

"In reading through the hearings and the Committee's report, we do not find sufficient evidence to support its conclusions . . . . Little or no evidence was uncovered where a polygraph examinee had been falsely accused or otherwise harmed through a polygraph examination administered by a Federal Agency."

Before, during, and in the wake of the Moss Subcommittee hearing, Alaska, Hawaii, Oregon, Washington State, Massachusetts, California, and Rhode Island, let witch hunts initiated by Mob-controlled labor unions, and other rotten-stinking sources, cause "elected" state representatives to enact ridiculous antipolygraph statutes of the flimsiest sort.

Contrarily, Illinois, New Mexico, Texas, Arkansas, Florida, Georgia, Virginia, and Kentucky, passed stringent educational, intern training, written examinations, moral requisites, plus a liability bond, to qualify a person to practice polygraphy.

But still, there were those uninformed and misinformed publicity-conscious politicians who invariably exploit every opportunity to show their constituents how "important" they are.

On August 26, 1966, Senator Sam J. Ervin, Jr., North Carolina, 89th Congress, 2d S.3779, introduced what since has been referred to as a "bill of rights" for Executive Branch employees. Section 1 (G) read:

"It shall be unlawful to require or request, or to attempt same, any employee of the United States serving in the depart-

---

*Hearings before a Subcommittee of The Committee on Government Operations, House of Representatives, Eighty-Eighth Congress, Second Session, Part 6, Thursday, August 19, 1965. Use of Polygraphs as Lie Detectors by the Federal Government.

ment or agency, or any person seeking employment in the executive branch of the U.S. Government, to submit to any interrogation or examination, or take any psychological or polygraph test which is designed to elicit from him information concerning his personal relationship with any person connected with him by blood marriage, or concerning his religious beliefs or practices, or concerning his attitude or conduct with respect to sexual matters."

Again, quite obviously, intelligent lawmakers ignored this asinine submission.

To put into law any such bill would automatically make illegal the questioning of a man for torturing or killing his wife, for theft, incest, rape, homosexuality, and blackmail, and for religious beliefs involving human sacrifice.

Doesn't our Congress, as well as our United States Supreme Court, already have enough of these kind of inferences attributed to it, among others?

There is one clear-cut and one subtle irony in the foregoing. We shall take the latter first.

For some strange reason, certain unions have publicly blasted polygraphy for years. Outwardly, this is their projection to the American public. So doing—playing on ignorance and fear—pulls members into their folds.

Yet, on July 13, 1962, a local of the Retail Clerk Union of America, AFL-CIO, sent the following letter to Truth Verification, Inc.:

> We . . . wish to authorize use of the polygraph to prove or verify the fact that a person in our union is telling the truth about the subject we wish verified.

So, also, a Texas UAW local at Bell Helicopter, Hurst, called in a nationally known polygraphist to resolve, after arbitration findings, accusations and denials between two employees of separate representative unions.

Test results were accepted as conclusive, approved by the local, and sent to UAW headquarters in New York where they were again accepted and approved, and the matter closed.

If every day a polygraphist can solve so many crimes, ranging from employe theft to murder, why can't a polygraph be used in combat situations to save American lives?

In October 1951 an American unit captured several North Koreans who had come toward their lines to surrender. Although intensively interrogated through an interpreter, these prisoners would reveal nothing more than their names, ranks, and service numbers. These prisoners were held in the forward area for a few hours before being sent to a rear stockade.

Later, a patrol was organized to obtain intelligence information. Not only was the patrol subjected to concentrated enemy mortar, machine gun and rifle fire, but the patrol suddenly had to cross an enemy mine field. All this resulted in both dead and wounded.

The North Koreans, who had earlier surrendered, knew enough about this mine field to pass through unharmed. There is no doubt that those North Koreans had also possessed other vital intelligence information such as the location of the gun emplacements and the extent of the enemy's troops in that area. If this information could have been learned from those prisoners, there would have been no need for that particular patrol.

In 1956 military intelligence decided to improve its information-getting programs, and brought polygraph into combat.

The first experimental examinations were conducted in a tent under field conditions. There was constant noise from nearby rifle fire, helicopters entering and leaving the area, shouting men and men going into and out of the tent.

In order to demonstrate the feasibility of examinations under the usual adverse conditions found in a combat situation, some of the prisoners examined had gone without food and sleep for an extended period. Despite these conditions, the experiments were successful.

Why didn't the noise affect the testing? Probably because the individuals being tested had become so accustomed to these conditions that they were no longer affected by them. As to the lack of food and extreme fatigue, the persons still reacted when lying because of what they considered the seriousness of their lies.

The first experiments of this nature were conducted at Camp

Pendleton, California, in 1956. Lt. Col. Regan Fuller, then intelligence officer for the Maine Corps Test Unit, and now a General, was contacted concerning the possibility of combat use of the polygraph. The commanding officer, Col. E. N. Rydalch, agreed to the proposal. Col. Rydalch, Lt. Col. Fuller and Major Bruce Myers then set up a series of hypothetical situations with which to confront Polygraphist Stephen L. Gardella, USMC, now with the San Diego, California, Police Department, during a maneuver that involved some 2,000 men and was to last five days.

The first prisoner brought in for examination was a captain. During the pretest interview he would state only his name, rank and serial number. His polygraph reactions revealed the following, and in this order:

1. The identification of his division, regiment and battalion.
2. The time of his unit's planned attack.
3. The direction of the planned attack.
4. The fact that the attack would be preceded by certain flare signals.

This examination lasted about twenty minutes.

The second prisoner was a Staff Sergeant who spoke only Spanish. During the pretest interview, this prisoner was instructed by an interpreter to answer all questions in the negative. The questions were written by the team and given to an interpreter to ask. Despite the language barrier, and the Sergeant's deliberate attempts to mislead Gardella, the following information was obtained within forty-five minutes:

1. The identification of his division, regiment, and battalion.
2. That he was the platoon sergeant of a rifle platoon.
3. That his platoon was operating with a tank force.
4. By use of a subdivided map, the area of the Aggressor's Command Post was pinpointed within a two hundred-yard area.

Since the first day's trials were so successful, more complicated problems were worked out for the second day of the exercise.

The first prisoner of this phase was a man who identified himself as Corporal Stanley J. Michael. Despite his efforts to confuse Gardella, Michael's polygraph reactions revealed that:

1. He had given his correct name.
2. He was actually a Lieutenant rather than a Corporal.
3. He was an Annapolis graduate, Class of 1953.
4. He was the Executive Officer of a rifle company.
5. His company was being supported by five M-46 tanks.

Several other prisoners were polygraphed. Colonel Rydalch was provided with the information obtained through the use of polygraphy. In each case he confirmed the accuracy of all the information.

In view of the success of the experiment in the hypothetical situations, arrangements were made, through the cooperation of Col. E. W. Durant, G-2 Officer, 1st Marine Division, for Gardella to examine naval pilots atending the survival course at Warner Hot Springs, California. The phase of the experiment began on March 16, 1956. Approximately eight pilots were processed when Gardella was given a pilot who remained completely silent throughout the entire examination. His test revealed:

1. The type of aircraft he operated.
2. That he was not operating from a carrier but was land based.
3. The armament of his plane.
4. That his aircraft had a nuclear capability.

The accuracy of these examinations was confirmed by Col. Durant and the naval officer present. In fact, the last examination was so accurate that Gardella's pilot testing was suddenly discontinued because of the extremely vital classified information he was learning.

As recently as 1965, during a large-scale Camp Pendleton maneuver ("Silver Lance"), our forces were still faced with basic questions when interrogating both prisoners and the local populace. These questions are basically those of establishing bona fides and in general consisted of trying to determine:

1. Is the individual actually who he says he is?
2. Does the individual actually do what he says he does?
3. Is the individual actually from where he says he is?

A member of General Krulak's staff, as well as officers of the First Counterintelligence Team of the First Marine Division, all verified the existence of the basic intelligence problem and confirmed the need of the polygraph in coping with it.

Following the critique of "Silver Lance," a recommendation was made to use the polygraph technique in South Viet Nam.

For his contribution via polygraphy, Stephen L. Gardella was awarded a Commendation by the U.S. Marine Corps. This high honor is very seldom bestowed upon a Reservist.*

*   *   *

In a speech delivered by Maj. Gen. Carl C. Turner, TPMG, to the American Polygraph Association on August 21, 1968, he cited some interesting cases:

> A quantity of firearms, including some automatic weapons, were stolen from a military unit over a weekend. An extensive investigation, which included interviews of every individual in the unit from which the weapons had been stolen, as well as the conduct of other investigative leads, did not result in the apprehension of the perpetrators of this crime or the location of the weapons.
>
> The investigators identified three individuals as possible suspects; however, a complete check of their background did not indicate that they were involved in the case. As a last resort, these three individuals were asked to undergo a polygraph examniation. This examination did not disclose that any of the three suspected individuals had committed the crime, but the polygraph examination of one of the suspects did reveal that about one month prior to the crime he had overheard a fourth individual mention that he had a market for stolen weapons. This fourth individual was apprehended and interrogated with negative results; however, a polygraph examination of this individual and subsequent interrogation resulted in his confession and the recovery of the stolen weapons.
>
> In this investigation, the polygraph was used to exonerate three suspected individuals and to locate the actual perpetrator of the crime, as well as the recovery of the stolen property.

General Turner continued:

> A few years ago, a fire, later determined as being ignited by an arsonist, occurred in one of the military stockades in an attempt by some of the prisoners to stage a prison break. Although investigation indicated that approximately twenty prisoners had the opportunity

---

*Arther, Richard O.: *The Journal of Polygraph Studies,* Vol. 1, No. 5, March-April, 1967.

to start the fire, only one prisoner admitted to having knowledge of the incident and he confessed to having ignited the fire.

Following his confession, this individual's fingerprints and a blood stain of the same type as that of the prisoner were found on tools located in the immediate area of the fire. Local legal authorities were of the opinion that they had sufficient evidence to warrant trial by general court-martial; however, the criminal investigator assigned to the case apparently possessed a sixth sense, as he was not satisfied with the evidence.

This investigator asked the prisoner to undergo an examination with the polygraph. Following consent by the prisoner, he was interviewed through use of the polygraph, which determined that he was untruthful in admitting his guilt to setting the fire at the post stockade.

Subsequent investigation, which included additional polygraphy, resulted in the identification and trial of the actual prisoners who had ignited the fire.

As it turned out, the prisoner who had made the original confession had been threatened with death by several other prisoners if he did not confess to igniting the fire. It has to be realized that the prisoner who made the false confession was a weak-minded, frightened individual, but the fact remains that if it had not been for the polygraph, it is possible that this prisoner could have been convicted and sentenced to a long term in prison.

Another case illustrated by General Turner goes thus:

Not too many years ago an individual of considerable stature in the military approached me and related that he was suspected of committing a very distasteful crime and that the CID had requested he undergo a polygraph examination. This gentleman complained that he was thoroughly insulted by such a request, and felt the examination would be degrading.

I had been briefed on this particular case and I knew that the legal authorities felt sufficient evidence existed for trial.

After a discussion with this party, during which time I explained that he could not be forced to undergo the examination, but the investigation had developed some very damaging circumstantial evidence, he agreed to submit to polygraphy.

The polygraph revealed no deecption on the part of this individual and the actual perpetrator was later apprehended.

Needless to say, this gentleman is still thankful that someone invented a polygraph.

Concluding his talk to the American Polygraph Association General Turner said:

Gentlemen, we have a common patriotic goal . . . to see that law and order replace lawlessness and violence as swiftly as possible. So I say to you, convey the true message about the polygraph to the misinformed, educate the ignorant about the polygraph, and above all, use the polygraph to harvest the truth in the fight against the force of evil.

X

JUDICIAL CONSIDERATIONS AND APPLICATIONS

DOUBTLESS, NOT WITHOUT exaggeration, is the following quotation from Francis Bacon, a leader (1605) in development of the "scientific method."

> In the year of our Lord, 1432, there arose a grievous quarrel among the brethren over the number of teeth in the mouth of a horse. For 13 days the disputation raged without ceasing. All the ancient books and chronicles were fetched out, and wonderful and ponderous erudition, such as was ever before heard of in this region was made manifest. At the beginning of the 14th day, a youthful friar of goodly bearing asked his learned superiors for permission to add a word, and straightway, to the wonderment of the disputants, whose deep wisdom he sore vexed, he beseeched them to unbend in a manner coarse and unheard-of, and to look in the open mouth of a horse and find answer to their questionings. At this, their dignity being greviously hurt, they waxed exceedingly wroth; and, joining in a mighty uproar, they flew upon him and smote him hip and thigh, and cast him out forthwith. For, said they, surely Satan hath tempted this bold neophyte to declare unholy and unheard-of ways of finding truth contrary to all the teaching of the fathers. After many days more of grievous strife the dove of peace sat on the assembly, and they, as one man, declaring the problem to be an everlasting mystery because of a greivous dearth of historical and theological evidence thereof, so ordered the same writ down.

Since 1923, the judiciary has been shying away from polygraphy. A general consensus of judicial opinions seems to have hinged on the assumption that polygraphy had not received sufficient psychological and physiological recognition.

Some courts have even side-tracked the issue with vaguely worded opinions.

In *State v. Cole* (354 Mo. 181, 188 S.W. (2d) 43, 1945) the court denied the defendant's request for a test upon all witnesses and himself. He was on trial for murder. A portion of the court's opinion is quoted thus:

> In our opinion, the day has not come when all witnesses in a case can be subjected to such inquisitorial and deceptive tests (or to drugs like scopolamine, or to hypnotism) without their consent. Furthermore, such dramatics before the jury would distract them and impede the trial. . . . No doubt the lie detector is useful in the investigation of crime, and may point to evidence which is competent; but it has no place in the courtroom.

The case of *Boeche v. State* (151 Neb. 368, 37 N.W. (2d) 593, 1949) is most interesting. The defendant had been accused of cashing a bogus check. Polygraph results were not admitted into evidence because, the court thought, "the vital function of cross-examination might be impared; that while the examiner could be cross-examined regarding his qualifications and the procedures, the machine itself would escape all cross-examination."

How could cross-examination be impaired by the admissibility of polygraphy? Does the court demand that the electrocardiograph instrument be cross-examined when its recording is submitted into evidence?

This court also said that it thought lie detector test results was "too subtle a task to impose upon an untrained jury."

Could we not fairly say, in this respect, that it is equally too subtle a task for an untrained jury to evaluate the power-ladden, subjective, often purely opinionated testimony of two psychiatrists who sit on a witness stand and testify in complete contradiction of each other on identically the same subject matter?

However, further exploring *Boeche v. State, we note that* Justice Chappell expressed a dissenting view that upon proof of an examiner's competency and evidence of general scientific recognition, the test results should be accepted by the courts. He was of the opinion that the failure of the judiciary to embrace aids of this type "will serve only to question the ability of the courts to efficiently administer justice."

Our last reference to this case includes another portion of the court's opinion: ". . . not yet received general scientific acceptance," and, ". . . that experimenting psychologists themselves admit that a wholly accurate test is yet to be perfected."

The implication contained in the foregoing quotes is almost inconceivable in a legal or scientific atmosphere. It seems ironic even to presume that judicial authority would admit into evidence any kind of a test conducted by "experimenting psychologists."

There is found much irresponsible subjectivity in so many psychological experimental adventures, which have few valid controls, that even the court's reference thereto appears totally incongruous.

In *People v. Wochnick* (98 Cal. App. 2d 124, 219 Pac. 2d 70, 1950) testimony of a lie detector examiner was rejected by the California Court of Appeal and a conviction reversed. The Court said:

> . . . . The evidence of the partial results of a lie detector test with respect to the defendant's reaction upon being shown the murder weapon was indelibly implanted on the minds of the jurors and could not but have had a prejudicial effect. . . .

In *Kaminski v. State* (63 So. 2d 339 Fla. 1953) the prosecutor tried to rehabilitate a witness's credibility by asking him if he had taken a lie detector test. . . .On appeal, the answering of the question was judged to be equivalent of an outright admission of the test results in evidence by the trial court.

With all due respect, let's formulate a brief analysis which explores another side of this situation. Again, in *State v. Cole,* we read the first sentence as quoted.

Correlation of the issue to the statement appears not to be present. Certainly scopolamine and hypnotism have not the slightest connection or association with the so-called lie detector test.

As we read the second sentence quoted, we wonder at its shallowness. It appears to have no interpretative foundation or meaning. Surely not even the most incompetent of all courts would dare entertain any such suggestion that a defendant or witness subject himself to an appendectomy, psychoanalysis, dental repair, hypnotism, injections of scopolamine, church service, much less the lie detector test before a jury.

The results of all of these, which are conducted in strict privacy, to one degree or another, is the main issue for consideration.

Whether or not the results are accurate should be the only question.

And now, we read the last quote which is even more confusing. By admission, the court recognizes the value of polygraph results which may point to evidence which is competent.

If John Doe willingly consents to submit to a polygraph examination and makes sepcific admission substantiated orally, or in writing, does not the polygraph aid in pointing to evidence which is competent?

Is it not possible that an x-ray may be shown in court without having to bring in the x-ray machine to "impede" the trial?

Must the guilty, if they are guilty, go free at the expense of the innocent, because of subjective suppositions based on minute technicalities which have no relation to the factual concepts of guilt or innocence?

In *Kaminski v. State,* we are somewhat astounded by the Florida Supreme Court's reaction to the prosecution's attempt at indirect use of lie detector test results. The witness was merely asked if he had taken a lie detector test. There apparently is no direct reference to results of the test in the question itself. The witness might have been permitted to say yes or no on the same basis of asking whether or not he took a bath that morning. Implication as to results of the lie detector test, or whether or not his bath cleansed his body, is hardly connected.

Perhaps the one case which created the greatest of all subsequent judicial consternation and skepticism relating to admissibility of polygraph tests, is the Federal case of *Frye v. United States* (293 Fed. 1013, D.C., 1923).

In this murder case, the court refused to allow Marston to testify concerning results of his "systolic blood pressure test." The court opinioned, in part:

> We think the systolic blood pressure deception test has not yet gained such standing and scientific recognition among physiological and scientific recognition among physiological and psychological authorities as would justify the courts in admitting expert testimony deduced from the discovery, development, and experiments thus far made. . . .

Therein, a rather sad precedent was established which has hampered investigations and thwarted punishment of the guilty.

We can't help but wonder if the court would have refused a doctor's testimony that he had recorded subject's systolic blood pressure. The same recording attachments are used, and systolic blood pressure exists whether taken by a polygraphist or a medical man.

Some forty-six years have gone by since then. Marston's "systolic blood pressure apparatus," and Father Summers' psychogalvanometer *(People v. Kenny,* 167 Misc. 51, 3 N.Y. Supp. 2d 348, 1938) have been refined into highly sensitive and very accurate polygraph recording instruments manufactured by Associated Research, Inc., and the C. H. Stoelting Company, both of Chicago, Illinois.

Nevertheless, these ancient cases are still delightfully played upon by defense attorneys.

Invariably, judges who have not informed themselves upon the factual issues of polygraphy as it exists today, fall back on outdated precedent. The obvious result is weakness in the true administration of justice.

With the increased crime rate, trial transcripts suggest the guilty are joyfully hiding behind judicial decision technicalities, e.g. mostly behind interpretation of minute parts of sentences in judicial interpretation of other interpretations. The innocent continue to suffer and pay an enormous price. Yet legislation, often times backed by the criminal and certain left wing elements, rambles on to create legal technicalities and obstructions based upon precedent compounded upon precedent.

Aspects of *State v. Lowry* (163 Kan. 622, 185 Pac. 2d 147, 1947) should first be considered. In this instance, a portion of the Kansas Supreme Court's decision read:

> . . . . Its usefulness (meaning polygraphy) has been amply demonstrated by detective agencies, police departments, and other law enforcement agencies conducting criminal investigations.

Now, let's take a look at some of the remarks in the *Frye v. United States* opinion:

. . . . Somewhere in this twilight zone the evidential force of the principal must be recognized, and while courts will go a long way in admitting expert testimony deduced from a well-recognized scientific principle or discovery, the thing from which the deduction is made must be sufficiently established to have gained general acceptance in the particular field in which it belongs.

Conflict in the two quotes is rather apparent. As we have seen, nearly every type of law enforcement agency, Governmental or otherwise, certainly has accepted the dual benefits of polygraphy. Simply add private industry.

How can there possibly be any question that polygraphy has "gained general acceptance in the particular field in which it belongs?"

In 1952 a symposium was conducted on "The Polygraph Truth Test" by Professor William Wicker, Dean of the University of Tennessee College of Law. The articles and comments presented at the symposium show that even then there was general scientific recognition that the polygraph possesses efficacy, and that reasonable certainty can follow from such tests.

At approximately the same time, the New York Bar Association Committee on State Legislation conducted investigations in the polygraph technique. The Committee found:

Investigations conducted . . . have indicated that the science of lie-detection has reached such stature that its aid should be made available in the process of judicial fact finding.

Accordingly, the Committee recommended that the New York Civil Practice Act be amended by adding a new section to provide, among other things, that whenever it shall be relevant to the prosecution or defense of a civil action or proceeding, or to a pretrial hearing therein, the court may order any party or witness to submit to lie-detector tests (NY State Bar Assoc. Circular 66, page 264, 1953). Thereafter, a bill was introduced in the New York State Senate on January 27, 1953, and committed to the Committee on Codes. It was not enacted into law.

The evidence is even more convincing today. As pointed out by Mordecai M. Merker, Deputy Director, Office of Emergency Planning, Executive Office of the President of the United States, in the December 1968 issue of the *New York State Bar Journal:*

The purpose of this paper is to suggest that the time has come for the courts to admit polygraph tests into evidence "in behalf of" a defendant in a criminal case. After establishing the proper foundation, the defendant should be permitted to present evidence of the results of his own polygraph examination, if he is willing also to submit to such examination by a qualified polygraph examiner of the prosecutor's choosing. . . .proof can be presented to show general scientific recognition that the polygraph possesses efficacy, and that reasonable certainty can follow from polygraph tests.

Today, the polygraph technique is playing major behind-the-scene roles in solving various domestic and paternity problems, both in and out of litigation.

In the *American Bar Association Journal,* Vol. 50, No. 12, December 1964, Roger Alton Pfaff, Presiding Judge of the Consolidated Domestic Relations and Conciliation Court, Los Angeles County, California, (now retired) wrote:

It is my hope to clarify certain misconceptions about what I would prefer to call "scientific truth testing" by the use of the polygraph instrument utilized by a competent examiner.

We are all aware of the invaluable use the polygraph has been in criminal cases. But its use in civil cases has been largely overlooked, except in Cook County, Illinois, and Los Angeles County, California.

Lawyers and judges are familiar with the unpleasant fact that all too frequently in cases involving conflicts over children, parties in a divorce action make the most vicious accusations concerning moral character—accusations which are difficult, if not impossible, to refute.

Having the parties submit to a psychiatric evaluation is of limited value since psychiatrists have no built-in antenna to ascertain the truth or falsity of charges of immoral conduct, nor do judges for that matter.

This report is to demonstrate dramatically how the use of the polygraph by a competent examiner has saved untold hours of court time, amicably resolved bitter child custody and visitation rights, cleared blackened reputations, concluded conflicting contempt charges, repeatedly settled contested paternity suits without trial, and even brought about marital reconciliations.

Since March, 1962, the Los Angeles Superior Court has been utilizing the polygraph in domestic relations cases, first in child custody, and later in paternity cases.

Attorneys immediately were so satisfied and pleased with the results that now they, not the judge, suggest use of the polygraph. They voluntarily stipulate that the polygrapher's written report be received in evidence.

The simplest and most succinct way to explain how the Los Angeles system has worked is by explaining how it originated. . . .

Mrs. B. sued her husband for divorce, requesting in her affidavit for "pendente lite" orders that her husband be denied any visitation rights with the two daughters, ages 12 and 9, alleging that he had been committing incestuous acts with the older daughter for the past two years and had just recently been making suggestive remarks to the younger daughter.

The father vigorously denied the charges and volunteered, "I'll take a lie detector test!"

When Judge Pfaff asked the mother if she would stipulate to the daughter's taking a similar test if the husband's test indicated he was truthful, or if it was inconclusive, she agreed.

Lieutenant Warren King of the Burbank Police agreed to conduct the tests. He interviewed the mother and daughter by telephone prior to the husband's appointment. He interviewed the husband who denied any sexual relations whatsoever with his daughter.

The polygraph test was administered, and it definitely indicated he was untruthful. When Lt. King told him of this fact, he then admitted that he had lied, but stated he had not actually had sexual intercourse but everything short of it in order to explain such matters to her at her request.

That settled the question of visitation.

* * *

Mr. G, after a final decree of divorce, sought custody of his two daughters, alleging that the little girls had complained to him that their mother had been committing certain strange acts they couldn't understand with a woman who was living in the home. Alarmed, the father spied on the house and then brought the action for custody.

In chambers, the wife's attorney impugned the ethics of the husband's attorney in being a party to such a scurrilous and false accusation that the mother was a lesbian. Judge Pfaff suggested that all could avoid a nasty hearing if the parties would take polygraph tests. The wife's attorney instantly stipulated.

A week later, the polygraph examiner's report stated that the wife arrived, he interviewed her, and then commenced to prepare the instrument to give the test when she stated, "You don't have to give me that test. It's all true as reported, and furthermore I have no intention of giving up my girl friend."

* * *

Mr. and Mrs. P each brought contempts against the other for failure to comply with the court's order. The charges were diametrically opposed; one or the other was lying. The attorneys suggested they both submit to polygraph tests, which showed that the wife was untruthful on every count in her contempt, and the husband was telling the truth. The case was settled without further hearing.

* * *

Mrs. X was positive her husband had been engaging in an illicit relationship with her best friend. Mr. X emphatically denied the charge, stated he loved his wife and three children: he was distraught at the possibility of a divorce.

Judge Pfaff suggested polygraph. Both parties agreed. The test proved the husband truthful, which satisfied the wife. A reconciliation was effected, the divorce complaint dismissed.

* * *

In a society characterized by premarital sexual promiscuity (one of every six marriages involves a premarital pregnancy; 40 percent of teen-age marriages), lax morals and divorce (one of every four marriages), is it any wonder that paternity suits are common?

The polygraph can play a decisive role in paternity proceedings, particularly in those cases in which there is a direct conflict in the evidence and the blood test does not rule the defendant as the alleged father.

The real dividend in polygraph cases is that in most instances where the test shows the examinee untruthful and this fact is revealed to him, he then voluntarily admits he was not telling the truth and gives the examiner a true version of what occurred.

In a number of cases, the polygraph has indicated that the mother was untruthful and in several instances she then admitted that she had not had sexual relations with the alleged father during the period of conception; that she was not sure who the father was, but she liked the defendant better than any of the other suspects.

A paternity case is usually initiated upon the complaint of a mother who alleges that a certain man is the father of her child. By such action, the complaint seeks to have the accused man legally declared the father and required to pay for the child's support.

If it goes to court, the judge or jury must decide whether or not the defendant is the father. If found to be the father, each month he must pay a certain amount of support money or go to jail. Usually this support must be paid until the child becomes an adult.

When testifying, the alleged father usually invokes one of two defenses. First, he may deny that he had intercourse with the mother during the conception period. Second, he may claim that during this same period the mother also had intercourse with one or more other men. Thus, he should not be held responsible since one of the others could also be the father.

Almost always, the mother will claim that during the conception period the defendant was the only one with whom she had intercourse.

A paternity court may be able to have blood-grouping tests made of the mother, defendant, and the child. Even if such tests are conducted, they can only exclude the defendant as being the child's father. They cannot establish that any particular man is the father. Currently, blood testing will only detect some 55 percent of the false accusations.

Where blood tests are not yet used, or when they do not exclude the alleged father, the judge/jury is faced with an extremely difficult problem in determining truthfulness. Rarely for either side are there any witnesses to be heard, or physical evidence that can be introduced.

For over thirty years a great number of Chicago judges have consistently availed themselves of the services of a polygraphist to assist them in their decisions in all types of cases, including paternity. Both the defendant and mother take the polygraph examination, usually at the conclusion of testimony.

In 1959, the Orange County (Santa Ana), California District Attorney started a procedure of having polygraph and blood tests given, providing the alleged father would first sign an agreement and stipulation that such evidence would be admissible in court. That procedure continues today.

If he does sign the stipulation, the mother first takes the test, and if she is believed to be truthful, then blood tests are conducted. If she does not "clear" her polygraph test, there is no prosecution.

The results of both the polygraph and blood tests are given to the defendant's attorney. If the mother has been truthful, generally the defendant pleads guilty, thus eliminating the need for a court trial.

On the basis of a study made of 312 consecutive paternity cases handled at the Chicago polygraph testing suite of John E. Reid & Associates, 93 percent of the 589 tested parties orally admitted to the polygraphist that they had committed perjury when testifying in court.

Sometimes a witness will testify, usually a man, claiming that during the possible conception period he had intercourse with the mother. This is to prove false her claim that she had intercourse only with the defendant.

When these "witnesses" were examined, 57 percent of them confessed that they did not have intercourse with the mother during the conception period. In fact, a majority of them admitted that they never had intercourse with the mother.

The fact that 93 percent of the 589 admitted committing perjury is sufficient to establish that a jury/judge, without polygraphy, has an almost impossible task in deciding what is the truth.

The foregoing figures are based upon those persons who agreed to be examined. Various courts using this procedure report a large number of cases where, after the polygraph is suggested, for the first time the alleged father and/or the mother admits having lied. Often such admissions terminate the case and the polygraphist is not used.

In addition, 40 percent of the mothers confessed to the polygraphist that they had intercourse with others during the conception period.

To request polygraphy is often the defendant's only hope of proving his contention that he is not the father. Rather than accuse the man whom she believes to be the father, the mother often decides to accuse the man she loves (hoping that he will marry her), or she accuses a man with money, hoping the court will require him to give her a large amount of support money each month the next sixteen to twenty-one years.

In paternity cases, the best procedure is first to have the alleged father and then the mother take the polygraph examination, even when the man admits intercourse during the conception period. This should be done for several reasons.

Since almost always both parties are either deliberately lying or withholding significant information, the testing of both affords the polygraphist a much better opportunity of learning exactly what the truth is. Likewise, in the event one person's examination is inconclusive, the other's chart analysis may be sufficiently definite to form an opinion regarding at least some, if not all, of the basic issues.

The first contention—no intercourse during the conception period—is an oft-used defense. Of the ninety-eight alleged fathers in Chicago using the defense, seventy-one confessed to having intercourse with the mother.

The second contention—that there were others— is true many more times than alleged fathers and their attorneys really think it is. Not only did it occur 149 times out of 312 Chicago cases, but 128 women admitted it.

Frederic C. Martin, polygraphist for the Orange County District Attorney, obtained confessions to "other men" from 142 of the 144 women whose polygraph charts indicated they were lying.

If just blood tests had been used in these combined 293 cases, only some 160 mothers would have been shown to have filed a false complaint, versus the 270 mothers who orally admitted it.

Representative Cases

Intercourse Only with the Defendant

The defendant claimed he never had intercourse with the mother, that she was a prostitute, and that during the conception period he sent men to her house so she could have intercourse with them. His allegations were partially confirmed by the testimony of another man, who stated in court that during the conception period the defendant had sent him to the woman's house so he could have intercourse with her.

Defendant's examination: Before his first test, he confessed to the polygraphist that he had made up the story about sending men to the woman's house; he had instructed the witness to testify falsely, and he, himself, had intercourse with her during the conception period.

Mother's examination: There were indications of truthfulness when she claimed that during the conception period she had intercourse only with the defendant.

Intercourse with Others as Well as with Defendant

A 15-year-old girl claimed that when only 13 she became pregnant by the alleged father because he was the only one with whom she had ever had intercourse.

Mother's examination: During her polygraph test, this attractive naive-appearing girl admitted intercourse with five men during the middle (ninth) month.

No Intercourse with the Defendant

A 16-year-old mother named as the father a man who could not be located. From her polygraph charts, the examiner determined the alleged father to be a fictitious person. The girl then admitted that her stepfather was the only person with whom she ever had intercourse. Further testing indicated the truthfulness of her new claim.

Another mother swore in court that during the conception period she had only had intercourse with the alleged father, who denied having had intercourse with her.

Defendant's examination: Chart analysis indicated truth when he denied intercourse during the three conception months.

Mother's second polygraph interview: At this time, she confessed that during the three conception months she had intercourse 36 times with one man, 24 times with a second man, and 35 times with a third. When another chart series indicated she was still not telling the entire truth, she admitted having had intercourse during that same period with yet another two men.

False Accusation of Defendant

A most beautiful mother, who during her pretest interview also appeared to be one of the most convincing and sincere persons, testified in court and accused a church choir director of being the father of her child. The mother was single, and a member of the choir. The choir director was married, the father of two small children.

Defendant's examination: Polygraphy indicated his truthfulness when he claimed that he had not even kissed complainant, much less had intercourse with her.

Mother's examination: Following her tests, she admitted the accused never had intercourse with her. She said she was in love with him and had wished for several years that if she ever became pregnant it would be by him. When she became pregnant by another man, she wanted to "honor" the baby by having the choir director legally declared the father.*

* * *

From the foregoing, one now realizes that with the assistance of polygraphy, judges, juries, and attorneys have a much firmer basis on which to render a just decision.

However, this invaluable judicial aid will never become widely utilized until Federal and state laws provide for proper

---

*Arther, Richard O., *The Journal of Polygraph Studies*, Vol. II, No. 1, July-August, 1967.

licensing requirements for examiners, and make it unlawful for any unlicensed person to operate.

When that time comes, polygraphy will become a respected profession and its scientific work a constructive contribution to the administration of justice.

Perhaps that time has already started.

On Monday, October 21, 1969, the results of a polygraph test, so far never approved as evidence by any appeals court in the United States, were admitted in a trial in Hennepin County, Minnesota, District Court.

Judge Dana Nicholson admitted the evidence over objection of the prosecution in the case of Andrew Ferrando.

Ferrando was being tried by a jury for lurking in order to commit theft in a northeast Minneapolis bar.

Judge Nicholson told newspaper reporters he had studied the development of polygraphy and believes the instruments and techniques have reached a point at which they are scientifically reliable enough to be admitted as evidence.

Arthur G. Kirby, polygraph specialist in the University of Minnesota Police Department, and a member of a firm that gives tests for other agencies, testified about the tests given Ferrando. He said they indicated Ferrando was telling the truth when he said he was not near the bar in question the night a man was seen there.

David Kuebelbeck, who prosecuted the case, objected to Kirby's testimony, arguing that Kirby had not shown that the polygraph instrument used to test Ferrando was reliable.

The jury acquitted Ferrando. The prosecution cannot appeal the verdict, so Ferrando is free.

In February of 1970, Willie T. Lockett had a lucky day in a Phoenix, Arizona Superior Court. Judge Howard F. Thompson dismissed charges of robbery and assault with a deadly weapon against him.

Lockett, 22, of Houston, Texas, was arrested on October 25, 1969 and was in custody until released. At his trial before a jury on January 20, 1970, a store owner testified Lockett was the suspect who had come into his store, pulled a gun on him, and fled when the store owner frightened him off with a gun of his own.

The jury also heard that Lockett had just finished serving a prison term in California on an armed robbery charge and was going to see a brother in Tucson before returning to Texas to live with his mother.

Lockett claimed he had just arrived in Phoenix, eaten lunch at a restaurant, had gone to a movie and was going to his car when police stopped him as the suspect who had just run from the store in question.

The jury found Lockett guilty on both charges.

"I wasn't satisfied he was guilty after the jury returned the verdict," Thompson said. "I believed he was telling the truth so I postponed sentencing to February 26 and ordred the county attorney's office to administer a polygraph test. The results indicated he was telling the truth."

In vacating the jury's verdict, Judge Thompson said, "I will not let a man be convicted under these circumstances."

A prior conviction usually brings a minimum 10-year jail sentence.

INDEX

221

State v. Joseph Francis Shea, 61
State v. Willie Lee & Freddie Pitts, 50
Supreme Court, 56-58, 121, 208
Forgery, 79
Fort Worth, Texas, 5
Fourth Amendment, 8, 194
Fraleigh, Howard, 120
Franklin, L. C., 80
Frazier, Spencer, 117
Frye v. United States, 27, 208-210
Fuller, Gen. Regan, 200

G

Gallagher, C. E., 193-195
Galvanometers, 34
Garmire, B. L., 179
Gano—Downs Co., 106
Gardella, S. L., 200, 201
Gardner, Erle Stanley, vii-xi, 49, 50, 76
Georgia, polygraph legislation, 197
Gibson, Charles, 96
Gibson, Judge F. R., 8, 9
Gilbert, Bill, 20
Goodhart, David, 96
Goodman, Ralph, 96
Grant, Daniel, 122
Great Britain, 11, 12
Greenberg, Jack, 56
Greene, Alec E., 86
Gregory, Alex, 49, 50, 76, 77, 106
Griffin, Clyde, 67, 68
Griffin, R. P., 193
Grover, Floyd Jr., 50, 51, 55
Gustafson, L. A., 25

H

Hampton, M. K., 65-69
Handbook on the Law of Evidence, 30
Hanscom, C. B., 45, 76, 87, 88, 112, 113
Hardison, I. L., 119
Hardy, Porter Jr., 193, 195
Harrelson, Leonard, 74
Harvard Business Review, 25
Hawaii, polygraph legislation, 197
Hellman, David, 97
Hennepin County, Minnesota, 42
Herbert, K. R., 93
Hightower, Cato, 5
Holley, Judge C. R., 58-60

Hollis, Charles, 108-109
Holmes, Justice, 27
Holmes, S. F. Jr., 146, 148, 155, 161
Holmes, Warren, 55, 57, 61, 64-66, 69, 97, 117-119, 123-128
Homicide, 19, 27, 34, 51, 61, 65, 80, 81, 82, 90, 92, 95, 99, 102, 105, 106, 107, 111, 112, 114, 116, 122, 123, 124
Hubbart, P. A., 56, 58, 60
Hynek, J. A., 114
Hypnotism, 206, 207

I

Illinois, People v. Berkman, 28
polygraph legislation, 197
rape, 70
Supreme Court, 28, 29
Inbau, F. E., 193, 194
Intercourse, 214-218
Internal Revenue Service, 186

J

Jacobs, I. R., 96
Jaspan, Norman, 162
Jeffers, R. N., 126, 127
Jewelry employment, 146-147
Jewel theft, 188
Johnson, Paul, 125
Jones, Charles, 172-179
Jones, K. E., 99
Juvenile delinquency, 79, 91
Justi, Ray, 61

K

Kaminski v. State (Florida), 207, 208
Kansas
State v. Lowry, 209
Supreme Court, 209
Kaufman, Judge Irvin, 29
Kaufman, Victor, 45
Keeler Polygraph Institute, 74
Keeler, Arthur, 117, 120
Keeler, Leonard, 49, 188
Kennedy, Robert F., 7
Kenny v. People (New York), 209
Kentucky, polygraph legislation, 197
King, M. L. Jr., 7
King, Warren, 89, 212
Kirby, A. G., 219

Schindler, Raymond, 49
Scopolamine, 206, 207
Seattle Times, 22
Security World, 143
Selby, Virginia, 117, 120, 121
Semet, B. N., 60
Sex crimes, 23, 71, 76, 87, 188
Shea, J. F., 62-64
Sheppard, Sam, 66
Simon, Tobias, 56
Smiley, Joseph, 94
Smith, G. D., 117
Smith, Tom, 49
Snyder, Dr. LeMoyne, 30, 31, 49
Sosa, P. B., 92
South Miami Hospital, 96
South Viet Nam, 202
Speck, Richard, 7
Specter, Arlen, 22
Spencer, Monroe, 65-68
Spinelli, William, 7, 8
Spotter, Raymond, 70-76
State v. Cole (Missouri), 205-208
State v. Lowry (Kansas), 209
Steeger, Harry, 49
Stephens, Dr. Elvis, 130, 163
Sternbach, R. A., 25
Steward, Cecil, 55
Stoelting, C. H. & Co., 209
Storer, John, 150
Summers, Father, 209
Systolic blood pressure, 208, 209

T
Teague, O. E., 17
Ten second minimum, 35
Texas, 179
  aid & compensation, 46
  Aquilar v. Texas, 8
  Board of Polygraph Examiners, 92
  Cruz, J. G., 93
  Department Public Safety, 78, 92
  forgery, 79
  homicide, 80, 81, 82, 92, 99, 103, 105, 107
  Law v. State, 80
  McIllwain, R. E. v. Texas, 108-110
  Pittman v. State, 102
  polygraph legislation, 197

Powell, McKinley Jr. v. Texas, 81
Rangers, 79
robbery, 78, 89
Supreme Court, 110
Tillis, J. E. v. Texas, 91
UFO, 113
Thaniel, Fred, 81
Thibedeau, Philip, 64
Thomas, J. R., 65-68
Thompson, H. F., 219, 220
Thompson, Laura, 124-128
Tillis, J. E., 90, 91
Tillis, Lee, 90
Tindell, Claude, 125
Titusville, Florida, 68
Tomlinson, Virginia, 68
Truth Verification Inc., 180, 187, 198
Tubbs, D. M., 170
Tucker, Donald, 94
Tucson, Arizona, 171, 178
Turner, Major General C. A., 202-204
Turner, W. F., 53-58

U
Unidentified flying object, 113-114
United Auto Workers, Texas, 198
United Nations, 150
United States
  Agriculture Department, 185, 186
  Agriculture Marketing Service, 185
  Air Force
    Amarillo Air Force Base, 107
    Camp Pendleton, California, 200, 201
    Office of Special Investigations, 62, 107, 108, 185, 186
    West Palm Beach, Florida, 62
  Atomic Energy Commission, 186
  Army, 185, 187-189
  Army, Criminal Investigation Division, 52, 53
  Central Intelligence Agency, 185-187
  Coast Guard, 187
  Congress, 12, 198
  Defense Deaprtment, 196
    budget allocation for polygraphy, 188
    Defense Atomic Support Agency, 185, 186